Paul's Model Art
MINICHAMPS®

Dear Collector,

to our surprise and delight we learned that a group of japanese friends had published a book on MINICHAMPS.

We take this as an indication of the world-wide popularity of our brand and are pleased to present this edition in english language for collectors that are interested in gathering informations for their own collections.

We hope you will enjoy reading through it.

Paul's Model Art GmbH & Co. KG - A company with an exemplary development

1990 — Foundation of Paul's Model Art GmbH & Co. KG by Paul-Günter Lang on May 1st, 1990. China is chosen as production site. The product range concentrates mainly on model cars of the DTM. Creation of the first MINICHAMPS die-cast model in 1/43rd scale: Audi V8, driver Hans-Joachim Stuck, 1990 German Touring Car Champion.

1991 — The product range is expanded by high-quality replicas in 1/24th scale as well as classic and modern road cars.
Creation of the first classic car replica in 1/43rd scale: 1955 Karmann Ghia.

1992 — The excellent quality of the die-cast models attracts the attention of car manufacturers. As a consequence, the first orders are placed by the automobile industry. Creation of the first Formula One replica in 1/43rd scale: Benetton B 192, driver Michael Schumacher, 1992 Belgian GP winner.

1993 — The success of Michael Schumacher sharply boosts public interest in Formula One racing in Germany. The Formula One field in 1/43rd scale is added to the product range. Creation of the first Formula One replicas in 1/18th scale: Benetton, Williams, Ferrari. Production of the 1.000.000th model.

1994 — The product line includes replicas in all major collector's scales. Particular focus is laid onto the development of road cars and racing cars in 1/18th scale. Creation of the first road car in 1/18th scale: 1993 BMW 3 Series Saloon.

1995 — Accessories such as helmets, key rings and figurines join the model cars. Creation of the first Formula One driver helmets in 1/8th scale: Heinz-Harald Frentzen and Damon Hill. Production of the 5.000.000th model.

1996 — Upon request of the BMW Company MINICHAMPS enters new territory in developing motor bike models. Photo-etched brake discs and wheel spokes are typical quality features of these replicas from the beginning. BMW honours such high quality standard by its decision to have motor bike models developed and manufactured exclusively by MINICHAMPS. Creation of the first motor bike replica in 1/24th scale: BMW R 1100.

1997 — Creation of the first replica in 1/12th scale: 1988 McLaren Honda MP4-4 Ayrton Senna. Production of the 10.000.000th model.

1998 — Mercedes-Benz entrusts MINICHAMPS with the development of a truck replica in 1/43rd scale. This spurs the development of an extensive range of very detailed truck replicas in the following years, also including race trucks. - Creation of the first truck replica in 1/43rd scale: Mercedes-Benz Atego.

1999 — By developing the first classic car in 1/18th scale a further market niche is occupied. Cars of German origin constitute the main area of that product range. Creation of the first classic car replica in 1/18th scale: 1964 Porsche 904 GTS. Production of the 15.000.000th model.

2000 — At the International Toy Fair in Nuremberg the first military vehicle in 1/35th scale developed by MINICHAMPS is being presented. A further première is taking place with the presentation of the first racing motorbike made by MINICHAMPS, a model that stuns with its unequalled level of detail. Creation of the first motor bike replica in 1/12th scale: Ducati 996.

2001 — Further expansion of the product range of classic cars and military vehicles; introduction of a Magirus Deutz S 6500 fire engine with extractable aerial ladder. The great success of the Ducati model leads to co-operation with other motorbike manufacturers, such as Honda, Suzuki and Yamaha.

2002 — Special gag: First model of a racing car with sound chip ('Pink Pig'); 'Model of the year'-Award for Setra S8 coach with Magirus fire engine runner-up; Formula One Pit Stop Crews of several teams; a 1/12th scale model of the Triumph Bonneville 650 T120 fitted with real wire spokes; introduction of the JAMES BOND Collection in 1/43rd scale and racing helmets in 1/2 scale.

2003 — First 1/18th scale replica of a classic truck worldwide: Mercedes-Benz L 6600 with functional doors, bonnet, steering, trailer coupling, flatbed loading planes and suspension. Its seats are even covered with genuine leather.
The model is half a meter long and has a weight of 2.5 kgs.

Contents
The world of Minichamps

4 The Color of Art
The world of color: Minichamps

The Passion of Red

Force of Yellow

Individuality of Blue

14 Road cars of Minichamps
- 16 Ferrari
- 24 Porsche
- 42 Mercedes-Benz
- 54 BMW
- 66 German Cars
- 74 British Cars
- 76 Italian Cars
- 80 French Cars and others
- 84 Minichamps at real car dealerships
  Porsche / BMW / Mercedes-Benz / Audi / Smart

92 Visit of Minichamps head office & Interviews
Managing Director: Paul G. Lang

- 96 Minichamps trivia

99 Rare Models Museum

106 Racing machines
- 108 Formula 1
- 124 DTM
- 136 Le Mans 24h
- 144 McLaren F1 GTR Series
- 146 Porsche Cup Series
- 148 Jägermeister Collection
- 150 Other Race Cars

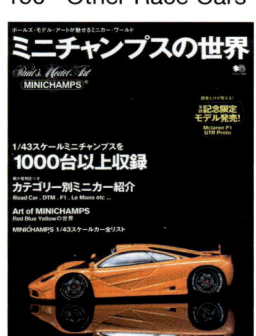

This book has been translated from the japanese book "Minichamps' World" published by EI Publishing. Co. Ltd.

All right reserved. No part of this publication may be reproduced, stored in a retrieval system, or transmitted, in any form or by any means, electronic, mechanical, photocopying, recording or otherwise, without the prior permission of the publisher.
ISBN4-87099-815-7

Red is the most commonly found body colour of cars in the Paul's Model Art / Minichamps range. A red body gives a car a sporty emphasis. Scale model fans and motorists alike would all want to own a red car at least once.

The Passion

of RED

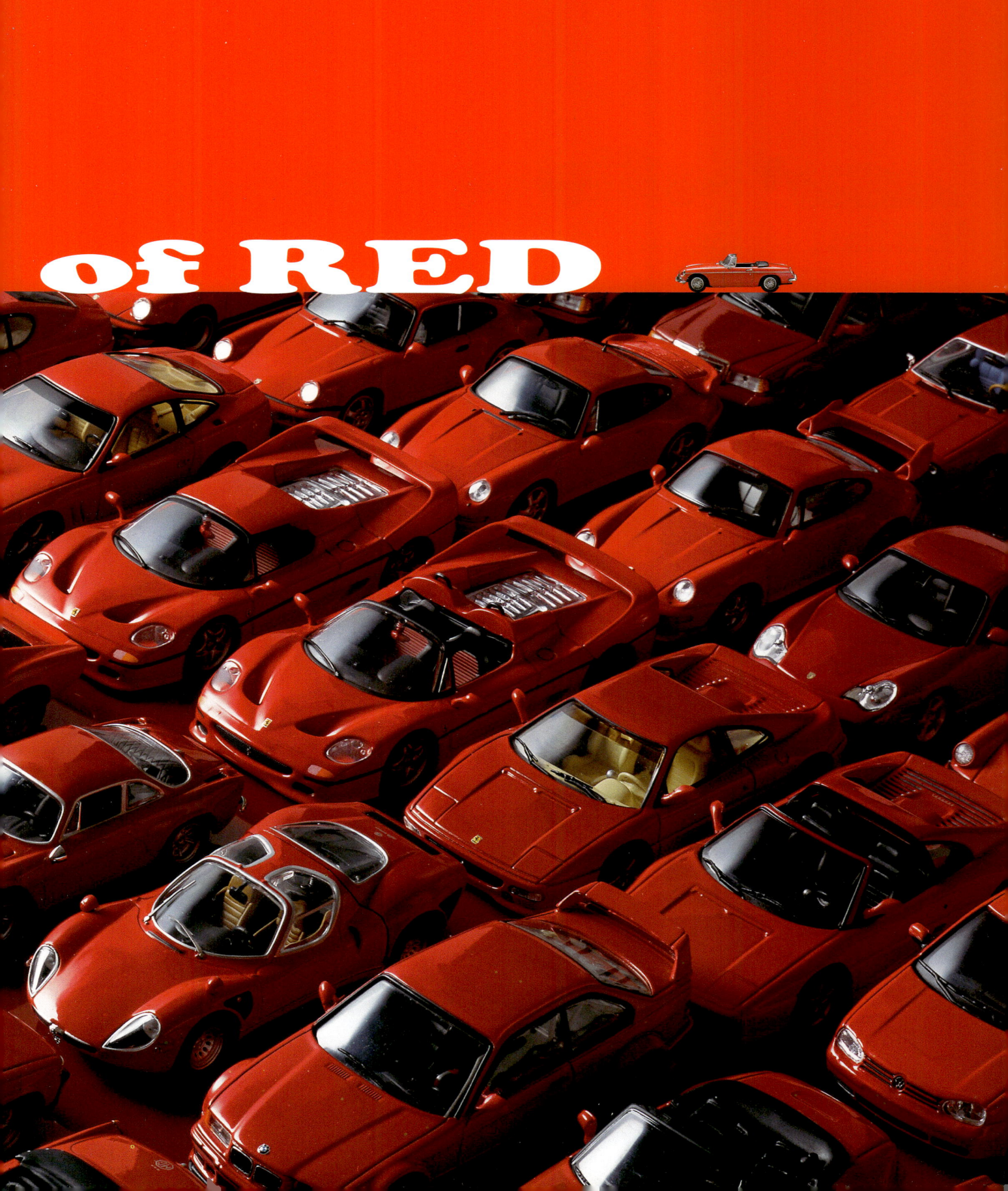

Red Minichamps Cars
The Passion of RED

Ferrari 333SP 1994 Presentation 430 947400	**Fiat X1/9 1972-78** 430 121660	**Volvo 121 Amazon saloon** 430 171000	**BMW M1 Street 1978-81** 430 025022
Mercedes-Benz C-Class Sports Coupe 2001 430 030000	**Porsche 911 1964** 430 067121	**Ford Escort RS Cosworth 1992** 430 082104	**Ford Mustang Cabriolet 1994** 430 085632
Lancia Stratos Street 1972-78 430 125022	**Alfa Romeo 147 2001** 430 120000	**Mercedes-Benz 280SL Cabriolet 1968-71** 430 032231	**Melkus RS 1000 1972** 430 010120
Ferrari 512 TR 1992 430 072500	**Chevrolet Corvette 1997** 430 142620	**Porsche 356 A Speedster 1956** 430 065532	**Alfa Romeo Tipo 33 Stradale 1968** 436 120920
Peugeot 406 Coupe 1996 430 112620	**Ford Capri RS 2600 1972-73** 430 085802	**MGB Cabriolet 1962-69** 430 131030	**VW 1600 Variant 1966** 430 055310

MINICHAMPS

Ford Focus 3-Door Saloon 1998 430 087000	**BMW 507 Cabriolet Soft-Top 1956-59** 430 022520	**Porsche 911 Turbo 1999** 430 069304	**VW Polo 1975** 430 050500
Triumph TR6 1968-76 430 132572	**Jeep Grand Cherokee 1993** 430 149662	**Lotus Super Seven 1968** 430 135632	**Mercedes-Benz E190 Evolution1 1990** 430 R03000
Audi Quattro 1981 430 019420	**Alfa Romeo 155 Saloon 1992** 430 120402	**Ferrari F50 Spider 1995** 430 075162	**Opel Kadett A Limousine 1962-65** 430 043002
BMW M3 GTR Street 1993 430 023382	**VW-Porsche 914 1969-73** 430 065665	**McLaren F1 Roadcar 1993** 530 133432	**Ferrari 550 Maranello 1996** 430 076020
Porsche 911 Speedster 1988 430 066130	**Fiat Barchetta Cabriolet 1996** 430 121930	**Volvo P1800 ES 1971** 430 171615	**VW 1200 Beetle oval window 1953-57** 430 052102

Of a wide variety of possible colours for a car, red remains the most popular. Red is not a favoured colour for racing machines; but for road cars red can be striking, and looks exceptionally good. The models on show are obviously not the extent of the Paul's Model Art / Minichamps range of red cars, but they do serve to show some of the depth of the collection. Passionate red. Please enjoy.

From first view, one can sense the joy of driving such models

RED

Force of

YELLOW

Despite the dominance of red among sports cars, a great many are also painted yellow. Yellow provides a certain vividness that can be simply breathtaking. Yellow cars can be very eye-catching, emitting a prominent radiance from display cases. Yellow is also very much a colour that befits the sports car.

Yellow Minichamps Cars
Force of YELLOW

AMG-Mercedes-Benz C 36 1993 430 032161	**Dodge Viper Cabriolet 1993** 430 144030	**Opel Kadett A Limousine 1962-65** 430 043000	**Porsche 356 A Speedster 1956** 430 065535
Ferrari 512 M 1994 430 074121	**BMW 318is 1994** 430 024300	**Porsche 911 Carrera RS 1995** 430 065100	**Ford Escort 1300L 1971** 400 081000
Ferrari F 355 1994 430 074020	**Lamborghini Miura 1966** 430 103005	**Mercedes-Benz W123 Limousine 200 D 1975-85** 430 032200	**Ferrari F 50 1995** 430 075151
Dauer Porsche 962 Street Version 430 064001	**Ferrari 550 Maranello 1996** 430 076022	**BMW 1600-2 1966-75** 430 022101	**Lamborghini Countach LP400 1974** 430 103101
Renault R8 Gordini 1964-68 430 113552	**Porsche 911 GT3 Road Car** 430 068001	**Lancia Stratos 1972-78** 430 125020	**BMW Z3 Roadster 1999** 430 028234
Karmann Ghia Coupe 1955-1959 430 005004	**VW Concept Car Cabriolet 1994** 430 054031	**Ford Capri RS 2600 1972-73** 430 085801	**Opel Rekord P1 Caravan 1958-1960** 430 043210

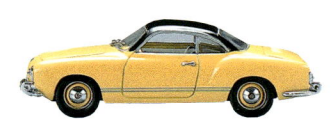

For sedans, a cream-like yellow is favoured, whereas for sports cars, a more bright and striking yellow is used. The great variety in shades of yellow can be surprising. Some 1/43-scale models have been painted yellow, but it is less easy to appreciate the full presence of a yellow car in miniature form.

Yellow – from subtle to striking

Yellow

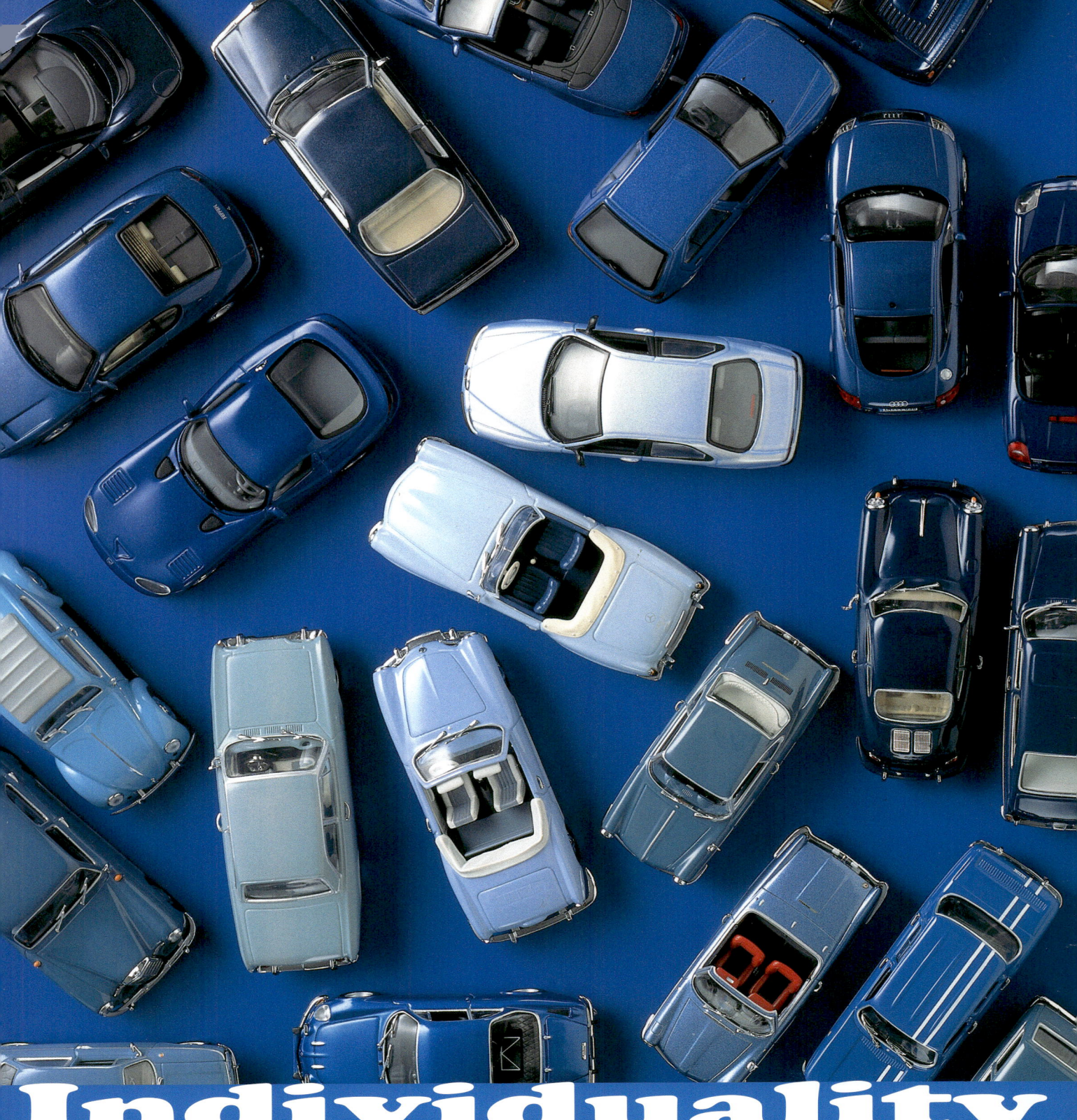

Individuality of Blue

There are also a great many shades and tones of blue. Cars with an air of individuality often come in blue. Sports cars will tend to come in a strong blue; sedans will use a more formal blue; and convertibles a more breath taking blue. Blue has many different shades and tones, with the particular variety used dependant on the preference of individual owners.

Blue Minichamps Cars
Individuality of Blue

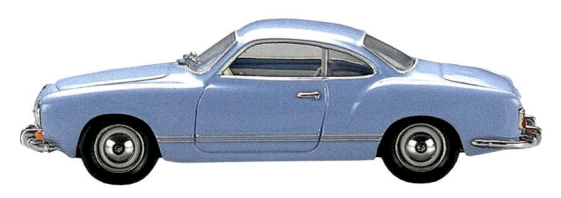

Karmann Ghia Coupe 1955
430 005001

Lamborghini 350 GT 1964
430 103200

Opel Rekord P1 Caravan 1958-1960
430 043211

NSU 1000 L 1964
430 015200

VW Beetle "split window" 1949-53
430 052002

Opel Kadett A Caravan 1962-65
430 043011

Porsche 911 1964
430 067126

Ford Taunus 1960
430 085106

Karmann Ghia Cabriolet 1964
430 005031

Mercedes-Benz SL 2001
400 031030

Mercedes-Benz W123 Break 280 TE 1975
430 032212

Renault Alpine A 110 1963-67
430 113600

Porsche 356 C Coupe 1963-65
430 062320

BMW M Roadster
80 42 9 421 763 (Dealer Version)

Peugeot 306 4 Door Saloon 1995
430 112571

Ferrari 456 GT 2+2 1992
430 072402

Jaguar XJ 220 1992
430 102220

12 MINICHAMPS

Mercedes-Benz W 123 Coupe 280 CE 1977-85	**Alfa Romeo 156 Saloon 1997**	**Renault R 8 Gordini 1964-68**	**Audi TT Coupe**
430 032222	430 120702	430 113550	433 017225 (Dealer Version)
Mercedes-Benz 190 SL Cabriolet 1955-62	**Dodge Viper Coupe 1993**	**VW Delivery Van 1963**	**Alfa Romeo Alfasud 1972**
430 033136	430 144021	430 052200	400 120100
Bugatti EB 110	**NSU Spider 1964-67**	**Porsche 911 Coupe 1993**	**VW 1600 TL Fastback 1966**
430 102110	430 019230	430 063008	430 055320

Toyota MR2 Cabriolet 2000	**Mercedes-Benz 180 1953-57**	**NSU Sport Prinz 1959-67**
430 166960	430 033102	430 019221

Ferrari F 355 SPIDER 1994	**Porsche 356 C Cabriolet 1965**
430 074033	430 062334

The colour feature section concludes here with refreshing blue. In blue, sedans appear formal, convertibles joyful, and sports cars striking – all cars achieve a different look. Blue goes particularly well with convertibles and cars with sunroofs. Blue scale models can conjure up blissful images of driving under a clear blue sky with a light breeze on your face.

Here we show 34 blue models, but there are obviously a great many more Paul's Model Art / Minichamps models in blue. Indeed, one could make a wonderful collection of blue cars alone.

The colour of fresh driving

Blue

Road Cars of MINI

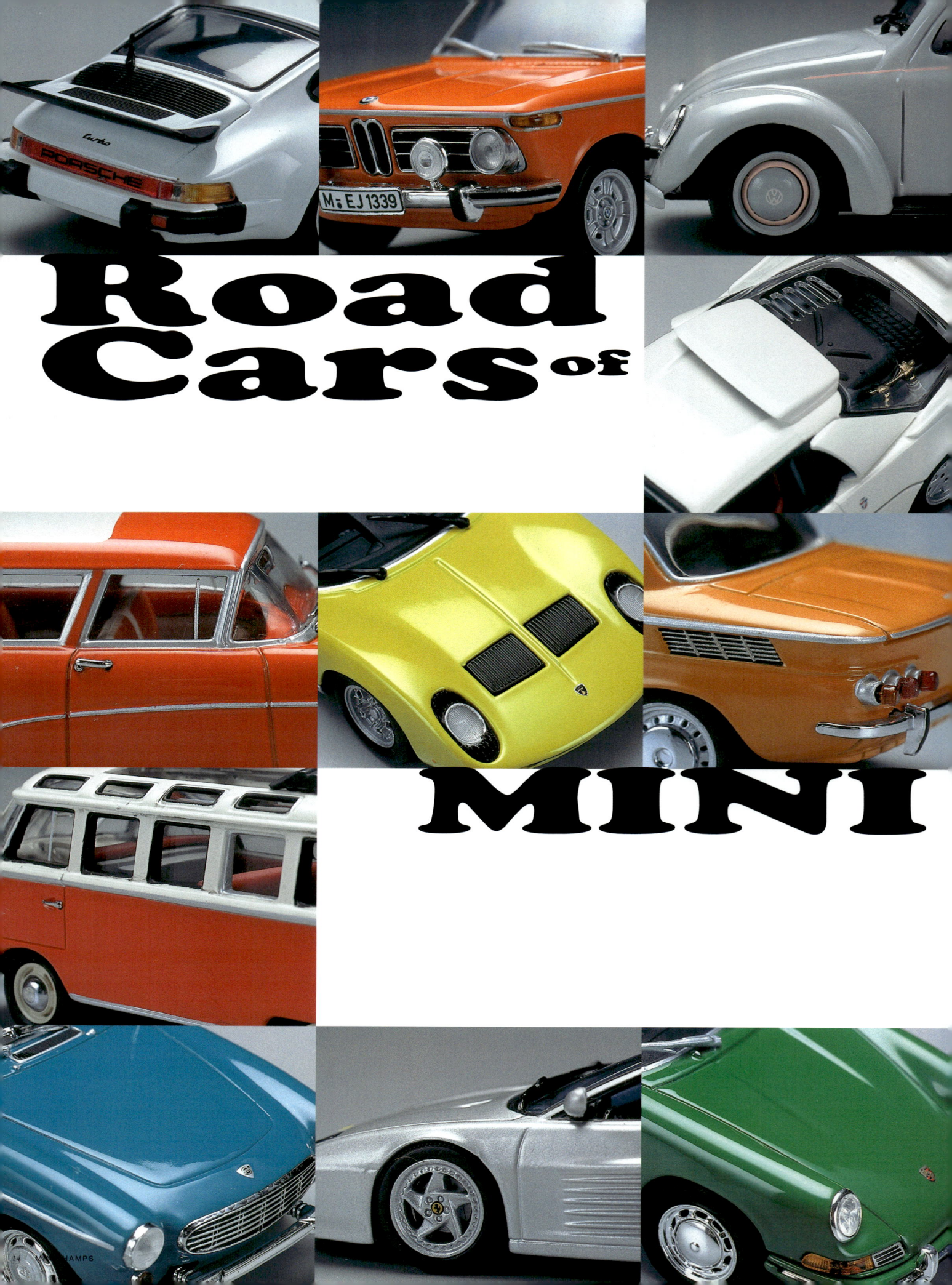

CHAMPS

The joy of collecting

Paul's Model Art / Minichamps produce many different models with many colour variations for you to collect. The joy in collecting road car models is that you can own your dream car, or several of your dream cars, in addition to owning your real car.
Let us now introduce you to the many attractive 1/43-scale road car models from Paul's Model Art / Minichamps.

Ferrari

The stampeding of the Prancing Horse.

Our hearts will always pound at the sight of the Prancing Horse emblem.
On hearing the distinctive sounds from a Ferrari exhaust either on the racetrack or the roads, minds will drift to off to the side of the track in Fiorano.
Although it may be just a dream to own an actual Ferrari, the glamorous body of the car can still be yours to hold in miniature form.

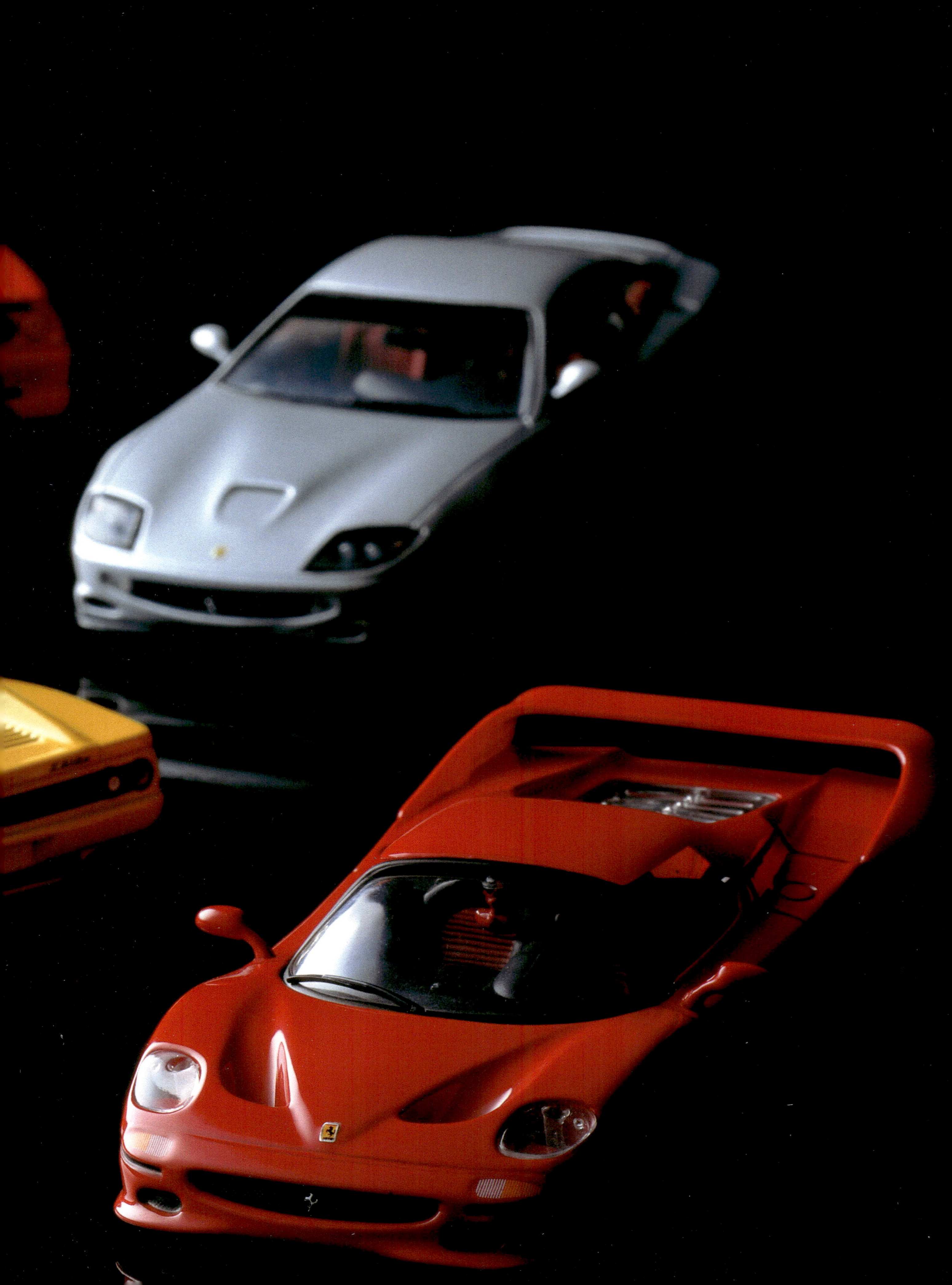

F50

The meanest looking Ferrari ever, graced with Formula 1 technology.

The F50 was initially released as an anniversary model, celebrating the 50th year of Ferrari. The latest Formula 1 technology was applied, and the F50 was to become the 'meanest' Ferrari road car yet. The engine is the 4.7l V12, with a massive 520bhp, with the same bore pitch as the F1 machine of the early 1990's. The chassis is made of a carbon Monocoque and the body is a compound of both carbon and kevlar. The engine is mounted directly to the Monocoque.

The double wishbone suspension is mounted directly atop the engine, as per the Formula 1 machine. This is proof of just how serious Ferrari's commitment to making the model was. The F50 was to be a flagship model of Ferrari, and was so popular that many manufactures made miniature models of it in the late 1990's. Of the many miniatures made, the Paul's Model Art / Minichamps version stands above the rest. The glamorous form, realistic air ducts and sharp edge of the rear spoiler are truly impressive. Note also the original centre lock wheel of F50, the traditional gear shift gate and various other detailed parts.

With the real model, you can enjoy having the roof either on or off, with the Spider or Barchetta versions. The miniature comes with a total of six variations, with both car types coming in 3 different colours.

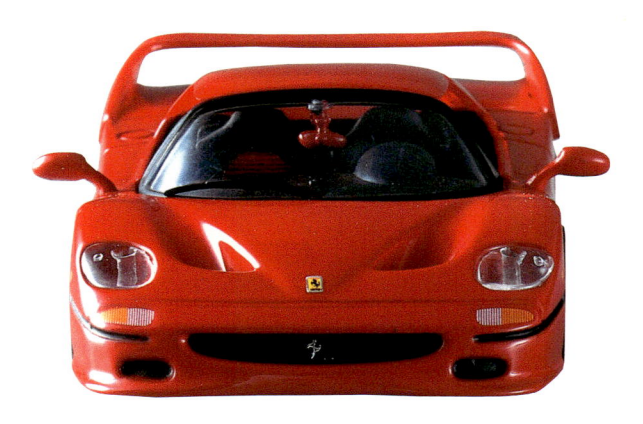

Note how close to the ground the front spoiler is, just like on the real F50. The headlights have been replicated wonderfully, and the wide tyre tread is reminiscent of F1 machines.

Sharp lines are very important in miniature models for authenticity. The Paul's Model Art / Minichamps miniatures are produced with utmost professionalism, doing justice to the F50's sharp form. The Prancing Horse emblem shines from the car's rear.

Coupe / / / / /

Ferrari F50 1995 red

430 075152

The most popular miniature model along with 512TR is the red F50. It is, however, very difficult to find in shops.

Ferrari F50 1995 yellow

430 075151

The F50 was also released in yellow, with yellow seats to match the colour of the body.

Ferrari F50 1995 silver

430 075150

The F50 was first released in silver, and this is the easiest colour in which to find the F50 in shops, however the coupe only comes in silver.

Spider / / / / /

Ferrari F50 Spider 1995 red

430 075162

The red spider was the third and final colour variation to be released in the series. The delicate details of individual parts have been captured well.

Ferrari F50 Spider 1995 yellow

430 075161

The most ostentatious F50 is this yellow Spider. Note how clearly the instrument panel can be seen.

Ferrari F50 Spider 1995 black

430 075160

The first colour that the spider was released in was black. Black can appear very aggressive, and many people prefer it to red.

Ferrari F355

A mid-engined V8 was first applied to the 308 series, and then repeated in producing the 328 series. These two series were manufactured for over ten years. The huge success was then bolstered by the 348 series with transverse transmission and Monocoque chassis.

In 1994, full-scale modifications were applied to the 348 series, resulting in the F355 series. The V8 engine had 5 valves per cylinder with titanium connecting rods, the same technology that was applied to Formula 1 machines. The 3.5l engine produces 380 bhp, over 100 bhp per litre.

The F355 is distinctive due to its curved exterior. The circular taillights, and oval shaped front grille are features traditionally associated with Ferrari.

The F355 had as many variations as the 348. The GTB has a coupe body, the GTS has a detachable roof, and the Spider is available as a convertible. Paul's Model Art / Minichamps also offer a closed top convertible version.

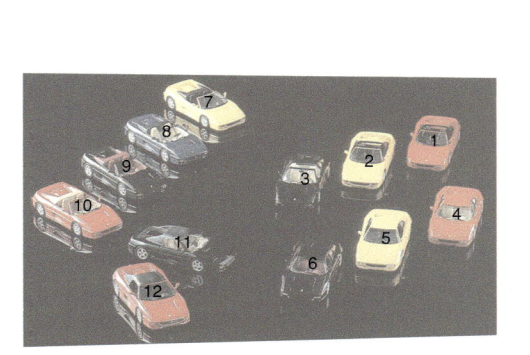

- F50
- F355
- 512TR
- 512M
- 550 Maranello
- 456GT

#	Code	Description
1.	430 074052	Ferrari F355 GTS 1994 red
2.	430 074051	Ferrari F355 GTS 1994 yellow
3.	430 074050	Ferrari F355 GTS 1994 black
4.	430 074022	Ferrari F355 GTB 1994 red
5.	430 074020	Ferrari F355 GTB 1994 yellow
6.	430 074021	Ferrari F355 GTB 1994 black
7.	430 074031	Ferrari F355 Spider 1995 yellow
8.	430 074033	Ferrari F355 Spider 1995 blue
9.	430 074030	Ferrari F355 Spider 1995 black
10.	430 074032	Ferrari F355 Spider 1995 red
11.	430 074040	Ferrari F355 Spider softtop 1995 black
12.	430 074042	Ferrari F355 Spider softtop 1995 red

F355

The Modern Super Car: mass-produced yet high-tech

The F355 was released after Luca di Montezemolo took charge of Ferrari. The car was an answer to the needs of the market, and its immense potential was realised with huge sales.

512TR

The 12-cylinder SEITOUHA

The ever-popular Testarossa was refined to become the 512TR. The V12 boxer engine originates from the 12-cylinder mid-engined model, the 365GT4BB. There are 3 colours available, including the much-favoured red. The 512TR is, however, very hard to find in red.

The car's Testarossa origins are visible from the side air intakes and accompanying fins.

The wide and glamorous rear end is very appealing. The 512TR and F512M can be distinguished by their differing tail-lights.

Ferrari 512 TR 1992 red
430 072500

Ferrari 512 TR 1992 yellow
430 072501

Ferrari 512 TR 1992 black
430 072502

512M

The last of the Boxer engines

The 512TR was later to become the 512M. Ferrari are keen to continually evolve and improve their cars. The last of the Ferrari Stradale, which is a mid-engined model, uses a V12 boxer. This model is available in silver, yellow and red, with red proving as always to be the most popular colour.

The headlights were altered to correspond with the American market. Notice even the small spoiler is replicated well in the miniature model.

The round taillights traditionally used by Ferrari were implemented on the 512M. These lights are responsible for the difference in looks between this model and the 512TR.

Ferrari 512 M 1994 red
430 074122

Ferrari 512 M 1994 yellow
430 074121

Ferrari 512 M 1994 silver
430 074120

550 Maranello

The ultimate luxury Ferrari

The 550 Maranello is the high performing front engined based Barchetta, with a 456GT based engine. The unique fixed positioned headlights are the distinctive feature of this Pininfarina designed model. Miniature models come in the traditional red as well as yellow and silver, these being the three most popular colours for Ferrari.

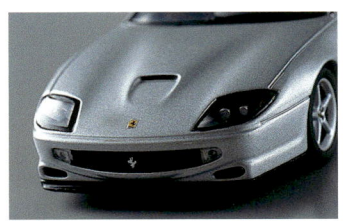

The 550's unique front mask is well captured in the miniature model, particularly if you look at the lights behind the light-covers, and also the indicators.

The steering wheel and instrument panel are captured in excellent detail.

Ferrari 550 Maranello 1996 red
430 076020

Ferrari 550 Maranello 1996 yellow
430 076022

Ferrari 550 Maranello 1996 silver
430 076021

456GT

The 12 cylinder 4 seater model

In 1992, the top end 4 seater model made its debut. It had a brand new chassis, coupled with Ferrari's traditional 12 cylinder engine. Pininfarina's design is captured well in miniature form, with the models coming in red, yellow, and dark blue.

The unique features, such as the air-ducts on the bonnet, are well crafted. It is essential for the lines of the model to be sharp to ensure authenticity.

The 456GT has plenty of boot space, and is a good car to take on a long trip. Ferrari's prancing horse emblem is noticeable here.

Ferrari 456 GT 2+2 1992 red
430 072400

Ferrari 456 GT 2+2 1992 yellow
430 072401

Ferrari 456 GT 2+2 1992 dark blue
430 072402

The Stuttgart precision machine

The air-cooled rear engine is an established characteristic of one of Germany's finest super sports cars – the Porsche. However recently, Porsche has switched to using water-cooled engines, as part of Porsche's ongoing commitment to progress.

Porsche 911 4S
Schwarz

Porsche 911 turbo
Indischrot

Porsche

The world of Turbo PART-1

911 TURBO 1977
930 Series

The leader of the super car era.

In the early 1970s, Porsche was very successful in competitive motor racing, with cars such as the 917/30 and Carrera RSR Turbo. The 911 Turbo benefited from all the technological expertise gained in motorsport. In 1973, the prototype was released in Frankfurt, and from 1975, the 930 Turbo went on sale. The newly designed 3 1itre engine was the basis of the car. With added turbocharger, the 930 Turbo had a massive 260 bhp, 50 bhp more than the 911.

The exterior was striking. Flared wing panels and a big rear spoiler made this car appear very aggressive. It was clear that this car was no ordinary 911 and its popularity soared. It was so popular, that its design was applied to some later non-turbo models. When the 930 Turbo was released, the rear spoiler was termed 'tray type', and was relatively small. But with its larger engine, an internal cooler was fitted on the new model and the rear spoiler was also made larger. These miniature models are the first series with a tray type rear spoiler. The wide rear bumper panels appear strong, and are well captured in miniature models.

In comparing the 930 Turbo and 911 Coupe, the difference is clear. There are 5 colours available, obviously including the ever-popular red. The interior design was a chequered metallic dark green and metallic light green, and was very popular.

The 930 Turbo's massive impact on the motoring world was predominantly due to its impressive performance, but the stunning appearance was also very influential in its success. The wide tyres ensure a lower centre of gravity, and the wing panels were widened to accommodate them. Large rear spoilers are another of the magnificent features of the 930 Turbo, which are represented very well in miniature form.

PORSCHE

① Porsche 911 Turbo 1977 grand prix white
430 069002

② Porsche 911 Turbo 1977 red
430 069000

③ Porsche 911 Turbo 1977 dark green metallic
430 069001

④ Porsche 911 Turbo 1977 meteor metallic
430 069004

⑤ Porsche 911 Turbo 1977 light green metallic
430 069005

The world of Turbo PART-2

911 Turbo 1990
964 Series

The new generation easy to drive turbo

When the new 964 series was released, the Turbo was initially dropped from the range. But in 1991, the Turbo was reborn. It was based on the new generation 964 and had all the sublime features of its predecessor, such as the extended wing panels and big rear spoiler, but the engine was slightly modified. The miniature model is based on the 3.3 litre model, the initial model. The metallic blue as seen in the photo is now very rare.

Porsche 911 Turbo 1990 blue metallic
430 069100

Porsche 911 Turbo 1990 turquoise metallic
430 069102

Porsche 911 Turbo 1990 green
430 069105

Porsche 911 Turbo 1990 red
430 069104

911 Turbo 1995
993 Series

The last, and ultimate, air-cooled Turbo

When the 993 series was released, the original Turbo was dropped from the production range yet again. The 993 series was the last of the air-cooled engines, released in 1995. The engine had twin turbo chargers and also 4WD. This air-cooled model was a flat 6 3.6l with two compact turbo chargers. The car was easy to handle, despite its immense 408 bhp. The 4WD system that manages this 408 bhp engine comes from the same technology applied to the 959. The multilink suspension is based on the non-turbo 993 and it was capable of high performance irrespective of road conditions. It is the ultimate high-speed cruiser. The miniature model comes in six colours, including black. Details such as the small air vent placed in the spoiler are well captured.

Compared with the 930 Turbo, it looks gentler. However the body is 60mm wider than the non-turbo 993, with both front and rear wheels being 18 inches, and the big rear spoiler.

911 Turbo 1999
996 Series

The rebirth of the traditional flat 6 Turbo

When the 996's engine became water-cooled, the Turbo engine followed suit. The car had 420 bhp and a top speed of 190 mph. The super sport had a refined 4WD system and the original AT was equipped with Tiptronic S. It was initially released in metallic red, a colour that exudes calm. There are also many air vents around the car, for enhanced cooling.

It seems every bit as aggressive as the real car, with big 18 inch wheels endowed with red callipers. However this car is slightly lower than the 996.

Porsche 911 Turbo 1999 red metallic
430 069300

Porsche 911 Turbo 1999 frosty blue
430 069302

Porsche 911 Turbo 1999 red
430 069304

Porsche 911 Turbo 1999 purple metallic
430 069305

Porsche 911 Turbo 1995 black
430 069200

Porsche 911 Turbo 1995 green metallic
430 069202

Porsche 911 Turbo 1995 riviera blue
430 069204

Porsche 911 Turbo 1995 red
430 069205

911 1964 Narrow body

The Flat 6 NA engine is the essence of Porsche

The new generation of Porsche debuted in 1964. It carried a brand new air-cooled 2l flat 6 engine. Without flared wings it was very narrow, although there were criticisms on how wide and heavy the new model was compared with the 356. Today it appears surprisingly narrow on the road.

In 1967, the Targa with detachable roof was introduced. The first series also had a detachable soft rear window, which left the roll bar bare. The miniature models replicate the very first range with short wheelbase. There is a wide range of colours available owing to popularity, with seven different colours for the coupe and two for the Targa.

① Porsche 911 1964 white
430 067120

② Porsche 911 1964 red
430 067121

③ Porsche 911 1964 conda green
430 067122

④ Porsche 911 1964 yellow
430 067124

⑤ Porsche 911 1964 blue
430 067126

⑥ Porsche 911 1964 green
430 067127

⑦ Porsche 911 1964 purple
430 067129

⑧ Porsche 911 Targa 1965 red
400 061160

⑨ Porsche 911 Targa 1965 orange
400 061161

The 911 has a unique front, which appears somewhat 'frog-like'. And given its exceptionally high performance for the time, the tyres are surprisingly narrow.

Paul's Model Art / Minichamps miniature models pay great attention to the interior as well as exterior of the cars. The replication and decoration of the instruments is remarkable.

911 Carrera RSR 1973

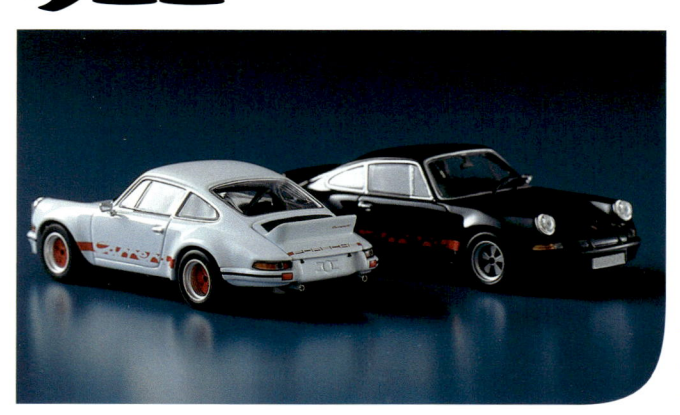

The Carrera RSR was introduced for as a group 4 homologation machine. The 2.8 litre engine was 100cc bigger than before, with a maximum output of 300 bhp. The weight was also reduced. Only 57 were made.

Porsche 911 Carrera Coupe RSR 1973 white
430 736900

Porsche 911 Carrera Coupe RSR 1973 black
430 736901

The wing panels are wider than the ones on the Carrera RS. The ducktail is a very distinctive feature.

911 Coupe 1978-88
930 Series

In order meet American safety standards, the new 911 (930series) was introduced, known as "big bumper". Many people consider this the archetypical 911. A 3 litre engine was fitted. The miniature models are the middle series 911SC, and they come in red, white and black.

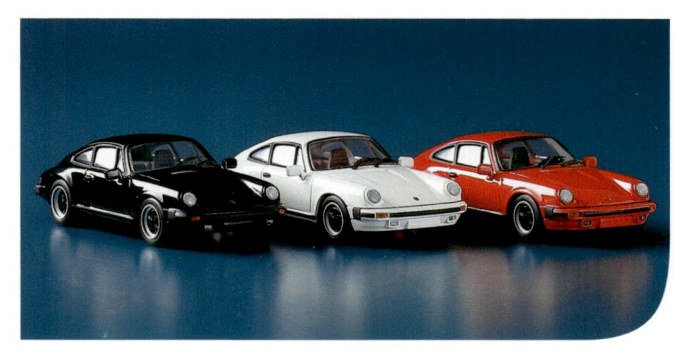

Porsche 911 Coupe 1978-88 red
430 062020

Porsche 911 Coupe 1978-88 black
430 062022

Porsche 911 Coupe 1978-88 white
430 062021

The unique "frog looking" front is unchanged. The big bumper, brought in for safety reasons, is well replicated.

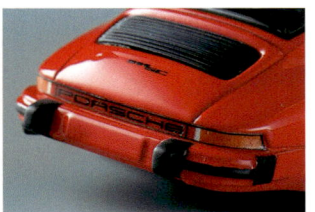

The rear decoration was a new feature of the 930. This design was used in many other cars. Maybe your car even has the same design!

911 Carrera 2/4 1992
964 Series

The 911was manufactured for 25 years without major changes. In 1989, the 964 series was released. It looks much the same, however, 85% of the parts are in fact newly designed. The traditional RS model, as well as the 4WD Carrera 4, were part of this range.

In 1992 the model was miniaturised. As with the real car, the miniatures are equipped with replication 17 inch cup design wheels and newly designed wing mirrors. They are available in yellow, anthracite, and metallic violet.

Porsche 911 Carrera 2/4 1992 yellow

430 062120

Without changing 911's image, a smooth rear bumper was fitted. This improved aerodynamics.

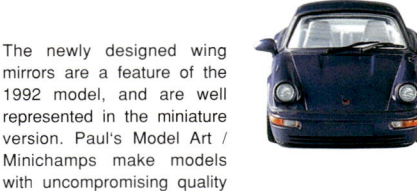

The newly designed wing mirrors are a feature of the 1992 model, and are well represented in the miniature version. Paul's Model Art / Minichamps make models with uncompromising quality and style.

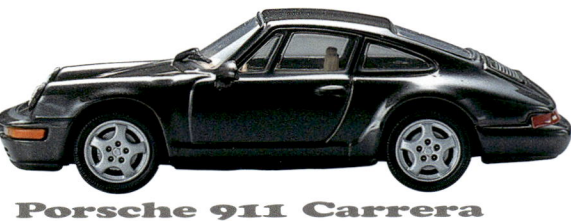

On the real cars, the rear spoiler pops out when the car exceeds 50 mph. On the miniature models, the rear spoiler pops out when the rear wheels are spun!

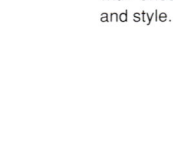

Porsche 911 Carrera 2/4 1992 anthracite

430 062121

Porsche 911 Carrera 2/4 1992 violet metallic

430 062122

Porsche 996 Series

The latest Porsche with comfort and speed

Since the advent of the 996, engines are now water-cooled. Since the introduction of the coupe model, several other variations have been added to the range. The GT3, the earliest model in the range, shared the same headlights as the Boxster. Other miniature models in the range are based on the most recent model, but with a slightly different front. The headlights are the same design as the Turbo.

Porsche 911
2001 grey metallic

400 061020

This is the 996's basic coupe model. Initially, the miniature car was released in grey, but in late 2002 metallic blue was added.

Porsche 911 4S
2001 black

400 061070

The wheels and spoilers on the 4WD Carrera 4S model are different to those of the basic coupe model, which was also later released in yellow.

Porsche GT3
1999 speed yellow

430 068001

The GT3 came in 5 colours, including silver and gold. A speed yellow GT3 was also later added.

430 068000 silver
430 068002 sauber blue
430 068004 black metallic
430 068005 green
430 068006 gold

Porsche GT2 Coupe
2001 red

430 060120

The GT2 came in 5 colours, including silver and gold. A speed yellow GT2 was also later added.

Porsche 911 1993 993 Series

There are many variations of the Porsche core models

The last series with air-cooled engine, the 993 series, has a very powerful engine and multi-link rear suspension, which enables the car to be rigorously driven at breath-taking speeds. The design is completely new, but from all angles it still looks like a 911. Only the bonnet and roofline are the same as other models prior to the 964 series.

There are many variations in the 993 series and almost all of them are present in the miniature model range. In the coupe range, the most striking model is the mint green one, which is a very suitable colour for the 993.

1. Porsche 993 Coupe 1993 black
   430 063000
2. Porsche 911 Coupe 1993 blue
   430 063008
3. Porsche 911 Coupe 1993 red
   430 063007
4. Porsche 911 Coupe 1993 mint green
   430 063002

Other than the models listed above, the metallic red coupe (serial No.063001) and Porsche authorized dealer model (in metallic blue) are on the market.

The rear end is bigger than on models prior to the 964 series. The rear spoiler, which pops out dependent on speed, is fitted to the miniature just as it is on the real car.

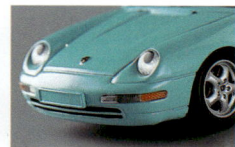

Rimless headlights can change a car's appearance. All new headlights on the miniatures have the lens cut just like the real car, with great precision.

911 GT2 1995

Compared to the normal 993, the GT2's blister bumpers and big rear spoiler make quite an impression. The GT2, true to its name, was made for GT2 class racing. The 993 Turbo has 4WD, but the GT2 uses 2WD to reduce weight. The engine was re-tuned to give a maximum output of 430bhp.

The miniature model comes in three colours. The bulging wings and rear spoiler have been replicated to a great degree of accuracy. Indeed there are many racing models, and it can be fun to line them up in comparison with one another.

Porsche 911 GT2 Street 1995 white
430 065000

Porsche 911 GT2 Street 1995 blue
430 065001

Porsche 911 GT2 Street 1995 red
430 065002

Huge spoilers symbolise high performance

When you see the car from the front, the rear wheel arch panels really stand out. The aggressive front of the car also appears unbelievably realistic on the miniature model.

The silver model with high rear spoiler is the Carrera RS, not the GT2. This is the original model by Kyosho that captured the real car spectacularly.

On the GT2, in order to match the wide wings, the front bumper is different from that of the normal 911. When you look at both cars, you can notice the difference.

The large rear spoiler is used to keep the car's immense power weighted to the roads. The bucket seats inside are well replicated in the miniature model.

Porsche minichamps ROADCARS 911 Series
- 996 Series
- 993 Series
- GT2
- Carrera RS

Porsche

34 MINICHAMPS

911 Carrera RS 1995

The lightweight street weapon

This model takes the traditional name "Carrera RS". All the luxury measures such as air-conditioning are eliminated in pursuit of weight reduction. The suspension is much stiffer than that of the previous model in pursuit of lighter footwork. The colour of the body and interior bucket seats are coordinated. The drilled disc brakes behind the 18inch wheel spokes look particularly realistic. Other than the three colours displayed on the left, there is also a silver model available (only sold in Japan with a high spoiler).

Porsche 911 Carrera RS 1995 yellow
430 065100

The European version of the 911RS has a small rear spoiler fitted, seen on the miniature model.

Compared with the GT2, the front spoiler on the miniature model looks less aggressive, just as it does on the real car.

Porsche 911 Carrera RS 1995 black
430 065101

Porsche 911 Carrera RS 1995 red
430 065102

Pure racing machine takes on road

Dauer 962 GT Street

Porsche's Le Mans winning 962C has since had a road version released. The bodyline is slightly different from that of the original 962C and it is captured well on the miniature models. Although it is becoming rare, you can still find them on the market.

Porsche Dauer 962 GT Street yellow
430 064001

Open to the Air PART 1
Porsche Convertible

When you drive a convertible, you can feel the wind in your face, and really notice the changing seasons. There are lots of people who prefer sports cars to be convertibles. There are many open-top models, such as Porsche's original detachable roof Targa, the convertible Cabriolet, and the lightweight Speedster. Almost all the Porsche open-top models sold on the market today are produced by Paul's Model Art / Minichamps. They are so attractive that collecting them can become a passion. With open-top models, you can see the interior much better than you can with a coupe. We look forward to seeing 944 and 968 convertibles with front engine layout.

911 Targa 1977

It feels like a convertible...
The new sensation, the Targa

With a rigid body structure yet also the comfort of an open-top, the essence of both types of sports car are present. The miniature models come with a detached roof. The sun-visors are replicated very realistically here. The Targa's large and round rear window is more noticeable when compared to the normal coupe.

Porsche 911 Targa 1977 Green metallic

400 061261

Porsche 911 Targa 1977 Blue

400 061260

The revival of the Porsche convertible, after an 18-year absence

911 Cabriolet 1983

This was the first Porsche convertible released since the 356C Cabriolet. The miniature models are based on the 1983 model, the 911SC Cabriolet, which had a production life of only one year.

Porsche 911 Cabriolet 1983 white
430 062030

Porsche 911 Cabriolet 1983 red
430 062031

Porsche 911 Cabriolet 1983 blue metallic
430 062032

911 Speedster 1988

The last model with the 930 body was the 2 seater lightweight convertible, the Speedster. There was a model with a Turbo-like appearance, however the miniature model is based on the normal Speedster.

Porsche 911 Speedster 1988 red
430 066130

The distinctive tonneau cover is captured well. This comes only in red.

The steeply angled front window is much lower than that of the Cabriolet

This attractive convertible was the most luxurious sports car of the time

356 C Cabriolet & 356 A Speedster

Apart from the lower front window and the bonnet, there are many other distinctive features of the Speedster in comparison to the 356A. The simple bumper structure without bumper overriders and set of 4 rear lights are examples of this. Note how realistic the painted wheels with metallic platecaps look.

The speedster, a popular model in the USA, has a simple hood structure. It comes in 5 colours, however black is very rare.

356 A Speedster **1956** black
430 065530

These are the very latest models of the 356C Cabriolet. Although they appear to be the same as the 356 convertible, some of the detaile parts differs.

356 C Cabriolet **1963-65** silver
430 062330

356 A Speedster **1956** red
430 065532

356 A Speedster **1956** willow green
430 065534

356 C Cabriolet **1963-65** red
430 062332

356 C Cabriolet **1963-65** blue
430 062334

356 A Speedster **1956** yellow
430 065535

356 A Speedster **1956** terracotta
430 065536

356 C Cabriolet **1963-65** black
430 062335

356 C Cabriolet **1963-65** blue
430 062336

Porsche Open to the Air PART-2
Open-top Porsche Part 2

911 Targa 964 Series

The traditional Targa style was carried over to the 964 series.

The Targa was on general release at the time of the Carrera 2's debut. The miniature models capture the image of the Targa as it was seen in the first series: distinctive square wing-mirrors and 7-hole alloy wheels.

Porsche 911 Targa 1990 black
400 061360

Porsche 911 Targa 1990 turquoise
400 061361

911 Targa & Cabriolet 993 Series

The glass-top Targa offers both comfort and the apparent freedom of an open-top

The 993 series Targa had a new electric powered glass top. The wheels are notably exclusive to the Targa. The ever-popular Cabriolet miniature model is now available too. The detail of the miniature is quite remarkable, even down to the windscreen wiper.

Porsche 911 Targa 1995 blue
Dealer Model

430 063061 red
430 063062 black metallic

Porsche 911 Cabriolet arena red
430 063034
430 063030 silver
430 063031 black
430 063032 red

Boxster

Proto

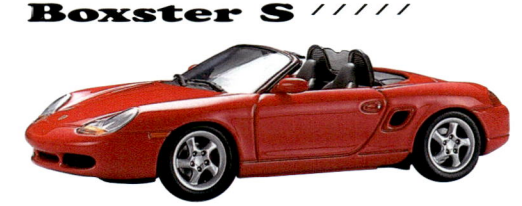

A rear-engined convertible that symbolises the new generation of Porsche

The miniature models here are the prototype that was unveiled in 1993 at Detroit motor show, and the high performing Boxster S. Although they may look much the same, you can notice the differences in detail if you look closely.

Boxster S

Porsche Boxster S 1999 blue
430 068034

Porsche Boxster S 1999 red
430 068032
430 068030 silver
430 068031 Ocean Blue metallic

Porsche Boxster 1993 red
430 063132

Porsche Boxster 1993 dark blue metallic
430 063131

Porsche Boxster 1993 silver
430 063130

38 MINICHAMPS

Carrera GT

A direct descendent of a racing machine – the secret weapon waiting for its debut

At the Paris motor show in 2000, the Carrera GT was released. This all-new super sports machine had an all-aluminium V10 engine with 558bhp. The engine was mid-positioned on the carbon chassis.

It is said to have much high-tech equipment in the cockpit. There is still time, however, before we will realise the full extent of the design of the car that will be sold.

At the moment, only black is being sold.

Porsche Carrera GT 2000 black
430 060230

Under the holed mesh is fitted the V10 engine, with a huge 558bhp. At present, it is only available in black.

911 Targa & Cabriolet
996 Series

The convertible version of the current 911

As soon as the Targa was released on the market, so was its miniature counterpart. The Cabriolet is of course an open-top model. The soft top is neatly folded and discreetly hidden, especially in comparison with the 993. The elegant rear is particularly attractive.

When you look closely at the interior, there are two dogs seated in the car. They are the pet dogs of Mr & Mrs. Lang, the president of Paul's Model Art / Minichamps. They are visible because the miniature model is a Cabriolet.

Porsche 911 Cabriolet 2001 blue metallic
400 061030

Porsche 911 Convertible with Dogs (Chicco&Kommadu) black
400 061031

Porsche 911 Targa 2001 black
400 061061

400 061060 red

39

Indulging into Old Porsche
Indulge into the older Porsche models and styles

356 C Coupe

The flat 4 is still a refreshing and invigorating drive

Professor Porsche's first production model was the 356. Although the prototype was a roadster with a mid-positioned engine, the production model had a rear layout with a flat 4 engine. The 356 began production, assembled by hand, from 1948, and continued until 1965. Several changes were made during the course of its production. This basic miniature coupe is the 356C. Although all the models are all called 356, the bodylines are different according to the model's production year, and this is even noticeable with the miniature models. They are available in 5 different colours, all of which are not difficult to find

When comparing this model with the 356A, shown on previous pages, one can notice that the body sculpting around the headlights is slightly different.

The rear of the car is rather cute. The plated stainless steel parts add to an overall air of quality.

Porsche 356 C Coupe 1963-65 dark blue
430 062320

Porsche 356 C Coupe 1963-65 silver
430 062321

Porsche 356 C Coupe 1963-65 red
430 062322

Porsche 356 C Coupe 1963-65 grey
430 062324

Porsche 356 C Coupe 1963-65 ivory
430 062325

356 Carrera 2

The super high performance sports car from 40 years ago

The Carrera 2 is the monster 356 with the reduced body weight of the 356B and the RS 61 engine, a pure racing engine. It is available in red and black. The black version comes with wheel caps, but the red does not. Such intricate little differences are part of the joys of collecting.

Porsche 356 Carrera 2 1963-64 red
430 062362

Porsche 356 Carrera 2 1963-64 black
430 062361

914

The product of a collaboration with VW – the lightweight mid-engined 2-seater

Using VW parts, a less expensive mid-engined sports car, the 914, was released. The miniature model has the VW flat 4 engine, but there was also a real model carrying the 911's flat 6, the 914/6. There are both convertible and hard-top models available, coming in seven different colours.

Porsche914 1969-73 lemon yellow
430 065660

Porsche914 1969-73 orange
430 065661

Porsche914 1969-73 conda green
430 065662

Porsche914 1969-73 silver metallic
430 065664

Porsche914 1969-73 red
430 065665

Porsche914 1969-73 black
430 065666

Porsche914 Hardtop 1969-73 blue metallic
430 065650

A rich history coupled with detailed craftsmanship, exemplifying the German tradition.

Mercedes-Benz is a leader in its field given its reputation for high-performance, attention to comfort, and a strong brand image. With its powerful legacy and pioneering technological innovation, Mercedes-Benz will remain a prominent manufacturer.

Mercedes

-Benz

Super Mercedes

Mercedes-Benz 500E Series

The V8 sedan with a touch of Porsche - the quintessential highway cruiser

At first glance, it appears to be an ordinary sedan. It is, however, produced in Porsche's factory and carries the same V8 engine used in the 500SL, the 'King of the Autobahn'. Indeed the miniature models are just as popular as the real car. The bumper panels and 4-seat interior are particularly well captured in the miniature models.

The difference between the normal W124 (left) and 500E (right) is more noticeable when you look at the bumper panels.

Mercedes-Benz 500E V8 Saloon black
430 003240

Mercedes-Benz 500E V8 Saloon anthracite metallic
430 003241

44 MINICHAMPS

Mercedes-Benz
Evolution 1&2

The racing machine of public roads is the cornerstone of DTM

In the 190 series came the 190E 2.5-16V carrying a Cosworth tuned engine. The Evolution 1 & 2 models were sold as homologation models before competing in and winning the DTM championship

These miniature models are one of the earliest models made by Paul's Model Art / Minichamps. The mean looking spoilers are very unique. Compared to more recent productions, the appearance may seem slightly less sleek. But they are still very rare to come by. It is available in metallic grey, metallic black, and red.

Mercedes-Benz 190E Evo1 1990 signal red

430 R03000

Mercedes-Benz 190E Evo2 red

430 R03100

1. Mercedes-Benz W123 Police Break
   430 032291
2. Mercedes-Benz W123 Police Saloon
   430 032290
3. Mercedes-Benz W123 Taxi
   430 032295
4. Mercedes-Benz W123 Taxi Break
   430 032296

W123 Break 200T red

430 032210

Mercedes-Benz Yesterday & Today

From Maybach to CL

Carl Benz and Gottlieb Daimler, two great innovators of the automobile industry, founded Mercedes-Benz, and the company maintains its

Luxurious Mercedes

Mercedes-Benz 560 Series

1980 saw the full-size sedan S-class W126 series become the new generation of motor vehicle. Despite being 2 generations old, its existence on the roads is still special. The miniature model shows the long wheelbase of the 560SEL's final version. It has a striking presence that makes quite a statement. The miniature model captures the original magnificently, and there are many colour variations to choose from.

A steering wheel with large diameter is a reputed characteristic of Mercedes-Benz, and the mouldings around the door handles are recreated in delicate detail.

560 SEL 1989-91 anthracite
430 039300

560 SEL 1989-91 petrol metallic
430 039301

560 SEL 1989-91 blue metallic
430 039302

560 SEL 1989-91 black
430 039304

560 SEL 1989-91 silver
B6 604 0244 (Dealer Version)

560 SEL 1989-91 dark blue
B6 604 0245 (Dealer Version)

600 SEC

The cyber coupe rich with cutting-edge technology

The 600SEC is a full size personal coupe. Notice the distinctive shape of the headlights. As it was at the top of the Mercedes-Benz range, the very best safety features and much new technology were applied. The "V12" emblem on the C-pillar indicates that this is a 600SEC.

600 SEC 1992 black
430 032600

600 SEC 1992 malachit green
430 032601

600 SEC 1992 smoke silver
430 032602

W124 Series

A middle class saloon known for its superior finish

Still popular, the W124's unique body sculptings are fully covered in this range. On this page is the final model of the E-class, but there are also earlier models. With some of the miniature models, you can open the bonnet and see the engine, and also open the boot. There are many variations for you to enjoy.

E-Class 1994 blue black metallic
430 033500

E-Class Coupe 1994 bormite
430 033522

E-Class Break 1992-96 blue black metallic
430 033540

E-Class Break 1992-96 blue metallic
430 033541

E-Class Break 1992-96 green
430 033542

E-Class Cabriolet 1994 blue metallic
430 033531

E-Class Cabriolet 1994 rose wood
430 033532

E-Class 1994 blue metallic
430 033501

E-Class 1994 imperial red
430 033502

450 Series

The flagship model blessed with great speed and luxurious comfort

All of the S-class miniature models are based on the SEL long wheelbase version. The Super saloon 450SEL6.9 is also available. The 450SLC is based on the SL with a longer wheelbase to comfortably accommodate 4 passengers.

450 SEL gold metallic
B6 604 0247 (Dealer Version)

450 SEL 6.9 1972-79 silver
430 039200

450 SEL 6.9 1972-79 smoke silver
430 039201

450 SEL 6.9 1972-79 silver green metallic
430 039202

450 SEL black
B6 604 0246 (Dealer Version)

450 SLC 1972-80 silver
430 033420

450 SLC 1972-80 green metallic
430 033421

450 SLC 1972-80 gold
430 033422

Stylish Mercedes

Mercedes-Benz 190SL Series

The roadster so loved in America

190 SL Cabriolet 1955-62 silver
430 033131

190 SL Cabriolet 1955-62 red
430 033132

190 SL Cabriolet 1955-62 black
430 033134

280SL Series

A mid range sports car with 3 variations

The 280SL was the successor to the 190SL, with its more modern design. The miniature models are convertible, soft-top and hard-top. Given the high demand, they are sadly already of limited availability.

The colours of the body and the interior have been co-ordinated, and the steering wheel has a design peculiar to the era.

280 SL Pagode 1968-71 gold
430 032250

280 SL Pagode 1968-71 white
430 032251

280 SL Pagode 1968-71 red
430 032252

280 SL Soft-Top 1968-71 red
430 032241

280 SL Cabriolet 1968-71 red
430 032231

280 SL Cabriolet 1968-71 dark blue
430 032232

280 SL Cabriolet 1968-71 light blue
430 032234

280 SL Cabriolet 1968-71 white
B6 604 0117 (Dealer Version)

MINICHAMPS

350SL Series
An enduring model which lasted 19 years

This SL series began in 1971 with the 350SL and continued up until the 560 SL of 1989. During its 19 years of existence, minor changes were frequently made.

The cars are still visible on the roads today, and Paul's Model Art / Minichamps make miniature models of the early models in the series in each of the convertible, soft-top and hard-top formats. It is rather difficult to produce and acquire all the many variations owing to their numeracy, especially if one includes the 450SLC and dealer versions.

Hard-Top

Mercedes-Benz 350 SL Cabriolet Hard-Top 1971-80 silver
430 033450

Mercedes-Benz 350 SL Cabriolet Hard-Top 1971-80 red
430 033452

Mercedes-Benz 350 SL Cabriolet Hard-Top 1971-80 brown metallic
B6 604 0185 (Dealer Version)

Soft-Top

Mercedes-Benz 350 SL Cabriolet Soft-Top 1971-80 white
430 033440

Mercedes-Benz 350 SL Cabriolet Soft-Top 1971-80 green metallic
430 033441

Mercedes-Benz 350 SL Cabriolet Soft-Top 1971-80 red
430 033442

Cabriolet

Mercedes-Benz 350 SL Cabriolet 1971-80 silver
430 033430

Mercedes-Benz 350 SL Cabriolet 1971-80 dark blue
430 033431

Mercedes-Benz 350 SL Cabriolet 1971-80 red
430 033432

The superiority of the C-class is based on the 190 series

The 190 series compact saloon typifies the renowned Mercedes-Benz quality, and was a great success world-wide. The miniature model made by Paul's Model Art / Minichamps is based on a Cosworth tuned 190E2.3 16V. Although the car has spoilers for better aerodynamics, they are subtle nevertheless. This is a very popular model and very difficult to find in today's market. The body colour comes only in metallic black.

Mercedes-Benz 190E 2.3-16 1984
blue black metallic
430 035600

Modern Mercedes

CL Coupe

A stylish highway cruiser

The most luxurious personal coupe of today is this CL. The latest 600SL carries a V12 twin turbo engine that produces an extravagant 500 PS! Needless to say, cutting edge technology is found everywhere in this car. The unique front mask and roofline of the miniature model mirrors that of the real car.

Mercedes-Benz CL Coupe 1999 grey metallic
430 038020

Mercedes-Benz CL Coupe 1999 dark blue metallic
430 038021

Mercedes-Benz CL Coupe 1999 black metallic
430 038022

Mercedes-Benz CL Coupe 1999 brilliant silver
430 038024

Mercedes-Benz CL Coupe 1999 blue metallic
430 038025

Mercedes-Benz CL Coupe 1999 purple metallic
B6 696 0301 (Dealer Version)

Smart

The city commuter car of the future available today

The Smart is only 2.5m long and its really compact body is filled with Mercedes-Benz technology. With the Cabriolet, you can enjoy the choice of 3 styles, and in miniature model, it also comes with an open body. The miniature model is as cute as the real car. The attractive colours of the body and interior respectively inspire one to collect these models.

Smart Cabrio 2000 silver/blue
430 039000

Smart Cabrio 2000 dark grey/silver
430 039001

Smart Cabrio 2000 yellow
430 039002

Smart Cabrio 2000 light white
430 039004

Smart Cabrio 2000 green
430 039005

Smart Cabrio 2000 black
430 039006

C-Class

The most popular model in Japan, the C-class, expanding the great name of Mercedes-Benz

The 190 series, a compact Mercedes-Benz, became the new C-class. Its relatively compact body and high quality production were widely welcomed by Japanese consumers and soon became a best seller. The first C-class came in both sedan and station wagon (T model) formats. The current C-class has sedan, station wagon and compact sports coupe versions. The miniature model of the sedan is awaiting imminent release.

The sculpture of the Paul's Model Art / Minichamps model is very accurate, with great care being taken in capturing every detail.

Mercedes-Benz C-Class Sports Coupe
brilliant silver metallic
B6 696 1916 (Dealer Version)

Mercedes-Benz C-Class T-model
brilliant silver metallic
B6 696 1919 (Dealer Version)

Mercedes-Benz C-Class T-model 2001 black
430 030110

Mercedes-Benz C-Class T-model blue
B6 600 5724 (Dealer Version)

Mercedes-Benz C200 T-model
green metallic
B6 600 5746 (Dealer Version)

C36

A fast and furious small machine tuned by AMG

AMG, now officially a partner of Mercedes-Benz, tuned up a C-class sedan and made the C36. It is perhaps not as striking as the ordinary sports car, but the body is subtly graced by spoilers and benefits from large wheels. The body of the car comes in three colours but metallic silver and metallic black are harder to find in miniature cars, owing to their popularity – as is the case with real cars.

1. Mercedes-Benz C36 AMG 1993 blue black metallic
   430 032160

2. Mercedes-Benz C36 AMG 1993 yellow
   430 032161

3. Mercedes-Benz C36 AMG 1993 silver
   430 032162

Captures the spirit and technology of Bayern

In the cross-shaped BMW emblem, blue signifies the sky, white signifies propeller blades to show that BMW began as an aircraft engine manufacturer. BMW cars are characterised by the strong body form and reliable power unit. Once you put your foot down on the accelerator, surrounding views of the world can literally be swept away.

BMW

M's Legend

BMW has always been involved in motor sport. In 1972, BMW founded a subsidiary company named BMW M GmbH in order to meet the demand for racing engines and various other parts for racing drivers and teams. A BMW machine sporting an "M" emblem indicates that BMW M GmbH tuned it.
The same body as the normal 3 series, 6 series and so forth are used, with the technological knowledge obtained from competitive racing applied to the engine. This is especially the case with the M3, a car based on the 3 series that has competed in many races. The M3 is very popular today. Paul's Model Art / Minichamps makes miniature models of all M3s. Here we shall take a look at them.

M3 Street E30

Born to win
The Touring Car Championship

The first M3, the E30, was built in order to compete in Group A races. The straight 4 engine was based on the F2 machine. Paul's Model Art / Minichamps has twice released miniature models of the E30. The first occasion was when Paul's Model Art / Minichamps first began. It was an M3 based homologation model, the M3 Sport Evolution. The second time was in 2002 when the normal M3 was released. The difference in exterior is the larger rear wing and bigger wheels. Photos above right are the Evolution model, and below the normal model. Notice and enjoy the differences between the two models.

BMW M3 Street 1990 black metallic
430 B02000

BMW M3 Street 1990 white
430 W02000
430 R02000 red

BMW M3 E30 black
430 020300

BMW M3 E30 red
80 42 0 149 841 (Dealer Version)

M3 Street & GTR
E36

The best seller that announced the M3's potential to the world

The E36 based M3 was fundamentally different from E30 by virtue of it being built for road use rather than the race circuit. It carried BMW's favourite straight 6 engine. The miniature models are made in great detail; the wing mirrors and wheels look exceptionally real. The M3 GTR was released as a racing model. Its appearance is unique, notably the wide bumper panels and a large rear wing. The road version is very popular and hence in shorter supply today.

BMW M3 GTR 1993 Street Version white
430 023380

BMW M3 GTR 1993 Street Version black
430 023381

BMW M3 GTR 1993 Street Version red
430 023382

BMW M3 Coupe 1992 black metallic
430 022301

BMW M3 Coupe 1992 mugello red
430 022300

430 022302 Daytona violet 430 022303 Avus blue
430 022304 Dakar yellow

M3 Coupe & Cabriolet
E46

The matured high-performance 'M'

The new M3 came out based on the same concept as the M36, yet more luxurious and faster. With this miniature model, you can open the bonnet and see the well-replicated straight 6 engine inside. Along with coupe, the M3 cabriolet was also released. As it is a very popular model, more variations are likely to follow in the near future.

BMW M3 Coupe 2000 black
431 020020

431 020021 yellow

BMW M3 Coupe Ltd.Edition Japan
80 42 0 137 691 (Dealer Version)

BMW M3 Cabriolet 2001 red
431 020030

431 020031 blue metallic

BMW M3 GT 2001 50 Jahre BMW Hanko
80 42 0 151 436
(Dealer Version)

The M3 GTR is the racing machine with a V8 engine. The colour of this model is available by special order and a limited number of only 750 were produced.

The Japanese original M3 model

The internet store, "Omoshirobuhinsouko", is selling two versions of specially ordered M3's. The body colours are Alaska blue and Dakar yellow. The popular Alaska blue has a black interior. The Dakar yellow is a revived and improved dealer version. A limited number of only 1008 pcs are to be sold for both models. The photos shown left are prototypes and minor changes may be made when they come out in the market.
http://gazoo.com//shopping/omoshiro

The Beginning of BMW

BMW had been building engines for aircrafts, but also had developed advanced technology in building automobiles. However, after the Second World War, Germany was divided and they were subsequently restricted to only building automobiles. In addition, the Allied Forces had confiscated all the machinery and blue prints for aircraft engines.

But the strong passion of engineers revitalized BMW. The great resurgence is shown by the fact that BMW is now one of the most prestigious automobile manufacturers in the world. Let us look at some of the models that came out after the war, from the 1950's to 1970's.

502 V8

The multi-cylinder model that shocked the public

A V8 saloon, the 502 was released in the luxury car market stating BMW's dignity in revival. The design was based on the 326 with its elegant curves and graceful presence. It was nicknamed 'The Baroque Angel.'

BMW 502 V8 Limousine 1954-61 white
430 022400

BMW 502 V8 Limousine 1954-61 black
430 022401

BMW 502 V8 Limousine 1954-61 dark red
430 022402

2000 Tii Touring

A significant step towards the middle saloon

The 2002 series was popular for its compact size and vibrant performance. The touring version, based on the 2002 series, has a spacious cabin and a rear hatch door for easy access.

Paul's Model Art / Minichamps made the miniature model of the higher-class 2000tii. The bright orange colour and athletic design of the rear is quite unique.

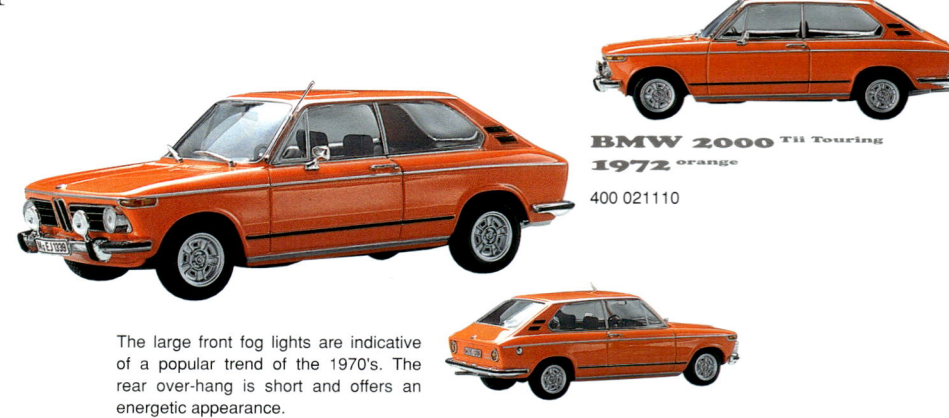

BMW 2000 Tii Touring 1972 orange
400 021110

The large front fog lights are indicative of a popular trend of the 1970's. The rear over-hang is short and offers an energetic appearance.

1600/2

The best pre-empting the success of the 2002 series

The 1600/2 coupe made its debut as a successor to the 700 series following a trend of BMW's continuous success in producing compact saloons. Like the previous model, it was a lightweight vehicle with 1.6 litre straight 4 engine. After several changes, the 2002 series was released.

Paul's Model Art / Minichamps released the very first set of the 1600/2 in orange, yellow, light green, and white. The white was the most recent addition to the collection.

1. BMW 1600/2 Saloon 1966-75 orange
   430 022100
2. BMW 1600/2 Saloon 1966-75 yellow
   430 022101
3. BMW 1600/2 Saloon 1966-75 light green
   430 022102
4. BMW 1600/2 Saloon 1966-75 white
   430 022104

700LS

The compact saloon that guided BMW out of crisis

The 700 series saved BMW from its financial crisis after the failure of the 502. Amazingly, this lightweight car carried the engine from a BMW motorbike, the R69.

The miniature model is based on the long wheelbase version, the 700LS. The colours of the car's body came in metallic anthracite, cream and silver. These colours are very rare today.

BMW 700LS Saloon 1960-61 anthracite metallic
430 023700

BMW 700LS Saloon 1960-61 cream
430 023701

BMW 700LS Saloon 1960-61 silver
430 023702

Comfortable BMW
A representative of German high quality

BMW gained popularity and grew from a producer of the compact saloon to the field of large luxury saloons, despite once failing. Today there are many variations, of which some are rather unique. We shall now look at some of the newer models.

7 Series

The best and most recent model - BMW's flagship

The latest 7 series is the flagship model of BMW, rich with high-tech equipment, bringing a new perspective to driving. In the miniature model, the newly designed headlights and luxurious interior is well captured. Under the bonnet, the engine can be seen.

BMW 740i
2001 green
431 020201

E1

The electric vehicle that promised to play a major roll in the near future

The electric vehicle, with a body 3.5m in length came in 1991 carrying a motor. It was expected and hoped to be released in the market as a city commuter car. They are not found on the roads today, but they can be seen and enjoyed as miniature models.

BMW E1
1993 red
430 023002

BMW E1
1993 mystic grey metallic
430 023006

X5

BMW's luxurious 4WD off-roader

In the era of the SUV, BMW's answer was the X5. Although it is an off-roader, it has a very high level of driving performance both on the road and off. New miniature models, such as this one, have engines under the hoods. It would be fun to line up the X5 next to the Porsche Cayenne, its main rival.

BMW X5
1999 purple metallic
431 028475

M635 Csi

A high-class sport coupe with an M1 engine

The M635, later renamed as M6, appears to be an ordinary luxury coupe - but it carries the same engine used in the M1, 3.5 litre straight 6. The base car, 635CSi, was a winning machine in touring car races.
There are silver and black miniature models, but the black is hard to find. The then-popular BBS wheels are made in great detail, to good effect.

BMW M635 CSi
1982-87 black
430 025121

MINICHAMPS

3 Series

The basic BMW that was explosively popular in Japan

The 3 series is the predecessor to the famous 2002 series, and continued its success by becoming the benchmark sedan against which all other manufacturers in the world must measure up against.
As it is the sedan that represents Germany, a full line-up of miniature models are being produced: 4 door sedan/ 2 door sedan, coupe, touring, and cabriolet. Miniature models also differ according to grades.

E36 4 DOOR

BMW 3-Series Saloon
1992 black
430 023301

E36 COMPACT

BMW 3-Series Compact
2000 black
431 020071

3 Series Saloon

BMW 3-Sereis
1975-83 orange
430 025400

BMW 3-Sereis
1975-83 light blue metallic
430 025401

BMW 3-Sereis
1975-83 copper metallic
430 025402

323i

BMW 323i Saloon
1975-83 silver
430 025470

BMW 323i Saloon
1975-83 red
430 025471

BMW 323i Saloon
1975-83 green metallic
430 025474

BMW 323i Saloon
1975-83 black
430 025475

323i Touring

BMW 328i Touring
1999 green metallic
431 028310

328i Touring

BMW 328i Touring
1999 steel grey
431 028311

BMW 328i Touring
red
431 028312

Splendid BMW
The splendid driving experience of BMW

BMW, along side Mercedes-Benz, is renowned for building luxury cars. Many feel that BMW has a somewhat sporty image, the driver's car of choice. The potential for high performance with a BMW is great, even with a more standard model. Let's take a look at some of the high performance models from the older to more recent versions.

2002 Turbo
The super car boom ignited by the rugged sports car

Renowned for its great chassis, a turbo charger was added onto the 2002 series. It became the first turbo model to ever be sold. The exterior had been fitted with spoilers and wide fender panels. The miniature models look as tough and mean as the real car. The attractive silver is unfortunately very rare.

The decor on the front spoiler of the 2002 series makes an intimidating statement to the car it is tailing, as if to say, "get out of my way!"

BMW 2002 Turbo
1974 cream
430 022200

BMW 2002 Turbo
1974 silver
430 022201

507 Hard-Top
The V8 sport with aluminium body

BMW released a roadster, the 507, to compete with the success of the Mercedes-Benz 300SL in the American market. With some modifications, the car was based on the V8 engine used in the 502. Paul's Model Art / Minichamps, known for producing a wide range, produced a 507 with an optional hard-top. The elegant sculpture, long nose and short base have been captured in good detail.

The appearance is quite elegant. On the real car, an aluminium body was used. The model's optional hardtop offers a rather different appeal.

Steel plated parts, widely used at that time, were used all around the car. BMW's trademark kidney grill is very unique.

BMW 507 Hard-Top
1956-59 red
430 022530

BMW 507 Hard-Top
1956-59 silver
430 022531

BMW 507 Hard-Top
1956-59 cream
430 022532

3 Series

The front engined layout that brings real driving pleasure

BMW is one of the few manufacturers who continue to apply the front engined layout. This is particularly noticeable with the current 3 series E46 – carrying the ultra smooth silky 6. Practicality was combined with joyful driving.

The alternative lightweight 4 cylinder E36, 318Ci was quietly popular because of its athletic handling. Out of the many models, Paul's Model Art / Minichamps really know the finest cars fit for

328 Ci ////

**BMW
328 Ci Coupe**
1999 light yellow metallic

431 028322

**BMW
328 Ci Coupe**
1999 green

431 028324

318 iS ////

**BMW
318 iS**
1994 yellow

430 024300

Z8

The 2 seater sports car as seen in the James Bond 007 film

Some of the essence of the design of the Z8 is shared with that of the 507 series. The photo you see is the hard-top miniature model. If you look closely at the design of the kidney grill and side air-outlet, they are similar to that of the 507 series. There is also a miniature V8 engine hidden under the bonnet.

**BMW
Z8 Hard-Top**
2000 silver metallic

431 028750

M1

The ultimate stylish sports car

With its unique appearance, the M1 with straight 6 mid-mounted engine stands out among other BMWs. This was the beginning of M series. The miniature model captures the distinctive wedge design and disc wheels. You can still find them on the market today, and you really should have it in your BMW collections! They are available in both white and red.

BMW emblems are placed on both sides of the rear end, which is a feature unique to the M1. Ital Design are responsible for the design of this machine.

**BMW
M1 Street**
1978/81 white

430 025020

**BMW
M1 Street**
1978/81 red

430 025022

Open to the Air
BMW driving with an exhilarating breeze

One has come to expect high quality saloons from BMW, but they also have a long history of creating many attractive open top models. The Paul's Model Art / Minichamps range includes the 507 that came out just after the Second World War, in the midst of chaos, as well as the latest Z8. We cannot, unfortunately, show you every model but will feature some of the best known models.

507 Cabriolet & Soft-Top

The simple open style, still popular today

When struggling after the Second World War, following the release of the flagship saloon 502, BMW released a luxurious sport car – the 507. Basic components and engine were based on the 502, but the difference was the 507's elegant body. The actual car came out as a convertible but Paul's Model Art / Minichamps made soft-top and hard-top miniature models. Notice the body sculpture, and the fact that the wheels are painted in same colour as the body in the miniature models. It is important not to miss the intricate details, such as the white wall tires on soft-top models.

BMW 507 Cabriolet
1956-59 red
430 022507

BMW 507 Cabriolet
1956-59 silver
430 022508

BMW 507 Cabriolet
1956-59 cream
430 022509

BMW 507 Cabriolet Soft-Top
1956-59 red
430 022520

BMW 507 Cabriolet Soft-Top
1956-59 black
430 022521

BMW 507 Cabriolet Soft-Top
1956-59 green
430 022522

2002 Cabriolet

An attractive variation added to the 2002 series

There was a cabriolet model in the popular 2002 series range. It was able to seat 4 passengers and still enjoy an open top. This concept is still being applied to the 3 series cabriolet.

The miniature model is quite distinct with its simple appearance yet beautiful steel plated parts and round taillights. Note the interior indicative of the trend of the 1960s.

BMW 2002 Cabriolet
1971 blue
400 021130

When we look at it today, the front design could be described as "cute". It is simple, yet still makes a statement.

64 MINICHAMPS

Z&M Series

The open top that typifies the series

The Z3 became a best seller as a stylish roadster. Along with the Z3 came the M roadster with an M3 engine, and the elegant and lavish convertible Z8. Paul's Model Art / Minichamps has a wide variety of such miniature roadsters. They even make different interiors according to the grade of a model. Noticing the differences can bring a smile to the face.

Z8 /////

BMW Z8
1999 metallic blue

431 028740

Z3 /////

BMW Z3 Roadster
1999 green

430 028232

Z3 2.8 /////

BMW Z3 2.8 Cabriolet
1997 red

430 024330

BMW Z3 Roadster 2.8
yellow

430 028234

M Series /////

BMW M Roadster
1996 orange

430 024360

328i Cabriolet

The comfortable 4 seater convertible

The 3 series traditionally have convertible models. We shall take a look at the current model, the E46. One can have fun with a 2 seater Z series, but with a 4 seater convertible it is possible to combine fun with comfort. Despite being a 4 seater, the body sculpture is still elegant. It would be interesting to juxtapose this miniature model to a sedan or M3 cabriolet.

BMW 328i Cabriolet
2000 red metallic

431 028030

An invitation to the arena of the road car

Our miniature cars are delicately created with exceptional care and workmanship. If you are fond of cars, then it is a natural desire to hold such attractive models in your own hands – particularly those cars for which you have a special affinity. Fortunately, Paul's Model Art / Minichamps makes a wide range of miniature cars that come from variety of different countries, including those from Paul's Model Art / Minichamps country of origin, Germany. Let us introduce you to some of the most attractive and all time favourite road cars.

German Cars of MINICHAMPS

German Cars of Minichamps

The first automobile was created in Germany. Germany has a long heritage of automobile production, and has graced the world with many remarkable cars. Owing to its German derivation, Paul's Model Art / Minichamps is very keen on producing German models and offers a wide range to choose from.

VW

"Volks Wagen" means "people's car" in German. The so-called 'KdF'-car of World War II - created by Dr. Porsche and nicknamed 'Beetle' - became a worldwide bestseller. Paul's Model Art / Minichamps covers a wide range of Beetles, a car that ranks surely as one of Germany's greatest creations. In addition, Paul's Model Art / Minichamps also covers a host of other VW models.

Beetle Series   The enduring character of the Beetle, still prominent today

1200 "Split Window"

The very first series of Beetle has a very distinctive feature - the rear window is divided into two (known as a "split window"). The blue and black models come with a canvas top.

VW 1200 Beetle "split window"
1949-53 black
430 052000

VW 1200 Beetle "split window"
1949-53 grey
430 052001

VW 1200 Beetle "split window"
1949-53 blue
430 052002

1200 Cabriolet Soft-Top & Cabriolet

This model is the reincarnation of the early 4 seater Cabriolet, crafted by Karmann in the 1950's. The colour coordination of the main body and canvas create a dynamic look.

1. VW 1200 Cabriolet Soft-Top 1951-52 red
   430 052040
2. VW 1200 Cabriolet Soft-Top 1951-52 black
   430 052041
3. VW 1200 Cabriolet Soft-Top 1951-52 green
   430 052042

VW 1200 Cabriolet
1951-52 anthracite metallic/cream
430 052034

VW 1200 Cabriolet
1951-52 green
430 052030

VW 1200 Cabriolet
1951-52 red
430 052032

VW 1200 Cabriolet
1951-52 grey
430 052031

Hebmueller

These Cabriolets produced by Hebmueller are the more personal 2 seater models. The difference in design between the Soft-top and 4 seater is distinct.
Both Cabriolet and Soft-Top are on sale. Note the differing paintworks of each model.

Although it is a Cabriolet, Hebmueller made a 2 seater model, which has quite a different hood and soft-top design.

VW Hebmueller Cabriolet
1949-50 black/red
430 052130

VW Hebmueller Cabriolet
1949-50 black/cream
430 052131

VW Hebmueller Cabriolet Soft-Top 1949-50 black/cream
430 052140

VW Hebmueller Cabriolet Soft-Top 1949-50 grey
430 052141

VW Hebmueller Cabriolet
1949-50 black
430 052132

VW Hebmueller Cabriolet
1949-50 red/cream
430 052134

1200

In this model the rear window is broader to increase visibility - the so-called "Oval window" model. It is this model that typifies the original design of the Beetle.

VW 1200 Beetle
1953-57 green grey
430 052100

VW 1200 Beetle
1953-57 blue
430 052101

VW 1200 Beetle
1953-57 red
430 052102

1302 & 1303

The Beetle's final models, the 1302 & 1303, with larger indicators, are equipped with many modern features. The various details of the bumpers have been accurately recreated.

VW 1303 Saloon
1972-74 light green
430 055102

VW 1302 Saloon
1970-72 willow green
430 055004

VW 1303 Saloon
1970-72 moss green metallic
430 055104

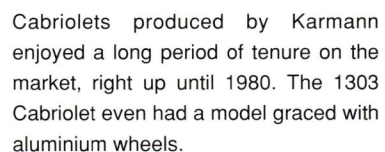

VW 1303 Saloon
1972-74 willow green
430 055004

1302 & 1303 Cabriolet

Cabriolets produced by Karmann enjoyed a long period of tenure on the market, right up until 1980. The 1303 Cabriolet even had a model graced with aluminium wheels.

VW 1303 Cabriolet
1972-80 marin yellow
430 055135

VW 1302 Cabriolet
1970-72 yellow
430 055035

VW 1303 Cabriolet
1972-80 black
430 055130

The 1 millionth Beetle anniversary model

In recognition of the gross production of the Beetle reaching 1million units, the anniversary miniature model was produced complete with gift box. It is now, however, very difficult to acquire, owing to its popularity and scarcity.

The beautiful paintwork and accompanying photo are very unique. Limited units of 9999 were sold, with each model being engraved with serial numbers.

VW 1200 1million 1953-57 gold
430 052103

Beetle Concept

This is the Beetle that was, at the time, paraded as a concept car in motor shows. But as we all know, it was later to become a popular production car.

VW Concept Car Cabriolet 1994 yellow
430 054031

VW Concept Car Cabriolet 1994 blue
430 054030

VW New Beetle
1999 blue
430 058004

VW Concept Car Cabriolet 1994 red
430 054032

67

German Cars of MINICHAMPS

- VW
- Opel
- NSU
- Auto Union
- Audi

Samba Bus & Delivery Van
The ever popular VW bus & van series

With its matchless style, the Type 2 is still popular today. Both the commercial Type 2, and the 'Samba Bus' vehicle, are available as miniature models. It is interesting to compare the Samba Bus, a vehicle with many windows and a sunroof, with the Type2, a vehicle based on the virtues of simple practicality.

Whether or not the canvas top can opened or closed differs according to the body colour of Samba Bus. The interior, as you would expect from all Paul's Model Art / Minichamps products, is delicately and skilfully crafted.

Delivery Van

VW Delivery Van
1963 blue
430 052200

VW Delivery Van
1963 grey
430 052201

VW Delivery Van
1963 green
430 052202

Samba Bus

VW Samba Bus
1958-60 grey/blue
430 052300

VW Samba Bus
1958-60 green/light green
430 052301

VW Samba Bus
1958-60 red/cream
430 052302

Golf Series
The new generation of VW - a focus on comfort

Ever since Beetle production declined, the Golf became VW's standard bearer. Paul's Model Art / Minichamps offers you the complete range of Golf 4 variations, including 4 door, Variant and Cabrio models. The satisfaction gained from owning such a car for oneself is truly marked.

VW Golf IV Cabrio
black
430 058330

VW Golf IV Variant
1999 black
430 056010

VW Golf IV Cabrio
blue
430 058332

VW Golf IV
1997 gold metallic
430 056008

VW Golf IV
1997 red
430 056000

VW Golf IV
1997 Jazz blue
430 056001

VW Golf IV
1997 silver
433 056003 (Dealer Version)

VW Golf IV
1997 green metallic
433 056004 (Dealer Version)

Polo & Lupo
A VW initiative - the small size commuter

The first Polo model became central to VW's product range. The model has progressed and endured, shown by the existence of the current Polo.

VW Polo
1975 yellow
430 050501

VW Lupo
1998 black
430 058102

Scirroco
The stylish VW of 1970's

The Scirroco is a stylish hatch back coupe designed by Karmann. In its miniature form, the original simple 4 headlight front mask is well captured.

VW Scirroco
1975 green metallic
430 050420

VW Scirroco
1975 yellow
430 050421

1600 & 411 Series
The classic flat 4

The 1600 and 411 models were created using parts from the Beetle. There are several variations of these, such as the Saloon, Fastback and Variant.

Fastback
VW 1600 TL Fastback
1966 blue
430 055320

VW 411 LE
1969-72 blue
400 051100

Saloon
VW 1600
1966 Cream
430 055300

Variant
VW 1600 Variant
1966 red
430 055310

Karmann Ghia
A specially made VW

Based on the Beetle chassis, Ghia designed a special model released as the Karmann Ghia Paul' Model Art / Minichamps recently released the early models of these with new colour varieties. The miniature models come in coupe, cabriolet and soft-top.

Soft-Top
Karmann Ghia Soft-Top
red
430 005062

Karmann Ghia Soft-Top
cream
430 005061

Karmann Ghia Soft-Top
green
430 005060

Coupe
Karmann Ghia Coupe
black
430 005000

Karmann Ghia Coupe
light blue
430 005001

Karmann Ghia Coupe
red
430 005002

Karmann Ghia Coupe
yellow/black
430 005004

Karmann Ghia Coupe
dark blue/cream
430 005005

Open model
Karmann Ghia Cabriolet
black
430 005030

Karmann Ghia Cabriolet
light blue
430 005031

Karmann Ghia Cabriolet
red
430 005032

Karmann Ghia Cabriolet
1957 green metallic
430 051034

Karmann Ghia Cabriolet
1957 pacific blue
430 051036

Karmann Ghia Cabriolet
1957 white
430 051039

181 Kuebelwagen
The VW with the atypical body

A body reminiscent of the military Kuebelwagen has been placed atop a Beetle chassis. Such simple body panels are well captured in the model's miniature form

VW 181 Kuebelwagen
1969-79 orange
430 050030

VW 181 Kuebelwagen
1969-79 olive green
430 050031

Opel

Opel, one of the world's oldest automobile manufacturers, was founded in 1899. Opel was known at the time for its 6 months warranty and thorough test-driving. In the early 1900's, Opel had won many motor racing championships. Opel produced a wide range, from family car to luxury car. Paul's Model Art / Minichamps covers this range comprehensively. Much of the range have an endearing simplicity, which is part of the attraction of the Opel range.

Kapitaen
The full-size retro style model

Opel Kapitaen
1951-53 ivory
430 043305

1. 430 043300 Opel Kapitaen 1951-53 dark red
2. 430 043301 Opel Kapitaen 1951-53 black
3. 430 043302 Opel Kapitaen 1951-53 grey
4. 430 043304 Opel Kapitaen 1951-53 savona green

1. 430 04000 Opel Kapitaen P2 Saloon 1959-63 black
2. 430 04001 Opel Kapitaen P2 Saloon 1959-63 turquoise

Olympia
The dignified front facade with an imposing look

Opel Olympia Saloon
1952 black
430 040400

Opel Olympia Convertible
1952 blue
430 040430

Rekord Serise
The original upper middle-class car

The Rekord series were targeted for general usage as middle-class cars, with the Kapitaen as the flagship model. In addition to the P1, P2 and A series models, there are also coupe, caravan and saloon models. Lively colours contribute to the effervescent character of the cars.

P1 Limousine

1. 430 043200 Opel Rekord P1 Limousine 1958-60 green
2. 430 043201 Opel Rekord P1 Limousine 1958-60 blue
3. 430 043204 Opel Rekord P1 Limousine 1958-60 red
4. 430 043202 Opel Rekord P1 Limousine 1958-60 grey

Opel Rekord P1 Limousine
1958 black/white
430 043205

P2 Limousine & Coupe

Opel Rekord P2 Coupe
1960-62 silver
430 040220

Opel Rekord P2
1960 white
430 040200

Opel Rekord P2 Saloon
1960 red/grey
430 040201

1. 430 043211 Opel Rekord P1 Caravan 1953-60 blue
2. 430 043210 Opel Rekord P1 Caravan 1953-60 yellow
3. 430 043212 Opel Rekord P1 Caravan 1953-60 red

P1&P2 Caravan

P1

Opel Rekord P1 Caravan classic
1958-60 white
430 043216

P2

Opel Rekord P2 Caravan
1958-60 grey
430 040210

Opel Rekord P2 Caravan
1958-60 white
430 040211

A & C Series

The standard model with widespread popularity

Rekord A /////

Opel Rekord A
1963 silver
400 041000

Opel Rekord A Coupe
1963 aero blue
400 041020

Opel Rekord A Caravan
1962 granada red
400 041010

Rekord C /////

Opel Rekord C 2-Door
1966 lago blue
430 046102

Opel Rekord C Break
1966 white
430 046110

Kadett

A stylish family saloon

If the Kapitaen, Admiral & Commodore are considered as high-class model, the Kadett should be considered a family car. It has a 1 litre class engine, and the Kadett A sold more than 650,000 units in just 3 years. Paul's Model Art / Minichamps covers a wide range of these cars in miniature form.

1. 430 043001 Opel Kadett A Limousine 1962-65 blue grey
2. 430 043002 Opel Kadett A Limousine 1962-65 red
3. 430 043000 Opel Kadett A Limousine 1962-65 yellow

A Limousine /////

Opel Kadett A
1962-65 ivory
430 043004

Opel Kadett A
1962-65 royal blue
430 043005

Opel Kadett A
1962-65 dark red
430 043006

Kapitaen, Admiral & Commodore /////

Opel Admiral Saloon
1969-77 iceland green
430 046061

Opel Kapitaen
1969-77 black
430 046001

Opel Commodore A
1968 dark red
430 046161

A Caravan /////

Opel Kadett A Caravan
1962-65 grey
430 043010

Opel Kadett A Caravan
1962-65 blue
430 043011

Opel Kadett A Caravan
1962-65 white
430 043012

Kadett C /////

Opel Kadett C Caravan
1973 green
430 045615

Opel Kadett C Swinger
1975 yellow
430 045605

Others

The reliable compact car with a global marketing strategy

Opel focuses today on producing compact cars. Paul's Model Art / Minichamps also has an extensive range of small cars. The often-present front grille, which is fast becoming a mainstay of Opel cars, and unique body sculpture, are both well captured in the model's miniature form.

Opel Corsa
2000 star silver
430 040301

Opel Zafira
1999 silver
430 048002

Opel Astra Coupe
2000 blue
430 049120

Opel Astra Coupe
2000 black
430 049121

Opel Astra Cabriolet
2000 silver
430 049130

Opel Agila
1999 magna red
430 049001

NSU

The German company NSU started off as a motorcycle manufacturer. NSU is best known by many not for its cars, but for the creation of the first rotary engine, the Wankel unit. As a compact car manufacturer, NSU first became successful after its release of the Prinz in 1960. With the subsequent Ro80, NSU unsuccessfully attempted competing in the upper-class market. In 1969, NSU merged with Audi.

1.	430 015300	NSU TT Saloon	1967-72	orange
2.	430 015302	NSU TT Saloon	1967-72	blue metallic
3.	430 015301	NSU TT Saloon	1967-72	silver

TT
The concept of compact size - which greatly influenced Japanese car production

Beneath the compact and sharp sculpted body, the TT carried a 1 litre class engine. It represents one of NSU's finest hours. The actual car is rather old but it was only recently that Paul's Model Art / Minichamps created a miniature model of TT. They are now widely available.

NSU 1000L
1964-72 blue
430 015200

NSU 1000L
1964 red
430 015201

NSU 1000L
1964 dark blue
430 015202

Ro 80
The rotary saloon that reigned throughout the 1970's

NSU had aimed to enter the upper-class market with its trump card, the Ro 80 - the car with a rotary engine. However the car was not as reliable as it should have been, and hence failed to sell. It was then that NSU had lost its momentum, prompting the merger with Audi.

NSU Ro 80 Saloon
1972 targa orange
430 015401

NSU Ro 80 Saloon
1972 iberic red
430 015402

Spider & Sport Prinz
An exceptionally driveable compact sport

Before NSU merged with Audi, it was very successful as a small car manufacturer. The Prinz was the car that made NSU famous. The miniaturized model is the Bertone designed Sport. The engine was less than 600cc but the bodyweight was around 500kg, yet it was still a vibrant drive.

1.	430 019220	NSU Sport Prinz	1959-67	silver metallic
2.	430 019231	NSU Spider	1964-67	silver

NSU Sport Prinz
1964 muscari blue
430 019221

NSU Spider
1964 gemini blue metallic
430 019230

The Bertone designed Spider & Prinz are beautifully sculpted. The essence of the lightweight sports car is well captured, coupled with its beautifully made interior.

Wartburg
The classic model that exuded cool

Wartburg is a lesser known brand from the former East Germany. Even after the Second World War, it kept on manufacturing cars at a former BMW state-run factory. In 1956, they began manufacturing the 311 as a Wartburg brand. They produced cars more distinguished than the of Trabant.

Wartburg A312 Saloon
blue/white
430 015900

Wartburg A312 Coupe
grey/white
430 015920

Wartburg A312 Coupe
black/white
430 015921

Wartburg A311/2 Cabriolet
1959 red/white
430 015931

Wartburg A311/2 Cabriolet
1959 blue
430 015932

DKW
Advanced front engined technology applied to family cars

Before the Second World War, Germany's automobile industry had many prominent manufacturers. DKW was one of many who specialized in small cars, and was later to become a part of the Audi Corporation.

DKW Junior de Luxe
1961-63 dark red
400 011500

Auto Union

The immense Auto Union was formed in 1932, a time of recession in Germany, initially with DKW and Audi's partnership, but later joined by Horch and Wanderer. The 4 rings of the Audi emblem symbolise those 4 manufacturers. At the time, there were 70 automobile manufacturers in Germany and within 4 years only 30 survived. Auto Union was efficient. Each company made a different category of car. Such efficiency underlines the essence of the company's manufacturing ethic today.

Paul' Model Art / Minichamps fine craftsmanship, detailing particularly the inside panels and various intricacies around the front and rear of the body encapsulate the great character of the past.

1000SP
A unique 2 door saloon with a 2 cycle unit

Audi was the most innovative quarter of the Auto Union, and was responsible for the 1000 series. The sporty coupe and convertible also comes in miniature form, but the backbone of this series was undoubtedly the saloon. This car emotively captures the history of the German automobile industry.

Auto Union 1000SP Coupe
1958-61 cream
400 011020

Auto Union 1000SP Convertible
1961-65 red
400 011030

Audi

Audi and Auto Union withstood the storm of recession. They continued to survive after the war, when Allied forces occupied Germany. But in 1965, VW became the majority shareholder and subsequently the most prominent brand. Audi had always been good at making middle-class cars and the current A series enjoys a range of diverse characteristics. Today, Audi has both the TT and S series to satisfy sports car fans, and is now ready for further market penetration.

A60
The backbone of Audi in the early 1970's

The 60 series was the backbone of Audi in the early 1970's. There were 2 door Coupe and Variant models. Audi was later to develop the 80 series.

Audi 60
1970 red
400 011300

Audi 60 Break
1970 cream
400 011310

100 Series
The high rolling 4 seater model with straight 4 unit

The 100 series entered production in late 1968. It was Audi's favourite middle-class saloon with a 1.8 litre straight 4 OHV unit and FWD layout. Paul's Model Art / Minichamps offers both the sedan and stylish coupe in miniature form for you to enjoy.

Audi 100 Saloon
1969 silver
430 019102

Audi 100S Coupe
1969-75 orange
430 019121

Audi 100S Coupe
1969-75 red
430 019122

A Series
Audi's mainstream model for the coming century

In the 1980's, the 80 and 100 series sold the most units for Audi. In 1994, the A4 made its debut. Now the diverse range includes models from the A8 to the compact A2. Paul's Model Art / Minichamps will be adding more models to their range to represent the diversity of the Audi range.

Audi A2 Saloon
2000 black
430 019002

Audi A3 4-Door
2000 black
430 010300

Audi A8 Saloon
1994 cashmere metallic
430 013001

Audi RS4 Avant
2000 yellow
430 019311

Audi A6 Saloon
2001 black
430 010200

Audi A6
2001 blue metallic
430 010201

Audi A6 Avant
2001 grey metallic
430 010211

TT
Audi's ambitious sports car project

Until the advent of the TT, Audi was not renowned for making sports cars. This 2 seater sports car comes as Coupe and Cabriolet. They are a recent addition to the range and widely available.

Audi TT Coupe
1998 white
430 017224

Audi TT Roadster
1999 green met.
430 017231

73

British Cars

The best-known British cars can be divided into two categories. The first is that of the compact lightweight convertibles such as the MG and Triumph; the second being that of the dignified saloons, such as Bentley and Jaguar. Two very different categories, yet both miniaturised in wonderful detail by Paul's Model Art / Minichamps There is a good range available, and Paul's Model Art / Minichamps manages to capture the dignified presence of each of the cars.

MG

The traditional open model

Over 500,000 MGBs have been made, with intermittent small changes, during its 18 year history. The miniature model is the 1962 model, MGB's debut model. There are both open and closed top models of the car.

MGB Cabriolet
1962-69 black
430 131030

MGB Cabriolet
1962-69 brithish racing green
430 131031

MGB Cabriolet
1962-69 red
430 131032

MGB Cabriolet Soft-Top
1962-69 cream
430 131040

MGB Cabriolet Soft-Top
1962-69 brithish racing green
430 131041

MGB Cabriolet Soft-Top
Softtop 1962-69 red
430 131042

Chrome plated parts are used in the miniature models just as they are on the real car, and the likeness of the miniature's cockpit to the original is phenomenal.

Lotus

The definitive open topped sports car still popular today

Lotus Super7
1968 british racing green
430 135630

Lotus Super7
1968 red
430 135632

The Super 7 was released as a high-spec model of the Lotus 7 and was in production until 1973. The Series 3, which debuted in 1968 enjoyed great popularity and the Caterham model is still based on it today. There are a great many small parts, and as such producing a 1/43 scale miniature is a demanding task. Nevertheless, Paul's Model Art / Minichamps produced it with the exceptionally high quality one would expect from the company.

McLaren

The pioneering 3 seater racing machine equipped with ultimate technology

Gordon Murray, a top designer in Formula 1, designed the McLaren F1. It is a 3 seater machine with the driver's seat in the centre, hence calculating optimum weight distribution. There are 5 colours available for the miniature models.

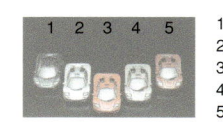

#	Code	Model	Year	Colour
1.	530 133430	McLaren F1 Road Car	1993	green metallic
2.	530 133431	McLaren F1 Road Car	1993	silver
3.	530 133432	McLaren F1 Road Car	1993	red
4.	530 133433	McLaren F1 Road Car	1993	Tag-Heuer
5.	530 133434	McLaren F1 Road Car	1993	red metallic

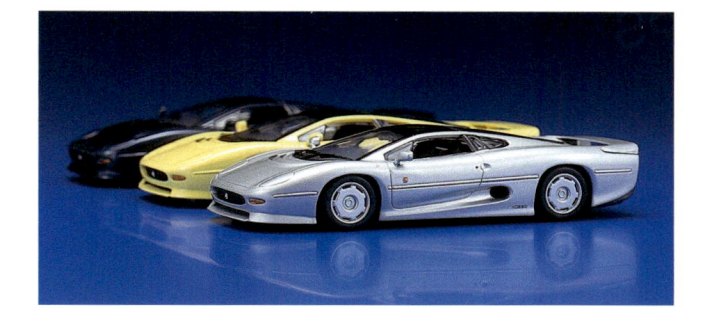

Jaguar

The dignified high performance animal

Jaguar, a luxury automobile manufacturer, has always been involved in motor-sport. The Mk II, a refined version of the Mk I, was very strong in the Tour de France. The XJ220, released in 1992, was the Ferrari F40 of Jaguar. It was a car of very high performance and a high price tag to match, and only a limited number were produced.

Mk. II /////

XJ220 /////

Jaguar XJ220
1992 blue metallic
430 102220

Jaguar Mk.II
1959-67 british racing green
430 130600

Jaguar Mk.II
1959-67 dark red
430 130602

Jaguar XJ220
1992 yellow
430 102221

Jaguar XJ220
1992 silver
430 102222

The 6222cc 60degrees V12 engine has been captured in particularly impressive detail. Because only 350 XJ220s were made, you will hardly ever see one on the roads. The miniature model's look is truly unique, and one that should be treasured.

Triumph

Famous for open top driving

As the name implies, the TR6 is the 6th generation of Triumph roadster. Karmann replaced Michelotti as the designer, and the TR6 subsequently proved to be a very modern model compared to the TR4 and TR5. The cockpit is replicated very realistically in the miniature model.

Triumph TR6
1968 british racing green
430 132571

Triumph TR6
1968 red
430 132572

Triumph TR6
1986 french blue
430 132579

Bugatti

Bugatti EB 110
red
430 102111

The super sports vehicle of a composite of different nationalities

Bugatti EB 110
blue
430 102110

Bugatti EB 110
black
430 102112

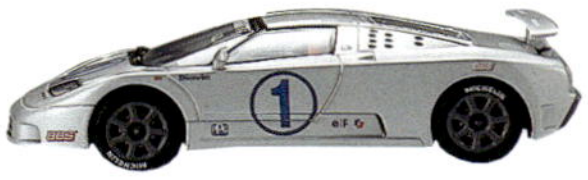

Bugatti EB 110
racing silver
430 102115

Bugatti EB 110
yellow
510 430012 (Schumacher Collection)

The EB110 came out in 1992 as a super high performance sports vehicle. The EB110 was named in commemoration of 110 years since Ettore Bugatti's birth. Note how realistic the V12 engine looks in the miniature model.

Bugatti had traditionally been a French luxury super sports brand. But in 1989, when making its revival, the headquarters was moved to Italy. Later Bugatti became a part of VW group and some now even consider it German. Bugatti can hence be described as a multi-national brand today.

Italian Cars of MINICHAMPS

The unique Italian design is seen here in magnificent detail. 1/43-scale models usually capture details well, and Paul's Model Art / Minichamps' Italian models are evidence of this.

Lamborghini

Ferrucio Lamborghini was a great car fanatic, to such an extent that he would even compete in the Mille Miglia. In 1963, using money made in his tractor manufacturing business, he founded a car company. His aim was to make cars that could out-perform Ferrari. However, in 1972 his tractor business made such huge losses that the majority of shares had to be sold to a Swiss investor. Since the company left the hands of Ferrucio, the ownership changed hands between a French company, Chrysler, an Indonesian conglomerate, and the Audi group. But the commitment towards making the best sports car possible always remained constant, irrespective of the company's ownership.

Miura
The mid-engined V12 fighting bull

In 1965, a bare chassis (apparently developed for racing use) was visible on the P400 model. A mid-engined layout was very rare at the time, and in the following year, the beautifully sculpted 'Miura' was officially released. The engine was a 60 degrees V12 unit. The flowing shape of the Bertone designed body has been well captured in the miniature model.

Gandini, 25 years old at the time, designed this elegant body. Paul's Model Art / Minichamps made 7 types including the popular red and black versions, with more variations hopefully to come.

Lamborghini Miura 1966-71 black 430 103000	**Lamborghini Miura** 1966-71 gold 430 103001	**Lamborghini Miura** 1966-71 red 430 103002	**Lamborghini Miura** 1966-71 light green exclusive for Kyosho 430 103004
Lamborghini Miura 1966-71 yellow 430 103005	**Lamborghini Miura** 1966-71 orange 430 103006	**LAMBORGHINI MIURA** 1966-71 viper green exclusive for Kyosho 433 103004	

Countach LP 400

The gull wing - a masterpiece

In 1974, the most famous Lamborghini, the Countach, was released after 15 years of production, with its remarkable looks, style and name. Despite a shortage of money for the development of newer models, the Countach was popular nevertheless. A later model was produced, which had spoilers and looked somewhat meaner. However Paul's Model Art / Minichamps presents the earlier range. The body sculpting is clean and simple in Bertone's original design, and it was very popular due in part to these reasons.

Lamborghini Countach LP400 1974 gold 430 103100	**Lamborghini Countach LP400** 1974 yellow 430 103101
Lamborghini Countach LP400 1974 black 430 103102	**Lamborghini Countach LP400** 1974 yellow - exclusive for Kyosho 433 103103

30 years on, the design of the Countach is still striking. In Japan alone, the yellow model came with a limited edition tan interior, whereas all other yellow Countach's were made with a black interior.

350GT & 400GT

The old sports car with the multi cylinder engine

Lamborghini's first production car on the market was the 350GT, with its particular selling point being the DOHC engine. Back then even Ferrari had an SOHC engine at that time.

2 years later, the 350GT became the 400GT, now with a bigger engine. Both models will be released with more colour variations in the near future.

Lamborghini 350GT 1964 blue metallic 430 103200	**Lamborghini 350GT** 1964 red 430 103201
Lamborghini 400GT 2+2 1964 silver 430 103300	**Lamborghini 400GT 2+2** 1964 green 430 103301

Alfa Romeo

Originally, Alfa Romeo made racing machines and more expensive cars. But after the Second World War, it suffered a financial crisis and had to diversify towards more mass-orientated production.

Early mass-production models were the Giulietta and the Giulia, each with DOHC engines. These models maintained the Alfa Romeo identity, and the company's innovative reputation remained in tact. In the 1970's Alfa Romeo re-entered F1 racing; however the company had never truly stabilised after the earlier financial crisis and was subsequently taken over by the Fiat group in 1986. Nevertheless, in keeping with its sporty image, Alfa Romeo manages to produce quite a diverse range of models today.

Tipo 33 Stradale
The racing car takes to the streets

The Tipo 33 Stradale originates from a pure racing machine, the Tipo 33. After the war, this kind of model was quite unique and unheard of. The engine is replicated in detail at 1/43-scale, and comes in a gift box.

Alfa Romeo Tipo 33 Stradale
1968 red in gift box
436 120920

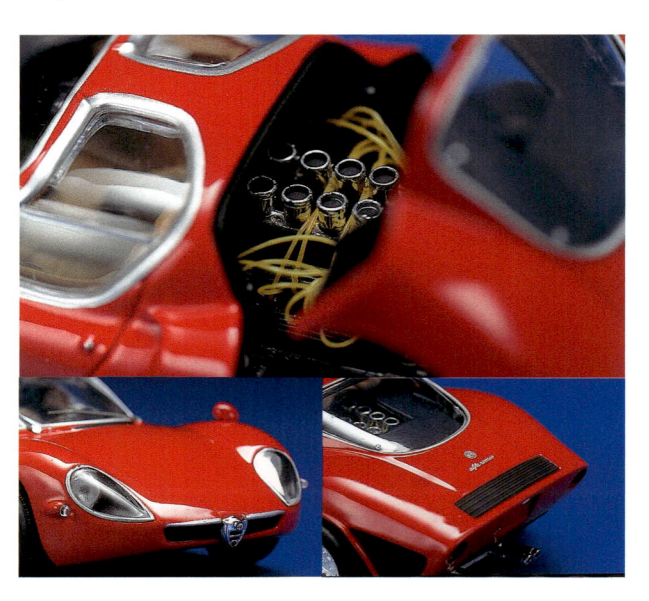

Alfasud & Alfetta GTV
Pithy exhaust tones

Amid the Italian government's plan to revitalize the country's southern states, a factory in Napoli was built to manufacture Alfasud. This model had an FWD layout that was unlike most other Alfas of the time, but it was reasonably priced and became very popular.

The Alfetta GTV had some of the essence of the Giulia and Giulietta models, and became very popular. Miniature models of these have just recently been released, with more colour variations expected to follow.

Alfa Romeo Alfasud
1972 green
400 120101

Alfa Romeo Alfasud
1972-77 blue
400 120100

Alfa Romeo Alfetta GTV Coupe
1976 light green metallic
400 120121

Alfa Romeo Alfetta GTV Coupe
1978 red
430 120120

155
DTM's high performing boxy sport

The 155 applied to a FWD layout predominantly for convenience reasons, allowing the shared usage of vital parts with Fiat and Lancia. Some feared that the FWD layout would damage the image of Alfa Romeo, but the 155's performance in the DTM carved a new and even better image. The miniature 155 is very popular, particularly in red. As such it is in short supply.

Alfa Romeo Alfa 155
1992 blue
430 120400

Alfa Romeo Alfa 155
1992 black
430 120401

Alfa Romeo Alfa 155
1992 red
430 120402

433 120404
155 TwinSpark red exclusive Kyosho

433 120403
155 QV red exclusive Kyosho

147 & 156
The modern Alfa that enthused the Alfisti

After the huge success of the 155, it seemed that Alfa had recovered from the financial crisis. Alfa was then able to release a successor, the 156, and a smaller model, the 147. These models have gained Alfa Romeo new customers, who were previously not keen. The attractive design is reminiscent of some of the older Alfa Romeo models, and the classic Alfa Romeo presence can even be felt from the miniature models, with red being the most popular colour.

Alfa Romeo Alfa 147
2001 red
430 120000

Alfa Romeo Alfa 156
1997 silver
430 120700

Alfa Romeo Alfa 156
1997 red
430 120701

Alfa Romeo Alfa 156
1998 nuvola blue
430 120702

Alfa Romeo Alfa 156 Sport Wagon black
430 120710

Lancia
The rally dynamo with a Ferrari V6 engine

Stratos /////

In 1972, Lancia released its special rally machine. It was described as "space-age" at the time, and the sculpting of the body on the miniature model shows this superbly.

1. 430 125020 Lancia Stratos 1972-78 yellow
2. 430 125022 Lancia Stratos 1972-78 red

Autobianchi
A fashionable and youthful generation of car

The Autobianchi A112 is sort of a diversion of the Fiat 127. In 1971, the Abarth version was released and gained renown as a 'hot hatch.' The miniature model is replicates the 1974 version of the car.

Autobianchi A112
1974 green
400 121100

The jovial rear view of this car has been influential in the design of many of today's compact cars.

Fiat
The master of lightweight sport

Fiat is famous not only for manufacturing family cars but also compact 2 seaters. There are the X1/9 (made throughout the 1970s and 1980s) and the Barchetta available in miniature form.

FIAT X 1/9
1972-78 red
430 121660

FIAT BARCHETTA CABRIOLET 1993 red
430 121930

The X1/9 was the mid-engined machine that used components from mass-produced cars – a method widely used today.

MINICHAMPS of other countries

There are French, American, Japanese, and Swedish cars in the Paul's Model Art / Minichamps range. There are unique cars from each respective country, and here we shall take a look at some of them. Note that Ford England and Ford Germany models are placed in the Ford America category.

Peugeot

One of the oldest automobile manufacturers in the world is Peugeot. They have a long history of collaborating with Pininfarina, who since 1955 have been their principal designers. These miniature models capture the beautiful form excellently.

504
A fashionable model based on a saloon

Peugeot 504 Coupe
1974-79 green metallic
400 112120

Peugeot 504 Cabriolet
1974-73 black
400 112130

406
Beautiful form designed by Pininfarina

Peugeot 406 Coupe
1996 lucifer red
430 112620

Peugeot 406 Coupe
1996 ecarlat red
430 112625

306 Series
Best selling French 2 door

Peugeot 306 2door
1998 silver
430 112800

Peugeot 306 2door
1995 green metallic
430 112500

Peugeot 306 2door
1995 red
430 112502

Peugeot 306 4door
1995 grey metallic
430 112570

Peugeot 306 4door
1995 blue metallic
430 112571

Peugeot 306 Cabriolet
1995 red
430 112532

Citroën

Citroën is well known for using many innovative techniques. Paul's Model Art / Minichamps has just released a Citroën range. The SM made its debut back in 1970 as luxury GT and it was the first model with a FWD layout that was capable of travelling at 200km/h.

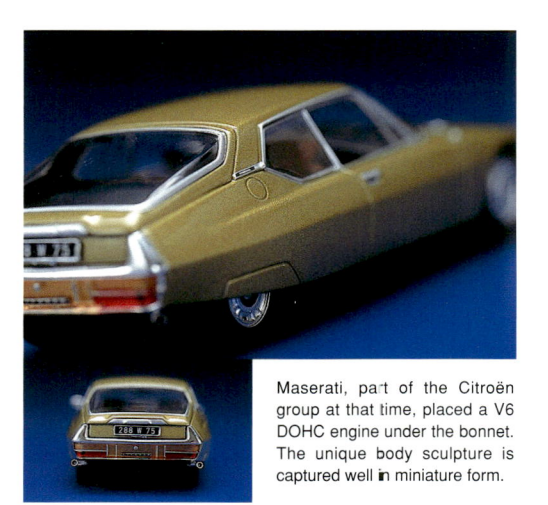

Maserati, part of the Citroën group at that time, placed a V6 DOHC engine under the bonnet. The unique body sculpture is captured well in miniature form.

SM
A unique form applied in FWD Grand Touring

Citroën SM
1970 gold metallic
400 111020

Renault

Renault is a representative of French automobile manufacturing. Paul's Model Art / Minichamps produces the Gordini tuned R8 and the Alpine A110, based on the R8. Many of these are specially tuned models.

R8 Gordini
The original racing cornerstone

Renault R8 Gordini
1964-68 blue
430 113550

Renault R8 Gordini
1964-68 yellow
430 113552

Renault Alpine A110
1963-76 blue metallic
430 113600

Renault Alpine A110
1963-76 red
430 113602

R16
A resurgence in popularity owing to the classic style

Renault R16
1965 white
400 113100

Alpine A110
The lightweight sports that triumphed even in rallies

Chrysler

In 1925, Chrysler was founded. Since its purchase of Dodge the company expanded, and was to become one of the American Big 3. In the 1970's, the company hit difficult times, but ultimately restructuring saved Chrysler. They have since merged with Daimler to become Daimler Chrysler.

Dodge Viper
The wild and venomous Viper

The Viper is a front engined sports car with a 400ps V10 engine. The coupe and cabriolet both feature in the range. See for yourself just how mean they look!

Dodge Viper
Indy 500 Pace car 1996
430 144023

Dodge Viper GTS
1993 blue metallic
430 144021

Dodge Viper GTS
1993 red
430 144022

Dodge Viper Cabriolet
1993 yellow
430 144030

Dodge Viper Cabriolet
1993 blue
430 144031

Dodge Viper Cabriolet
1993 red
430 144032

900
The harmony of high safety measures combined with environmentally friendly features

The 900 succeeded the 99, targeting the American market with a host of strong safety measures. In 1983, the cabriolet also joined the range.

9-5
The simple and sturdy middle-class saloon

The 9-5 is at the top of the Saab range, being more luxurious than the older 9000 model. Saab's very first station wagon, the Break, was also added to the range..

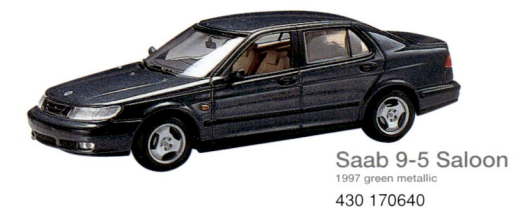

Saab

Saab was founded as an aircraft manufacturer, but began an automobile division after the Second World War. Saab ensures high quality and good performance by using aerospace technology. Saabs are generally not the most ostentatious cars, but in spite of this they have still managed to create a strong brand image.

Saab 900
1995 aubergine
430 170501

Saab 9-5 Saloon
1997 green metallic
430 170640

Saab 900 Cabriolet
1995 blue
430 170531

Saab 9-5 Break
1999 imola red
430 170811

Saab 9-3 Aero Cabriolet
1999 blue metallic
430 170830

Ford

Automobile magnate Henry Ford founded his company in 1903. He was keen on penetrating foreign markets, so he therefore founded Ford England in 1911 and later, Ford Germany. Ford also became very well known in the field of motor sport.

Mustang
The American Ford with a V8 engine sound

The Mustang, a specialty car, made its debut in 1964, nicknamed the "Pony Car". It is one of the most loved cars in American automobile history. The miniature model is based on the 1994 production car.

Ford Mustang Cabriolet
1994 blue metallic
430 085631

Ford Mustang Cabriolet
1994 red
430 085632

Capri
The stylish front engined car that won glorious victories on the racing circuits

The Capri could almost be described as the European version of the Mustang. It was a collaboration of Ford England and Ford Germany. The Capri RS is the homologation model for the touring car championship, and as such extensive weight reduction measures were taken.

Ford Capri
1969 silver
430 085500

Ford Capri RS 2600
1972-73 blue metallic
430 085800

Ford Capri RS 2600
1972-73 yellow
430 085801

Ford Capri RS 2600
1972-73 red
430 085802

Escort RS
The English-made rally weapon

In 1992, the Escort RS was released as the Group A standard rally model.
The name "RS" shows Ford's confidence in the model.

Ford Escort RS Cosworth
1992 red
430 082104

Ford Escort RS Cosworth
1992 black metallic
430 082100

Ford Escort RS Cosworth
1992 green metallic
430 082102

RS 200
The legendary Ford rally model

In 1985, the RS200 was released as a Group B WRC machine, a high performance 4WD.
But in 1986, production was curtailed due to an FIA call to eliminate Group B racing, because of fatal accidents that occurred. Only 200 were made, and as such they are rarely seen on the roads.

Ford RS 200 Road Car
1986 white
430 080200

Ford RS 200 Road Car
1986 red
430 080201

Puma & Couger, Focus
A new compact class from Ford

Ford produced several specialty cars that stem from family saloons. Examples include the Fiesta-based Puma and Mondeo-based Cougar (released under the brand-name Mercury). The Focus is making progress in WRC, and its sporty image is growing.

Ford Puma Coupe
1997 green metallic
430 086524

Ford Puma Coupe
1997 red
430 086521

Ford Cougar
1998 green metallic
430 088021

Ford Focus 3-Door Saloon
1998 red
430 087000

Lincoln
The expansive and opulent presidential vehicle

There are two types of the Presidential vehicle, the Lincoln Continental; one for President Kennedy and another for President Johnson. The attention to detail paid to each respective model is remarkable.

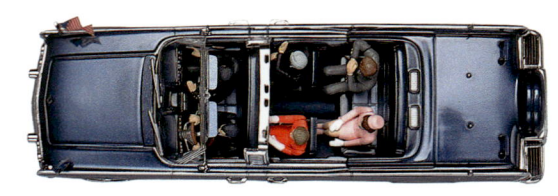

Lincoln Continental Presidential Plade vehicle
X-100 J.F.Kennedy 1961 Jaguar XJ220
430 086100

The detail extends beyond not only the car itself, but to the interior and even the figure of the president. It really is quite a work of art.

Lincoln Continental L.B.Johnson
1964 black
436 086101

Taunus
The sport saloon suited to the American consumer

The Taunus, manufactured until 1972, was Ford Germany's best selling model. Several small changes have been made throughout its time in production. The miniature model produced is the 17M model; so named because of its 1700 cc engine.

Ford Taunus saloon
1960 yellow
430 085105

Ford Taunus saloon
1960 white
430 085100

Ford Taunus saloon
1960 dark red
430 085102

Ford Taunus saloon
1960 turquoise
430 085106

Fiesta, Ka & Escort
Ford family saloons

The Fiesta and Ka are the smaller and basic models in the Ford range, with the Escort being the standard basic saloon. Paul's Model Art / Minichamps produces most of the European manufactured Ford's in compact 1/43-scale.

Ford Fiesta
1995 red
430 085002

Ford Fiesta
2001 red metallic
400 081101

Ford Ka
1996 purple
430 086401

Celica
The FF sport with fresh style

Toyota Celica SS-2 Coupe
1994 black
430 166620

Toyota Celica SS-2 Coupe
1994 red
430 166622

Toyota Celica
2000 black
430 168921

Toyota

Toyota is undoubtedly the leading automobile manufacturer in Japan. Paul's Model Art / Minichamps produce the models most popular in Europe, the Yaris and MR2. These are their export names, but in Japan, they are called Vitz and MR-S respectively.

MR2 — The lighter mid-engined convertible

Toyota MR2 Cabriolet
2000 blue metallic
430 166960

Toyota MR2 Cabriolet
2000 black
430 166961

Yaris, Corolla, RAV4 — Toyota's favourite top of the range compact cars

Toyota Yaris TS
2001 black
430 166060

Toyota Yaris TS
2001 blue metallic
430 166061

Toyota Corolla 2-Door
2001 blue metallic
400 166100

Toyota RAV4
2000 green metallic
430 166000

Volvo

Volvo is renowned for its high safety measures, and was the first manufacturer in the world to offer front seatbelts as standard. Sporty models such as the P1800 have been produced, but the saloon is the model that sold the most units.

V70 — 21st century neo-conservative Volvo

Volvo had always used a front engine layout and the V70 was the first Volvo that came with 4WD. The 1/43-scale model of the estate wagon is quite popular and there are V70, V70XC and 850 versions available.

Volvo V70 XC
2000 black
430 171270

P1800 — Even now the design appears cutting edge

The P1800 was released in 1960 as the first Volvo production sport car. Italian Carozzeria Frua designed the body.

Volvo P1800 Coupe
1969 grey
430 171624

Volvo P1800 Coupe
1969 green
430 171625

Volvo P1800 ES
1969 dark red
430 171614

Volvo P1800 ES
1971 red
430 171615

Volvo P1800 ES
1971 yellow
430 171617

Saloon Series

Volvo 850 Saloon
1994 smoke silver
430 171401

Volvo S40
2000 blue
430 171101

Volvo S60
2000 gold metallic
430 171261

Volvo S70 Saloon
1998 red metallic
430 171800

Volvo S80 Saloon
1999 cassis metallic
430 171901

MINICHAMPS AT REAL CAR DEALERSHIPS

PART 1 PORSCHE
PART 2 BMW
PART 3 Let's Get the Special Models!

1 - histrical collection   2 - heritage collection   3 - silver collection

MINICHAMPS AT REAL CAR DEALERSHIPS

A miniature model shop isn't the only place where your can buy Paul's Model Art / Minichamps models.
It is possible to purchase miniature models at a production car dealership. Indeed there are some models that are only sold at real car dealerships, and as such fans should be aware not to miss them!

Special Thanks to
Porsche Japan Setagaya
BMW Japan

PART 1 PORSCHE

In many import car dealerships, you can purchase the latest miniature models. Of course, many of them are manufactured by Paul's Model Art / Minichamps. There are some special models only sold at car dealerships. The quality of the German based Paul's Model Art / Minichamps' miniature models is very highly regarded, even by the automobile manufacturers themselves. The special models come in boxed distinctive cases. Their design is really quite remarkable. Specially ordered miniature models tend to have a unique or particular body colour and emblems, which are not available on general sale. For example, consider the Porsche: a silver body colour is popular on the actual cars and miniature models alike, but a silver coloured miniature model is seldom seen on the general release. But if you look at the 1/43-scale models sold in Porsche dealerships, you can often find models specific to that dealership unavailable on the market.

This photo is of the Setagaya, Tokyo's Porsche Centre. In the display cabinet, there are so many beautiful 1/43-scale models on show that it is hard for you to choose a favourite!

There are also certain models available in car dealerships that are not yet available on the market. For example, the Porsche Cayenne and BMW Z4 are only sold in dealerships as specially ordered models at present. Special models available at car dealerships include past and present favourites as well as certain racing machines. In order to complete a collection, one must acquire such models. New models come in frequently but as expected, popular miniature models sell out fast. It is useful to check your local car dealerships regularly for any rare new miniature models. Why not allow yourself trips to car dealerships to see the range of miniature models (and also admire the full size models!) at the weekends?

The special colour range elevates the status of the car

Porsche dealerships have packages of historical miniature models on sale, aptly named 'History Collection'. The Le Mans and Turbo ranges are included in those packages. They are not sold on the market, nor are they available individually.

Popular series sold only at dealerships include the GT3 and GT3R. These are some of the many 1/43-scale models specially sold this way.

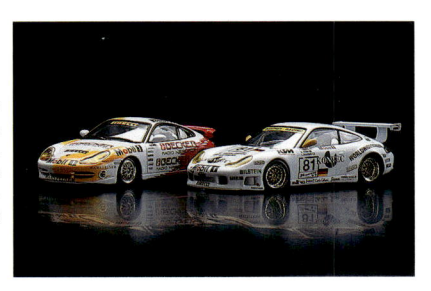

'History Collection' targeting on Porsches

Le Mans Set

These are the machines that battled many times at Le Mans. This set features miniaturized models of the cars exhibited in the Porsche Museum adjacent to the Porsche headquarters in Germany. The collection includes the 917K, the first Le Mans winner as well as the Martini striped markings of the 953/78. The collection is very attractive indeed.

917 Langheck-Coupe 
356 Leichtmetell-Coupe 1951 
936/77 Spyder 
917 Kurzheck-Coupe 1970 
956C Coupe 1982 
935/78 Coupe "Moby Dick" 1978 
993 GT1 1996

Turbo Set

The Turbo set covers the very first turbo model, the 930 Turbo, right up to the latest 996 Turbo. All of the 4 models come in silver and are housed by a beautiful specially made box. This set attracts great popularity.

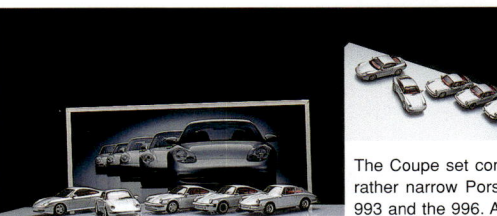

Coupe Set

The Coupe set consists of 5 models, the very first rather narrow Porsche 911, the 930, the 964, the 993 and the 996. All are made by Paul's Model Art / Minichamps, except the 996 (made by Schuco).

Targa Set

From the narrow Porsche 911 to the latest 996, 5 Targas are in the set. They come in silver with a red interior. The appearance is striking.

MINICHAMPS AT REAL CAR DEALERSHIPS

PART 1 PORSCHE
PART2 BMW
PART3 Let's Get the Special Models!

1 - histrical collection   2 - heritage collection   3 - silver collection

Porsche dealerships offer miniatures in silver as standard. And as mentioned earlier, the regular retail versions do not include silver models.

Porsche has always advocated selling miniature models at dealerships. Recently the 993 Coupe, Targa and Cabriolet models, in addition to the GT2, have been on sale at Porsche dealerships.

It is important to note that miniature models sold in Porsche dealerships are not the same as those sold on the main retail market.

Dealership models come in special colours that are not found elsewhere, and are not to be missed! At present, the recently re-vamped 996 and the Boxster are available in a variety of different colours.

In addition to road cars, many racing machines have been miniaturized for sale. The show models of 1/43-scale models, and presentation models, are particularly rare and valuable.

The Heritage Collection – the ultimate masterpiece

A range of Porsche convertibles are being sold as 'Heritage Collection'. The 5 series, the first Porsche 911, the mid-engined 356, the 356A Speedster, the 550 Spider, the RS60 Spider and 911 Speedster all feature in the collection. They are, however, completely sold out, and as such are exceptionally difficult to obtain today.

Porsche 911 GT1 "Black Window"

This 911 GT1 is the Le Mans winner of 1998. It was released as a special order model before going on general sale. There is no interior detail, hence the windows being blacked out. Notice also that the wheels are different from those of the models on general release.

Porsche 911 Super Cup Presentation Model

The 993 super cup model comes with stand. The presentation model has been miniaturized with a specially ordered body colour not found elsewhere on the market.

column

The Silver Collection – a new range

The BMW 2002 Turbo and Porsche 911 are sports cars that are representative of their era. They are both limited edition models, so purchasing soon to avoid disappointment is advised.

The polished body series were released as a new range of miniature models exclusive to dealerships. They are so well polished that one is hesitant to touch them. At present, the narrow Porsche 911 Coupe, Targa and BMW 2002 Turbo are on sale, with more exciting additions to the range hoped to be available soon.

Because the body sculpture is so beautiful and yet simple, it is important to apply delicate craftsmanship in the production of a Porsche miniature model. Such fine craftsmanship is a trademark of Paul's Model Art / Minichamps.

PART2 BMW

Wonderfully presented in a special box, great satisfaction is assured.

BMW is also enthusiastic about special order miniature models. There are many 1/43-scale models in BMW dealerships. There are many variations of miniature models past and present, including racing machines and F1 machines. Most of them come in colours exclusive to dealerships, and BMW fans should not miss out on them! Some may appear to have the same colour as a regular production miniature, but on closer inspection, delicate differences in detail can be noticed. Hence one must enjoy, but also be aware, of the many intricacies of the models.

Furthermore, certain models are often sold in dealerships prior to general release. For example the 2002 series, 1600 series Touring and Cabriolet, and latest Z4 have not yet been released by Paul's Model Art / Minichamps.

Indeed, it is both interesting and fun to see the actual cars and juxtapose them to their miniature cousins in the dealerships.

MINICHAMPS AT REAL CAR DEALERSHIPS

PART 1 PORSCHE
PART 2 BMW
PART 3 Let's Get the Special Models!

1 - colorful line up   2 - open air series line up   3 - F1 machine completeness rise

The colourful variations of new and old models will tickle the hearts of collectors

7 Series
This is the current 7 series, which has many high-tech features.

X5 4.4i
With the X5 you can enjoy BMW driving on and off road.

M3 Coupe Japan Original (E46)
This is the Japanese original, sold only in Japanese BMW dealerships.

M3 Coupe (E46)
This is the current M3 sold in BMW dealerships worldwide.

M3 (E30)
The black M3 (E30) is available on general release. The dealership model is red.

3 Series Coupe
This is the current 3 series Coupe, blessed with a beautifully sculpted body.

325 Ti Compact
This is the compact 3 series hatchback model.

318i Touring
The popular 3 series Touring model is also in the range.

635 Csi
The enormously popular 6 series is also on sale.

323i
This 3 series truly expanded BMW's popularity.

2002 Turbo
Notice the different colour of the spoilers on this model when compared to the general release version.

2000Tii Touring
You cannot find this colour available on general release.

1600
The famous 2002 series was based on this model.

1600 Touring
BMW's first Touring model, a model definitive of its era, is available in miniature form

1600 Cabrio
This model was never available on general market release and is exceptionally rare.

700
Only this miniature model comes in this format.

These are models that are only sold in Japan, exclusive to the Japanese market. They are understandably still attractive to foreign-based collectors. In addition to the distinct nature of the model itself, it also comes in a special box. Though it appears to be a simple black box, it can actually be folded in the middle to become an exhibition piece for the miniature model.

Miniature models of the past have the same casing, but come in different colours and have the model name printed on the base. Some boxes also come with beautiful drawings. They are available while stocks last.

BMW's dealership models come and go very quickly. If you are not careful, a new model may arrive and then sell out before you know it. The dealership is therefore a very good place to look for miniature models, especially because these models are particularly likely to become valuable in the near future.

The range also includes many convertibles.

Z8
Z8, BMW's leading convertible, has stunning body sculpting.

Z8 Cabrio
The Z8 miniature is also available with the roof down.

M Roadster
The M Roadster is the special convertible that comes with an M3 engine.

M Roadster (Open Ver.)
This is the same M Roadster, but with the roof down.

Z3 Roadster 2.8
The top of the range Z3 with high performance engine.

Z8 Safety Car
This is the miniature model of a Z8 used as safety car.

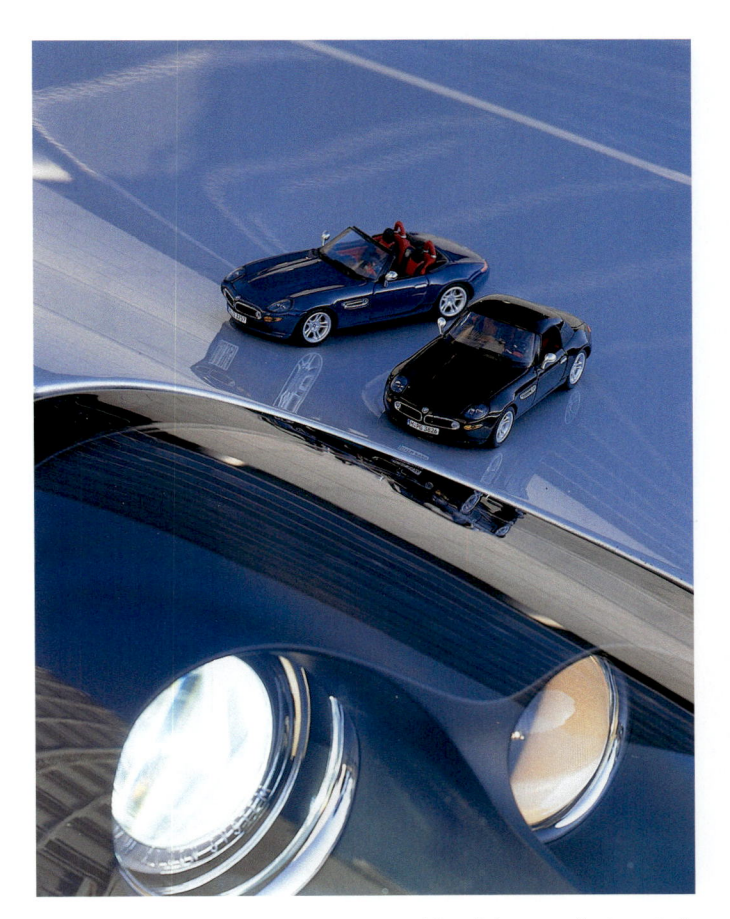

Even if the body may appear the same, there are subtle variations according to grades in dealership models. You have a good chance of finding a model identical to your own car.

---

column

Winning F1 machines made in such accurate detail

BMW are now supplying F1 engines to the Williams team. There are many F1 miniature models now available, including the very latest F1 machines. It is therefore a good idea for F1 fans to check dealership versions.

Williams F1 FW24
This is the 2002 Williams FW24. The original display is different from the retail version.

B 186
This is the Benetton B186. F1 machines of the past are continually being added to the range.

Williams F1 FW24
Though it may appear to be the same as the model on the left, the driver is actually different in this model.

792
This is the machine that has conquered F2. The wider range available at dealerships makes them good places to look.

MINICHAMPS AT REAL CAR DEALERSHIPS

PART 1　PORSCHE
PART 2　BMW
PART 3　Let's Get the Special Models!

1 - Porche by the dealer is possible　　2 - Let's Get the Special Models!

MINI ONE
This is the basic version of Mini One. This playful new Mini comes in several different colours.

Two Mini Coopers sit on the dashboard of a real new Mini. The 2 white stripes on the bonnet and large wheels are perfectly replicated.

column

You can also purchase classic racing car models at BMW dealerships

At BMW dealerships, there are road cars, Grand Prix machines and racing cars of past and present available in miniature form. Shown on the right are just a few of them. You are likely to find one you like at your local dealership.

BMW 507 Schauinsland Rennen winner 1959
The 507 Hard Top is the machine the legendary Hans Stuck drove.

M1 ProCar
One make racing version of the M1 mode was miniaturized.

635 Csi Gr. A
The 635CSi won many touring car races in Europe and various other countries.

BMW M3 GTR 2001
BMW's latest, mean-looking, racing machine with V8 engine.

PART 3 Let's Get the Special Models!

There are manufacturers other than Porsche and BMW that sell miniature models in their show rooms. Indeed most German manufacturers sell miniature models in their dealerships, Mercedes-Benz being a good example – having a wide range from the latest E-class to the classic models. However for brands like Audi, VW, and Opel, it is sometimes necessary to purchase straight from Paul's Model Art / Minichamps.

No matter which show room you look in, you will find miniature models of past and present cars. One could perhaps attribute this to the importance of historical development among European manufacturers.

In building a truly accomplished miniature collection, it is hence useful to visit dealerships as well as miniature model shops.

Mercedes-Benz

Here are some of the older Mercedes-Benz models. The 280SL and W123 estate car are fast becoming difficult to find, and not to be missed by the Mercedes-Benz collector.

Smart

Smart, the city commuter car manufacturer, also keep miniature models in dealerships. The photo shown here is of the retail version, however there are two dealership models, which each have two different colours to the body. It is a playful model, and the body colours are interchangeable.

230 SL Rallye Spa-Sofia -Liege 1963
This is the rally version of the SL. It is a very rare model indeed, and the simple body decoration is indicative of the time.

230 SL Around the world in 80 days
There are several versions of the rally model, sure to ignite the passions of any rally fan.

450 SLC 5.0 Rallye
The distinctive features, such as the huge grill-guard with fog lights and the spotlights, are superbly replicated.

Audi

Audi, also, has many models available at dealerships. We have featured the TT Coupe, but there are the new A8, popular A4, RS4 Avant, and RS6 also available in the range, with several colours available for each model.

Audi 450 SLC 5.0 Rallye

The COMPANY

Special Interview for MINICHAMPS

Minichamps Past, Present, and Future

Paul's Model Art / Minichamps continue to charm miniature fans the world over with their top quality models. But what kind of thinking and people are behind the product? The best way to find out is to go straight to the top! A team of reporters flew to Aachen, Germany where the Paul's Model Art / Minichamps company is based, and interviewed managing director Mr Paul G. Lang. What they discovered was a great passion for miniature models!

Reporter: Thank you for spending time with us. Paul's Model Art's / Minichamps' products have been on sale for 10 years now and instantly became the top miniature models brand when they were introduced. We as fans are very happy about this. Firstly, what has been the path of Paul's Model Art / Minichamps' growth?

Mr. Lang: In 1923, my grandfather, Johann Danhausen opened his shop in the town of Aachen. At that time he did not sell miniature models but bicycles and hardware goods… It was after the Second World War that he started to sell toys. It was then that people began to spend money on toys, which were generally regarded as hobby products. As a child I grew up in that particular environment. However I was not interested in selling toys and after graduating from university, I worked in the TV industry. It was in the '70's that I began helping in my family's business. My first assignment was to import and sell English made metal kits in 1972 and 1973. We were working with Western Model / England and AMR in Paris, a company we subsequently bought, and we became serious about selling model cars. In the end, we moved all the development facilities and factory to Hong Kong.

Reporter: We believe your product is very high quality. Is this the number one priority for Paul's Model Art / Minichamps?

Mr. Lang: Of course. High quality is our top priority. For example of this are that in 1991 we released a series of hand made DTM models, including Audi, Mercedes-Benz, and BMW M3 in Nuremberg Toy Fair.

Reporter: Is there a specific model that you particularly like?

Mr. Lang: I quite like the first production and sales model of the Audi V8's DTM car. I would class it 95% satisfactory by my standards. It was mass-produced using die cast, but the end result was still close to that of hand made models.

Reporter: This is it. [showing Mr. Lang the actual model, which had been brought by the reporter]

Mr. Lang: Oh! This is it! I am surprised you have it. I am sure there are some parts that need to be updated in comparison to the current model. However I have a special affinity for it.

Reporter: Can you sign it for me?

Paul's Model Art / Minichamps
Managing director, Mr. Paul G. Lang:

"Products that I wasn't satisfied with? None……that I can remember [he says, with a smile]"

This is the exterior of Paul's Model Art / Minichamps in Aachen. It is very clean and modern. The Mercedes-Benz at the entrance is Mr. Lang's limousine.

Mr. Lang: Of course.

Reporter: It appears that the miniature models by Paul's Model Art / Minichamps are made only on a limited scale. Is there a particular reason for this?

Mr. Lang: One of the reasons for it is that we are particularly concerned about the collector's market. The collectors like limited editions. We only produce each model once so that the market is not diluted by over-production. We want our product to be unique and we will not produce the same model again. Another reason is that, especially in the case of racing models, the market does not react kindly if we release them a number of times. So, if we talk about the racing machines of 2003, the models should be made once without much time delay. We believe this is very important for our sales.

Reporter: I see. On the other hand, you are releasing some old racing machines like McLaren and Chaparral. Is this to meet the demands of the market?

Mr. Lang: It is true that we still receive demands for these models. We recently signed a contract with McLaren to release all the McLaren series from the past.

Reporter: Internet auctions are becoming widely popular around the world. What is your reaction to Paul's Model Art's / Minichamps' products being auctioned on them?

Mr. Lang: We know that some of our products are traded at very high prices among collectors. We have no problems with such trade. On the contrary we are rather honoured to see our products valued like that. We will continue our efforts to release models that will appreciate in value.

Reporter: There are many people who appreciate the models released by Paul's Model Art / Minichamps. Have there been any models that you weren't really satisfied with?

Mr. Lang: There shouldn't be...[he says, laughing]. But if I were to pick a model, the quality of the W124(E-class) could have been better. It was sold in 1993.

Reporter: Really? That was extremely popular in Japan...

Mr. Lang Yes, so I heard. It was popular in Germany too. However I never liked the finish of the model. The demand for a remake is very high but we will not do it. After that model there wasn't anything I was unhappy with. Achieving 100% satisfaction level is a very difficult thing of course, but I believe we make no compromises in the quality of our products.

Reporter: What can we expect in future productions from Paul's Model Art / Minichamps?

Mr. Lang: We have a very wide and varied range now. We will be releasing more racing machines, the Senna collection, the McLaren collection, and so on. There will also be new models added to the ranges of tanks and motorbikes. Personally I like the old fire trucks, so I am hoping to add them to the portfolio.

Reporter: The tank series is something new to me. Are there any other new fields that you are planning to introduce?

Mr. Lang: At the moment we have no plans to enter new areas, such as aeroplanes for example. There are far too many competitors.

Reporter: With regard to the making decisions in terms of scheduling and releasing new models and innovations, are these made by you or do you make them based on discussions?

Mr. Lang: Basically, we make decisions based on discussions with our sales and development people. Ultimately however I make the final decisions. As old cars become less popular we tend to release

Managing Director Paul G. Lang

newer models. Releasing cars that I like, such as old fire trucks, motorbikes, and tanks have solely been my decision.

Reporter: I'm somewhat relieved to hear that even your favourite models are already among the established categories!

Mr. Lang: I cannot influence the company purely based on my hobby. We have a meeting twice a year where the distributors from all over the world gather to discuss the future and sales targets. As for the licensed models, we have to be very careful with the timing when it comes to production. There was a case where we made the miniature model 3 years after obtaining the license.

We also have to take into consideration certain characteristics of the miniature models. For example, German models sell best in Germany, American models sell best in America, and so forth. We have to understand the markets and carefully plan the volumes of models we make.

Reporter: What about models targeted the Japanese market?

Mr. Lang: It would be difficult to market Japanese cars worldwide. At the moment, we make some Toyota models, but competition in Japan is vast and the demand for Japanese cars in Europe is not great. Therefore we have no plans to introduce any new Japanese models at this point in time.

Reporter: Is there a competitor right now for Paul's Model Art / Minichamps?

Although the W124(500E) was popular in Japan, Mr. Lang was not very satisfied with the finish. This is a model hoped to be remade with the latest technology.

Mr. Lang: There are many competitors. But in 1990-1991, we moved our production to China and a great deal of effort was made in raising the quality. We gather information and do the research and development in Germany and then take this to China where the models are carefully produced. This is how we maintain our exceptionally high quality standards.

Reporter: Is it better for the collectors that only a few limited models are released each year.

Mr. Lang: Yes, you are right. If there are too many special models, there is no value or meaning to limited editions, and thus market interest will diminish.

Reporter: Speaking of collectors. They keep track of the collection by the serial codes. However with Paul's Model Art's / Minichamps' models the last digit of the serial number is sometimes not printed. Why is this?

Mr. Lang: It's for a very simple reason. The last number identifies the body colour. For example, the miniature models that automobile manufacturers sell (including those sold in dealerships) have the serial number 3, which is indicative of a special colour. This colour is not used in the regular models. So, with regular models, the number is simply not printed.
As for different numbers that are not printed on the regular models, it is either going to be added to the range or for some reason the model has been discontinued.

Reporter: I didn't know there were these reasons. Very interesting indeed. Now, I hear that you are building a museum right next to your offices. When will it open?

Mr. Lang: The building will be completed in May 2004 and the museum will open around the same time. It will be open to everyone and for all to enjoy. The space is limited, so we cannot display all the miniature models but we are in the midst of planning how we would exhibit some of them. The miniature models to be exhibited are already there.

Reporter: Do you have any comments for the Japanese fans?

Mr. Lang: I believe the Japanese fans have good taste and the collector market is well established here. We are happy to hear that Paul's Model Art / Minichamps is receiving positive and good acceptance in such a selective market. We will continue in delivering products that will satisfy customers' demands.

Reporter: I think the Japanese fans would like to see what they are familiar with.
For example, the F1 cars that raced in the Japanese Grand Prix and the models of the super car era. People like to have the models they remember seeing. And we cannot ignore the demand for Ferrari.

Mr. Lang: Is Ferrari necessary? If Paul's Model Art / Minichamps obtained a license to make Ferraris, do you think there would still be a market for them?

Here we are overlooking the entrance from the 2nd floor of the head office. The middle part of the building is a stairwell and behind it is the office. The office is brightly lit.

A new office is being built right next to the current building. This will be the office, stock room and exhibition space for Paul's Model Art / Minichamps products. The exterior has the same style as the current head office.

Special Interview for MINICHAMPS

Reporter: I am not sure if Ferrari would still be a massive sales success. However they are bound to become important items for the collectors. We would very much love to see the F40, 512BB and Dino246GT. There was a so-called "super car boom" in Japan, and the people of that era are now in their 30's. I am sure releasing cars of that era would meet a great demand.

Mr. Lang: When we released the Countach, there was a huge volume of orders from the Japanese fans. We will certainly consider your suggestions.

Reporter: Thank you very much for your time.

The Audi DTM machine, the first model, is a favourite. The racing models, especially DTM machines, contributed largely to the success of Paul's Model Art / Minichamps today.

MINICHAMPS trivia

Paul's Model Art / Minichamps produces a wide range of miniature cars.
The boxes and labels mark 10 years of heritage, and collectors should be able to enjoy the development.
Let's get to know Paul's Model Art / Minichamps more.

Chapter 1

Box & label

With a few exceptions, Paul's Model Art / Minichamps' miniature models are housed in a clear case presented in a cardboard box. As you already know, there are labels with the name of the model as well as serial numbers on one side of the box. We will always focus on the miniature models themselves, but there's so much information on the box and the label. We shall explain some of these features through photos.

Firstly, let us consider the box. The metallic dark grey box was used from Paul's Model Art / Minichamps' foundation until 1993. After that, the box was silver, without changing the design until it became black in 1997. Until then, both road car and racing machine had the same box. Currently road cars come in a black box, and racing machines come in the checker flag design box.

On the label, serial number, name of the car, and colour of the model are printed. We should take note of the serial numbers. Initially, it was a 4 digit number starting with "Best. Nr". After 1997, it was a 6 digit number starting with "MIN". Currently, the serial numbers are 9 digits.

Note, however, that these are purely observations, rather than official statements.

The early series

A metallic dark grey box was used from Paul's Model Art / Minichamps' birth until 1993. Today, there are Paul's Model Art / Minichamps stickers on top of a model's clear casing. If you do find such a box, you can be sure that the model is quite old.

The middle era

A silver box with the same design was used from 1993 until 1996. This box was used for both road cars and racing machines. The logic to the serial number was altered half way through this period to how it is known today.

Current model 1
Road Cars

The box in which current models come was first used in 1997. The design of the box changed to become black with white logo. From 2001, the URL was printed on the back of the box.

Current model 2
Racing Machines

The overall colour of the box is black, but it is decorated with a checkered flag – a very flashy box indeed! The URL is printed on the back of the box, as it is with road cars.

The early series

The serial number of the early series of road cars comes with 'Best. Nr' followed by a 4 digit number and a letter. The letter represents the colour.

The middle era

After 1997, the serial number was a minimum of 6 digits. The numbers can be interpreted in the same way as the current serial numbers' final 6 digit numbers.

Current models

The serial numbers for current models are 9 digit numbers. The font of the label sometimes differs between models.

Special releases

The first 3 digits given to regular models are always 430. In many cases, for special release models the number will be 433 instead of 430.

430 006900

The first 3 digits – 430 – show that the model is 1/43-scale. The next 3 digits denote the brand of the car. For example, 020 denotes a BMW and 030 a Mercedes-Benz. Some brands share the same code. The last 3 digits – for example 900 - represent the type and colour of the car. With the last digit, for road cars, 0 indicates that this model is in the original production colour. Numbering 1, 2, and so forth indicates the subsequent order in which the model's colour was added to the range. Sometimes, however, there can be no number at all.

Chapter 2
Dealer Version

Because of the high quality of Paul's Model Art / Minichamps miniature models, there are special versions ordered by request from the car manufacturers. Some are used for promotional purposes, and others are sold in dealerships worldwide. They are clearly separated, and usually known as the 'dealer version'. The dealership versions are often quite different models, also with distinct packaging. We will show you some of the examples below.

Benz — There are quite a number of models made for Mercedes-Benz. They currently come in dark grey, rough skinned boxes, and silver, smooth skinned boxes.

Porsche — The box is a brownish grey and has rough skin. The name of the car is printed both on the cardboard box and the base of the miniature model.

Audi — Audi uses a silver and white box. The cutting on the cardboard box is shaped like an arc, and is very unique. But then individuality is the essential.

BMW — Until recently the cardboard box came beautifully illustrated. Currently the models come in a black box, which opens up and becomes a display stand. The silver BMW emblem is quite impressive.

Volvo — The design is very simple. On the white box, the Volvo logo is printed in blue. On the base is the name of the miniature model.

VW — This black cardboard box has a very simple design. Its larger dimensions are particular to VW dealership versions.

Chapter 3
Special Box

At Paul's Model Art / Minichamps, special models come in special boxes, and limited editions come in commemorative gift boxes. These boxes are so beautiful you can spend hours looking at the boxes alone. Here are some examples:

To the left is the McLaren Can-am machine from the McLaren Collection. The McLaren F1 is on the right hand side with it's original box.

Around 1995, DTM models came in a box with a popular DTM car illustration on it. The box varies according to the season it was released.

Only Martini sponsored Alfa Romeos come in a special box. The finish on this box is as good as the box of a special version.

The F50 and 550 Maranello come in a distinctive blue box, which is specific to this set. Different models come in a red box.

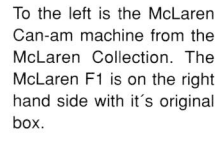

Original boxes are prepared for special models, MEETING POINT. On a white box, national flags tend to look particularly sharp.

This model, a limited edition with gift box, was made to commemorate Nicola Larini's winning of the DTM championship. A record of his race victories

The trendy design and decoration of this machine is quite unique. In fact, the sponsor was a condom manufacturer.

In 1994, this DTM Special Edition was in the catalogue. Other than the Mercedes-Benz shown above, there is a BMW M3 and an Audi V8.

Have the tyres got stuck to the base?!?

Sometimes, the tyres of old miniature models get stuck to the base. This is because some of the materials used in the tyres melt slightly during time and stick to the base of the box. But this will not affect the main body of the car. Do remember, though, that the screws that hold the model to the base of the box should not be too tight.

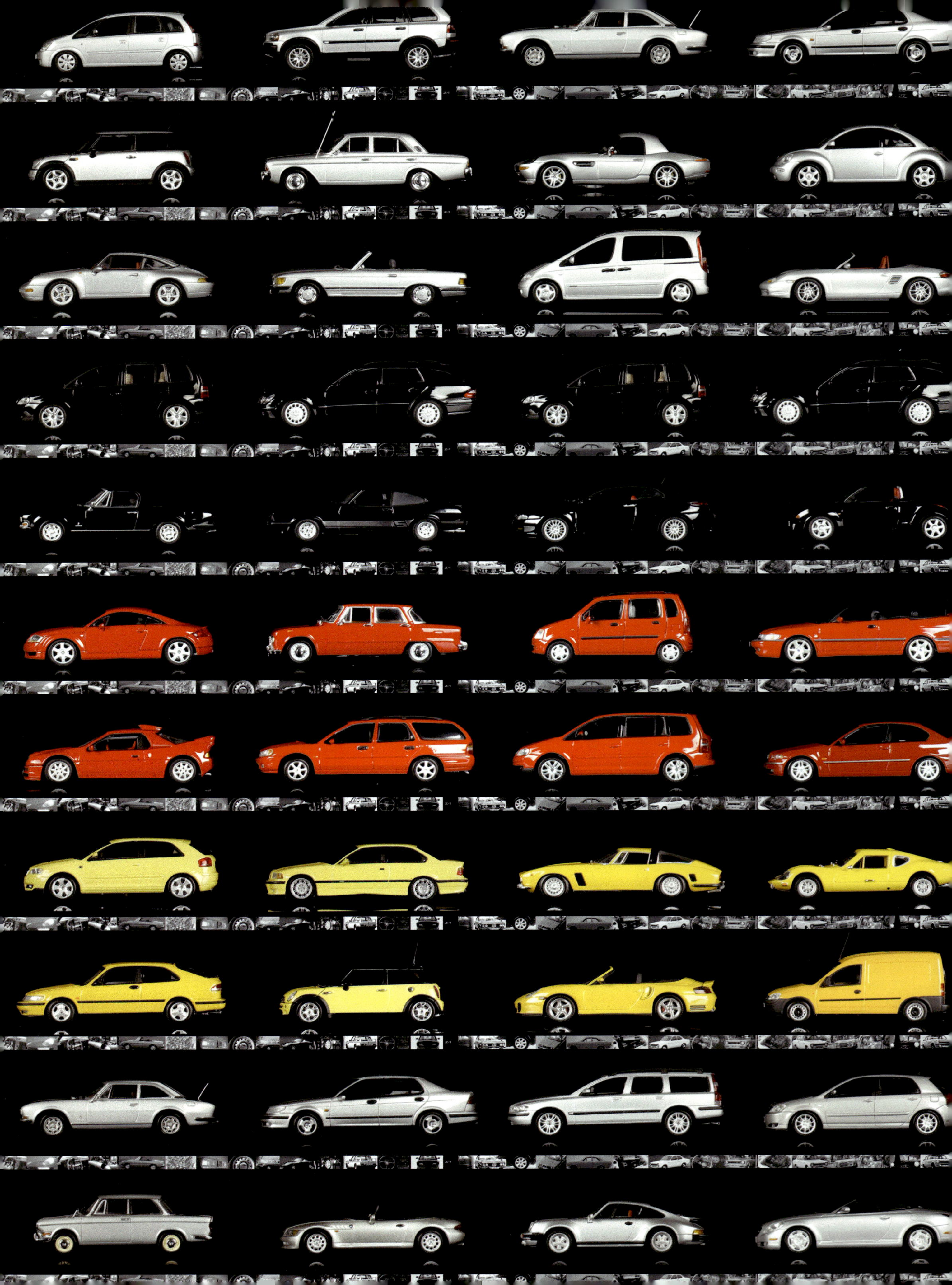

Rare Models Museum

MINICHAMPS

p 100   McLaren F1 GTR "WEST"

p 101   Audi V8 QUATTRO DTM "10 Jahre"

p 102   Dauer Porsche 962C & 911 RS "International Toy Fair Model"

p 103   Lancia Stratos "International Toy Fair Model"
AlfaRomeo 147 "IAA Model"

p 104   Porsche 911 Carrera 1973 "MODELL FAHRZEUG Version"
Porsche 911 GT1 "MODELL FAHRZEUG Version"

p 105   Lamborghini Countach LP400 "AUTOSTADT Version"
Ferrari 550 Maranello "Record Car"

The collecting of exclusive masterpieces

The miniature models of Paul's Model Art / Minichamps are made only once.
These models are very rare.
But there are models that were never released on general sale.
Fans would love to get their hands on these, the rarest of the rare.

Rare Models Museum

McLaren F1 GTR "WEST"

In the history of Paul's Model Art / Minichamps, no model ever produced is rarer than this one.

The McLaren F1 GTR won many races including The Le Mans 24 hours, which it did on its first ever entry at the race. This was the first time such a thing had ever happened at Le Mans. This race car was competing in the FIA BPR series, in which tobacco advertising was restricted. The car raced with the logo "East" instead of the tobacco logo "West". The miniature models sold by Paul's Model Art / Minichamps were released with the "East" logo. The model with the proper logo "West" is a special edition, shown here, and was made as a gift to be given to only a few close friends. It is somewhat of a phantom to collectors.

The difference with the market version is, of course, the logo. The "West" McLaren F1 GTR model does not have serial numbers printed on it. Because it is such a rare model, there are many fakes on the market, which you should be aware of at auctions.

To commemorate 10 years in business, the boxed Audi was given to a few close friends.

The Audi V8 is the first miniature model Paul's Model Art / Minichamps made. It is the favourite model of managing director Mr. Lang, and was resurrected as a gift version to commemorate Paul's Model Art / Minichamps' tenth anniversary.
Only 500 were made, and none were sold. It was a special gift given to close friends of Paul's Model Art / Minichamps. The photograph featured in the gift box is of the new Paul's Model Art / Minichamps Head Office. Every single one of the models has a serial number.

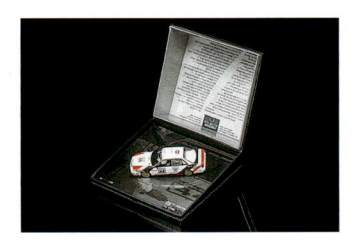

In addition to the beauty of the gift box and the rarity of the model, it stands as proof that in 10 years Paul's Model Art / Minichamps has continued to progress in terms of quality. The body sculpting is accurate and sharp, everything on this model seems flawless.

Rare Models Museum

Audi V8 QUATTRO DTM "10 Jahre"

Rare Models Museum

Dauer Porsche 962C & 911 RS
"International Toy Fair Model"

At the world's largest toy show, the Paul's Model Art / Minichamps special model is given to close friends.

The world's biggest toy fair is held annually from the end of January until early February in Nuremberg, Germany. New models are introduced at this fair, which is only open to retailers and related business personnel and not to the general public. The models given out here were never sold, they were only given out as business gifts.

Every year, a special model is made, with large "Paul's Model Art / Minichamps" and "Spielwarenmesse" logos printed on them. This is a model that Paul's Model Art / Minichamps fans would love to get their hands on!

A Dauer Porsche was handed out at the 2002 toy fair. The symbol on the front, as well as the checker flag-like design, is very unique. The Carrera RS comes with the usual hand-written style logo. If it were sold on the market, there would be no doubting its popularity.

The models are essentially the same as the retail versions. The logos are the distinguishing feature of the models that were given out at the toy fair.

This special model was handed out at the Nuremberg Toy Fair. The rocking horse, the symbol of the show, and the teddy bear logo, are both very cute. The authenticity of Paul's Model Art / Minichamps miniature models seen together with such logos is quite an interesting sight.

Rare Models Museum

Lancia Stratos
"International Toy Fair Model"

Teddy bear and rocking horse symbols
A rare model, which is extremely difficult to obtain

The checker flag sticker is even featured on the rear window of the Alfa Romeo 147, it was made for the 2001 toy fair.

The IAA Frankfurt Motor Show is also a place where new miniature models are released. Paul's Model Art / Minichamps, a German Company, makes many new models for this show. On the bonnet, the IAA symbol is printed to striking effect.

Rare Models Museum

AlfaRomeo 147
"IAA Model"

Paul's Model Art / Minichamps raises the spirit of the Frankfurt Motor Show

103

The Pink colour was chosen by the editor in chief. The Carrera RSR is a popular model. A limited number of only 1000 were made.

The German model car magazine, 'Modell Fahrzeug', releases many special order Paul's Model Art / Minichamps models. This photo is of the Carrera RSR with an ostentatious pink body, and it is undoubtedly the most striking model of the collection. The Porsche Carrera GT also comes in bright pink.

Rare Models Museum

Porsche 911 Carrera 1973

"MODELL FAHRZEUG Version"

The German miniature model magazine released a shocking pink 73 Porsche Carrera

The model itself is the same as the Le Mans version. But the road version comes in a refreshing metallic blue, which creates a different ambience.

The 911GT1 was made to win the Le Mans 24 hours in the GT class. There is a road version of the 911 GT1 but it was never miniaturized. This is a special order of the road version, which is sure to interest Porsche and Le Mans fans alike.

Rare Models Museum

Porsche 911 GT1

"MODELL FAHRZEUG Version"

The racing machine that can be driven on the roads
The almost non-existent Masterpiece

The model itself is the same as the regular version, having a yellow body with tan interior. The striking 'Autostadt' logo was tampo printed on the bonnet.

The release of the Countach was long awaited, and it became a massive success soon after release. This Countach is slightly different from the regular version. Only 400 models with the 'Autostadt' logo were produced. As such it is a very rare model, and is seldom seen.

Rare Models Museum

Lamborghini Countach LP400
"AUTOSTADT Version"

The Countach made by a German shop, bearing its logo

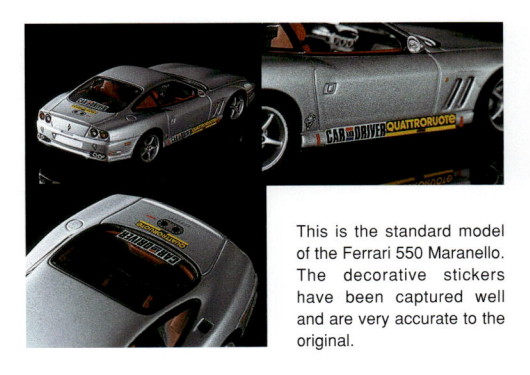

This is the standard model of the Ferrari 550 Maranello. The decorative stickers have been captured well and are very accurate to the original.

This 550 Maranello was made by the Seattle model shop 'Gasoline'. It is the miniaturized version of the 550 Maranello, which 'Car & Driver' tested for a speed record. There are many models made by individual shops the world over.

Rare Models Museum

Ferrari 550 Maranello
"Record Car"

The 550 Maranello made by a shop – the stickers bring originality

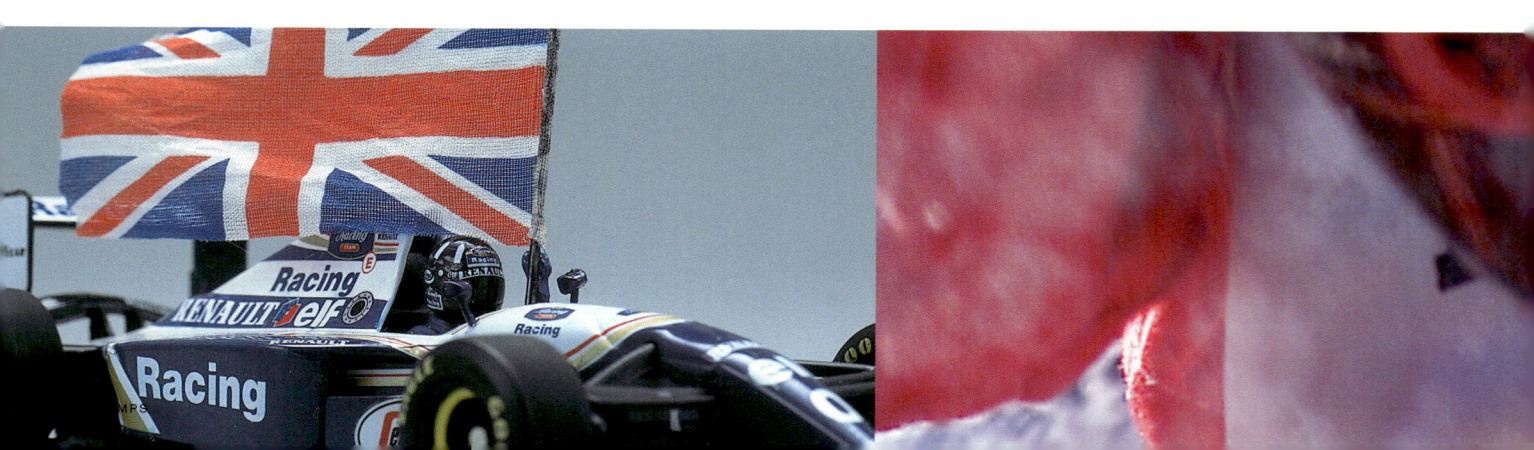

Racing Cars of MINI

CHAMPS

The joy of synergy between the unusual and the ordinary

If road cars are a collection of the ordinary, collecting racing cars is the pursuit of the unusual.
The speed and exhilaration of motor racing make the driver's heart pound while the car's exhaust roars.
Here we introduce you to the range of competitive racing vehicles released by Paul's Model Art / Minichamps.

Race Cars that have competed at the world's top racing circuits

Formula 1 - the world's finest racing machines driven by the world's finest drivers.

It is sometimes known as the "F1 Circus", with races being held all over the world, captivating new and existing fans alike.
The beautiful form of F1 machines is replicated fantastically in 1/43-scale models.

rmula 1

MICHAEL SCHUMACHER COLLECTION

F1 collectors dream of completing this, the Michael Schumacher collection

The Michael Schumacher collection began in 1994. His sensational victories in the Benetton paved the way for him to become a champion with Ferrari. The miniaturised models range from 1/12-scale to 1/64-scale models. There are fourty 1/43-scale models, the most extensive range in the collection. There are some models in the collection that are not F1, and Paul's Model Art / Minichamps hope you enjoy these too – the collection aims to capture the complete essence of Michael Schumacher, one of the finest racing drivers ever. They are all so popular that they sold out rapidly. As such it is now difficult to make a full collection. Models 16, 17, and 22 are traded at particularly high prices amongst collectors, owing to their scarcity. This is Paul's Model Art / Minichamps biggest collection, and as such the pursuit of quality and accurate replication is particularly meticulous.

Ed.1 Benetton Ford B192 GP Belgium 1992
510 430000

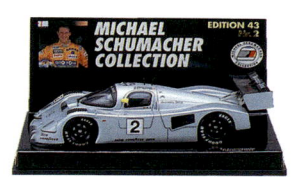

Ed.2 Sauber Mercedes C 291 Autopolis Japan 1991
510 430001

Ed.3 Mercedes-Benz 190 E Evo 2 1991
510 430002

Ed.4 Sauber Mercedes C11 Mexico 1991
510 430003

Ed.5 Ford Escort Cosworth 1992
510 430005

Ed.6 Kart
510 430006

Ed.7 Reynard F3 German Champion 1990
510 430007

Ed.8
Reynard F3
Macau
510 904304

Ed.9
Benetton Ford B193 Winner GP Portugal 1993
510 430009

Ed.10
Benetton Ford B193 194 Pres. Japan 1994
510 430010

Ed.11
Benetton Ford B194 GP Pacific 1994
510 944305

Ed.12
Benetton Ford B194 GP Germany 1994
510 944325

Ed.13
Benetton Ford B194 World Champion 94
510 944335

Ed.14
Benetton Ford B194/B195 Showcar 1995
510 954391

Ed.15
Bugatti EB 110
510 430012

Ed.17
Benetton Renault B195 GP France 1995
510 954318

Ed.16
Benetton Renault B195 GP Brasil 1995
510 954301

Ed.18
Benetton Renault B195
GP England 1995
510 954312

Ed.19
Benetton Renault B195
GP Germany 1995
510 954313

Ed.20
Benetton Renault B195
GP Belgium 1995
510 954314

Ed.21
Benetton Renault B195
GP Italy 1995
510 954315

Ed.23
Benetton Renault B195
GP Australia 1995
510 954317

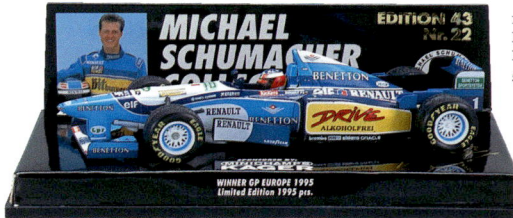

Ed.22
Benetton Renault B195 GP Europe 1995
510 954316

Ed.24
Benetton Renault B195
GP France 1995
510 954318

Ed.25
Ferrari 412 T2
Launch Version 1996
510 964391

Ed.26
Ferrari F310
1996
510 964301

Ed.27
Ferrari 456 GT
510 430014

Ed.28
Ferrari F 355
510 430013

Ed.29
Jordan 191
1991 1st Grand Prix
510 914332

Ed.30
Ferrari F310
1st GP-win with Ferrari Spain 1996
510 964311

Ed.31
Ferrari F310/2
1996
510 964321

Ed.32
Ferrari F310
Presentation 1997
510 974395

Ed.33
Ferrari F310B
1997
510 974305

Ed.34
Kart Set 1995/1996
510 954396

Ed.35
Ferrari F310B
GP Magny Cours 1997
510 974315

Ed.36
Ferrari F310 V10
Presentation 1998
510 984393

Ed.37
Ferrari F300
1998
510 984303

Ed.38
Ferrari F300
with Tower Wings 1998pcs.
510 984333

Ed.39
Ferrari F300
Fiorano Test car
510 984300

Ed.40
Tony Kart
1996
510 964304

111

Toyota

Climbing up the championship ladder, one step at a time – the power of Japan

Toyota entered F1 in 2002, taking the most challenging route possible - building everything from scratch. The Show Car is already difficult to find, but it is still possible to make a full Toyota F1 collection if you start now.

Panasonic Toyota Racing TF102 M.Salo
400 020024

Panasonic Toyota Racing TF102 A.McNish
400 020025

Panasonic Toyota Racing Show Car 2002 M.Salo
400 020074

Toyota F1 Debut 2002 Australia GP M.Salo
Panasonic Box

Panasonic Toyota Racing Show Car 2002 A.McNish
400 020075

Panasonic Toyota Racing TF102 M.Salo
403 020024

Panasonic Toyota Racing TF102 A.McNish
403 020025

Toyota F1 Debut 2002 Australia GP A.McNish
Panasonic Box

Panasonic Toyota Racing Show Car 2002 M.Salo
403 020074

Panasonic Toyota Racing Show Car 2002 without driver
400 020174

Arrows

The Orange typhoon – The creator of excitement in the battle for the middle positions

Arrows ended 24 years of F1 racing in 2002. There was an occasion in 1997 where Arrows had a chance to win a race, but still luck excluded them. This series consists of the recent cars, but there is also a car with distinctive front wing that never actually raced.

Orange Arrows Asiatech Show Car 2001 J. Verstappen
1 of 2.500 pcs.
430 010084

Arrows Yamaha FA18 D.Hill 1997
6th place British GP
433 970101

Arrows Hart 1998 Launch version

Arrows A19 Barcelona Test 1999 T. Takagi
430 990184

Arrows 1999 Show Car T. Takagi
430 990084

Arrows A20 1999 T.Takagi
430 990015

Arrows F1 Show Car 2000 P.De La Rosa
1 of 2.088 pcs.
430 000088

Orange Arrows Asiatech A22 Monte Carlo
400 010114

In order to achieve a lower centre of gravity at the city circuit of Monte Carlo, a distinctive front wing was developed.

Benetton

Benetton - the fashionable constructor that was an icon of the era

A team being owned by a clothing company was previously unheard of in F1. In 1986, the first year in which they competed, they won the Mexican GP and in 1995 they gained both available titles. In 2001, the team was taken over by Renault. Having won the Canadian Grand Prix, Alesi stalled his engine and jumped on Schumacher´s car during the cool down lap and waved from it. This miniature model is very popular.

Benetton BMW B186 1986
G. Berger
430 860020

Benetton Ford B193B Hockenheim 1993
GODE Model

Benetton Ford B192 M.Brundle
GODE Model

Benetton Ford B194 Hockenheim
J. Verstappen 1994
430 940906

On the sidepod, there was a Paul's Model Art / Minichamps logo, because Paul's Model Art / Minichamps was a sponsor of the Benetton team.

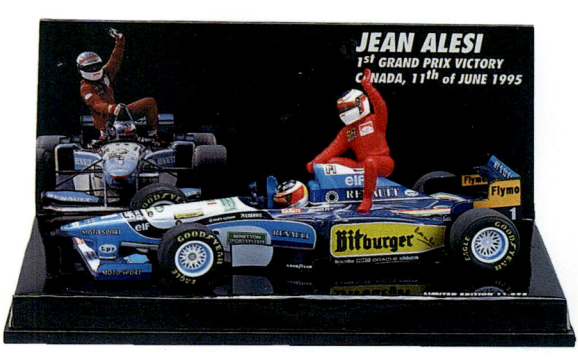

Benetton Renault B196
J. Alesi
430 960003

Jean Alesi 1st Grand Prix Victory Canada 1995
431 952701

Benetton Renault B196
J.Alesi Australian GP Box
433 960003

Benetton Renault B196
J.Alesi
430 960023

Benetton Renault B196
G.Berger
430 960034

Benetton PlayLife B198 A.Wurz
430 980006

Benetton 1999 Show Car G.Fisichella
430 990079

Benetton Renault B197 G.Berger
430 970008

Benetton Renault B197 G.Berger GP Japan 1997
433 970008

Benetton Renault Sport Show Car
2001 G.Fisichella
430010097

Fomula1 Auto Sports Model

113

McLaren

The Great McLaren - a creator of world champions

The McLaren team was founded in 1963 by Bruce McLaren. But it was not until the 1980s, when Ron Dennis became boss, that the team had a stable winning record. The engines used changed from TAG Porsche, to Honda, to Mercedes-Benz, but consistent victories showed the strength of the constructors. There have been many McLaren models released by Paul's Model Art / Minichamps, and they all enjoy great popularity. The McLaren Team Edition of the MP4 series comes with the tobacco logo, and is very rare. The "Black Star" version of the MP4/12 is one of the rarest F1 miniature models in existence.

McLaren MP4/4 Honda Turbo 1988
Ayrton Senna Collection

McLaren MP4/6 Honda V12 1991
Ayrton Senna Collection

McLaren MP4/7 Honda V12 1992
Ayrton Senna Collection

McLaren MP4/8 Ford 1993
A.Senna
530 934308

McLaren MP4/4 Honda V6 Turbo A.Prost
Vice World Champion 1988
530 884311

McLaren MP4/5 Honda V10 A.Prost
World Champion 1989
530 894302

McLaren MP4/9 Peugeot
M.Hakkinen
German GP 1994
533 944367

McLaren MP4/9 Peugeot
M.Hakkinen
British GP 1994
533 944377

McLaren Ford M23 J.Hunt 1976
with engine
530 764311

McLaren MP4/2B TAG Turbo 1985
A. Prost Worldchampion
530 854302

The logo uses just one colour - black. It is one of the most difficult ones to obtain.

McLaren Mercedes MP4/12
M.Hakkinen "Black Star"
533 974309

MP4/10 & 4/11

McLaren MP4/10 Mercedes
N.Mansell
530 954307

McLaren MP4/11
M.Hakkinen
530 964307

McLaren MP4/11
D.Coulthard
533 964308

McLaren MP4/11
M.Hakkinen
533 964307

MP4/12

McLaren MP4/12 Testcar
M.Hakkinen
530 974389

McLaren MP4/12
M.Hakkinen
530 974309

McLaren MP4/12
M.Hakkinen
Team Edition

McLaren MP4/12
D.Coulthard
Team Edition

MP4/13

McLaren MP4/13
M.Hakkinen
530 984308

McLaren MP4/13
D.Coulthard
Team Edition

MP4/14

McLaren MP4/14
D.Coulthard
433 990002

McLaren MP4/14
M.Hakkinen
B6 696 1901

MP4/15

McLaren MP4/15
M.Hakkinen
B6 696 1910

McLaren MP4/15
M.Hakkinen
Team Edition

McLaren MP4/15
D.Coulthard
Team Edition

MP4/16

McLaren MP4/16
M.Hakkinen
403 014303

McLaren MP4/16
D.Coulthard
403 014304

MP4/17

McLaren MP4/17
D.Coulthard
403 020103

McLaren MP4/17
Kimi Raikkonen
403 020104

Ferrari

The prestigious team that has led F1 through the years is still going strong

No team exceeds Ferrari's record in the number of team titles, total victories and the number of pole positions. There were tough times for the Ferrari team after Enzo Ferrari passed away, but the team stabilized after the return of Luca di Montezemolo, the former team manager. Currently, the team seems invincible. The miniature models of the machines driven by Niki Lauda, Gilles Villeneuve and Jean Alesi, as well as the Schumacher collection shown earlier, are all incredibly popular, and as such very hard to come by.

Ferrari 312T
1975 N.Lauda World Champion
430 750012

The 312T brought victory to Lauda. The unique induction box has been well captured in the miniature version.

Ferrari 126 C2
1982 G. Villeneuve
430 820027

The 126 was completely redesigned by Harvey Postlethwaite. The turbo engine had matured and Gilles Villeneuve's chances of winning the title would have been great, if it wasn't for that unfortunate accident.

Ferrari F93A
J.Alesi
430 930027

The F93A was released during tougher times for Ferrari. The suspension trouble never ceased. A white stripe was painted on the car to emulate the cars from times of former glory. The popularity of this miniature model is immense.

In the golden era of the late 1970s, the T4 was born, and was one of the most tenacious Ferraris ever. The advantage of the miniature models is that the shape of the ground clearance, the trend at that time, can be studied closely.

Ferrari 312T4
1979 G. Villeneuve
430 797312

Ferrari 412T
1994 J.Alesi
430 940027

Ferrari 412 T2
1995 G.Berger
430 950028

Ferrari F92A
J.Alesi
Gode Box

Ferrari Launch Version
1996 E.Irvine
430 960092

Ferrari 1997 Launch Version
E.Irvine
430 970096

Ferrari F310 V10
1996 E.Irvine Qantas Edition
433 960002

Ferrari F300 V10
1998 E.Irvine
430 980004

Many versions of Ferrari are released

The attraction of the F1 series is in its extensity. Collectors will be both tantalised and satisfied. Ferrari has the Schumacher collection, with special editions including the Qantas model. Sometimes they are cased in a special box like the one on the right, and sometimes are even released complete with Marlboro tobacco logo like 'West' for McLaren. There are cases of unauthorised shops putting stickers of the tobacco logos on these models, so be careful!

The retail limited edition model is the one on the left. Below is the model with tobacco logos. There are so many variations that it is hard to ever make a complete collection.

Minardi

Young drivers aiming towards that exclusive podium place

Giancarlo Minardi, the owner of a Ferrari dealership, founded his own Italian team in 1985. The team is not yet at the level of challenging for the championship, but their passion for the sport is immense. Opportunities are given to young, talented drivers in this team, and many successful drivers began their careers with Minardi. Minardi scale models are readily available.

Minardi M198
E.Tuero
430 980023

Minardi 1999 Show Car
M.Gene
430 990070

Minardi Ford M01
1999 M.Gene
430 990021

Minardi F1 Show Car
2000 G.Mazzacane
430 000071

Minardi European F1 Show Car
2001 T.Marques
430 010071

Williams

Ready to win back the title with two ace drivers standing by

Around the time of the 1970s, Williams was competing as a private team using second hand Brabham cars. The designer, Patrick Head moved from Lola and obtaining financial support from the oil industry, achieved victory for the team. In the 1980s, Williams started to climb the rankings and, by 2002, had won nine team titles. There are occasions when teams will release their championship-winning driver, but this is probably due to extreme confidence in their machines. The invincible cars with the Renault engines, the FW14 of 1992 and FW15 of 1993, are very popular in miniature form. The FW07 with detachable front cowl panel has just been released and it is still obtainable. This model is likely to become rare.

Williams F1 FW07
A.Jones 1979
430 790027

Williams F1 FW08
K.Rosberg 1982
430 820006

Williams Ford FW08C
K.Rosberg 1983
430 830001

Williams Ford FW08C
J.Laffite 1983
430 830002

Williams Renault
Welt Meister 1992
Gode Box

Williams Renault FW15 A.Prost
430 930002

Williams Renault FW15 A.Prost Hockenheim 1993
GODE Model

Williams FW15
A.Senna Estoril 1994
430 941002

The Rothman's decorated Williams was the last race car Ayrton Senna ever drove.

Williams Renault FW16 A.Senna
430 940002

Williams Renault FW16 D.Hill Presentation 1995
430 950095

Williams Renault FW16 Winner British GP 1994 D.Hill
433 940101

At the British GP at Silverstone in 1994, the British driver Damon Hill won first place in this British race car.

Williams Renault FW18 1996
430 960006

Williams Renault FW18 Winner German GP 1996 D.Hill
433 960205

Williams Renault FW18 Qantas Australian GP 1997
430 960006

Williams Renault FW18 1997 Launch Version J.Villeneuve
430 970093

Williams Renault FW19 1997 J.Villeneuve
430 970003

Williams FW20 MechaChrome 1998 J.Villeneuve
430 980001

Williams 1st Edition Promotional Show Car 1999 R.Schumacher
430 990096

Williams F1 SuperTech FW21 1999 A.Zanardi
430 990005

Williams Promotional Show Car 2000 R.Schumacher
430 000079

Williams FW 21 BMW Launch Car 2000
430 000099

Williams FW21 BMW Jenson Button
Motor Show Box

Williams FW21 BMW Launch Car 2000
80 42 0 017 591

Williams F1 BMW FW23
Williams BMW BOX

Williams F1 BMW FW22 Jenson Button
80 42 0017 595

Williams F1 BMW FW23 1st GP Win SanMarino R.Schumacher
400 010025

119

Lotus

The legacy of genius left behind by Chapman, one of the F1 world's brightest ever assets

Colin Chapman, the founder of Team Lotus blessed with many amazing ideas, applied many innovative new technological measures, such as the Monocoque chassis, ground effect, and others, to the cars he worked on. In 1982, Chapman died suddenly, but the team remained strong for a while. But its grip gradually slipped away, with 1994 being the last season for the team. Drivers like Nigel Mansell, Ayrton Senna, and the first Japanese F1 driver Satoru Nakajima had driven for the team. Paul's Model Art / Minichamps Lotus models remain very popular.

Lotus 72
1970 E.Fittipaldi 1st Win
430 700024

The 72 had radiators on both sides, which set a new standard. Jochen Rindt posthumously won the Formula One World Championship in 1970.

Lotus 72
1970 J.Rindt
430 700005

Lotus 72
1972 E.Fittipaldi World Champion
430 720008

Lotus 97T
Renault Turbo 1985 A.Senna
540 854312

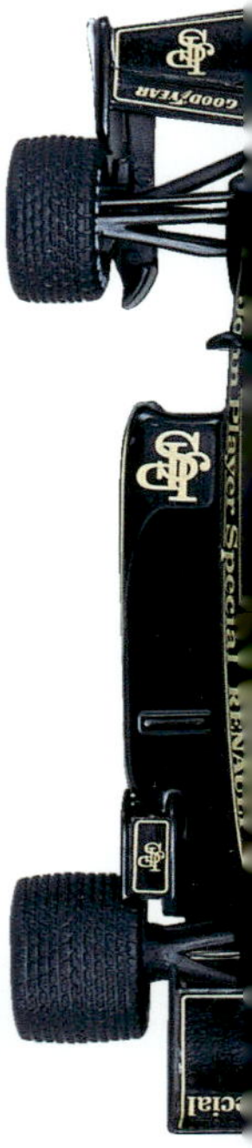

Lotus 79
1978 M.Andretti World Champion
430 780005

Lotus 79 Martini
1979 Carlos Reutemann
430 790002

Lotus 98T
Renault Turbo 1986 A.Senna
540 864312

Lotus 99T
Honda Turbo 1987 A.Senna
Lang Collection

Lotus 99T
1987 S.Nakajima
430 870011

Many people associate the JPS decoration with Lotus F1.

But from 1987, when Nakajima started driving, Camel took over as the main sponsor.

Set collection is F1's unique enjoyment

The set collection is made up of several ranges: constructors who won the title in two consecutive seasons, or two cars, or helmets, of a popular F1 driver. This kind of set is not really common among road car miniature models.

402 858601
WC Set 1985/1986 McLaren
Prost/Prost

402 888901
WC Set 1988/1989 McLaren
Senna/Prost

402 909101
WC Set 1990/1991 McLaren
Senna/Senna

402 929301
WC Set 1992/1993 Williams
Mansell/Prost

402 969701
WC Set 1996/1997 Williams
Hill/Villeneuve

402 989901
WC Set 1998/1999 McLaren
Hakkinen/Hakkinen

516 974303
Williams Renault FW19
J. Villeneuve Worldchampion

402 000119
Arrows Supertec Verstappen
GP Canada with Helmet Scale 1:8

Michelin Limited Edition

Recently, Michelin's concept materialized with limited sales of a set consisting of Bibendum and a race car.

Jordan

The Yellow Express - ready to excel in 2003

In 1991, Jordan made its debut and finished 5th in the constructors championship. It is one of the most successful new teams in recent years. In 1998, a glorious victory was won. As it is a relatively new team, almost all of its cars are available in miniature form.

Jordan Peugeot
EJR 195 R.Barrichello
430 950014

Jordan
191 Ford A.de Cesaris
430 910031

Jordan Peugeot
EJR 195 E.Irvine
430 950015

Jordan Peugeot
1996 Launch Version R.Barrichello
430 960081

Jordan Peugeot
196 M.Brundle
Total box

Jordan Peugeot
197 R.Schumacher
514 974311

Jordan Peugeot
197 G.Fisichella
430 970012

Jordan Mugen Honda 198
D.Hill
430 980009

Jordan Mugen Honda 198
Tower Wing D.Hill
430 980039

Jordan Mugen
Honda Test Car H.H.Frentzen
511 984310

Brabham

Everyone misses the disappearance of this prestigious F1 team

At the end of 1998, after having won a total of 35 victories, Brabham ceased competing in F1. A notable Paul's Model Art / Minichamps model is the BT46, which debuted in 1978. There was a unique feature to the car - a fan was fitted to suck air from underneath the body to gain downforce and increase traction. The BT52 was the turbo model, which brought victory for Nelson Piquet.

Brabham BT46
Fancar 1978 J.Watson
430 780102

Brabham BT52
1983 N.Piquet
430 830005

Brabham BT52
1983
80 42 9423 036

Stewart

The short-lived new team with real ability

The triple World Champion Jackie Stewart founded the Stewart F1 team in 1997, backed by Ford. In 1999, Johnny Herbert won his first race, but by then Ford's policy towards F1 had changed and the team was sold to Jaguar, who have been competing since 2000.

Stewart Ford
1997 SF-1 R.Barrichello
430 970022

Stewart Ford
1998 SF-2 J.Verstappen
430 980029

Stewart Ford
1998 J.Verstappen Limited Edition
433 980029

Tyrrell & BAR

Tradition of pedigree
Creating new legends

Ken Tyrrell, a former Matra team manager, founded this team in 1970. The following year, the first World Constructors Title had been won. But in the 1980's, the team slipped. Newcomer Alboreto's driving gained recognition, but was not enough to keep up with the leading performers. Japanese drivers Nakajima, Katayama and Takagi drove for the team, so it was consequently very popular in Japan. By the end of 1998, the team was bought by BAR. The Tyrrell P34, a race car with 6 wheels, was victorious in the late 1970's, and it is likely to become scarce.

Tyrrell P34
1976 6-wheeler J.Scheckter
430 760003

Tyrell 003
1971 J.Stewart
World Champion
430 710011

Tyrell 006
1973 J.Stewart
World Champion
430 730005

Tyrell P34 FNCB Monte Carlo
1977 6 wheeler
R.Peterson
430 770003

Tyrell P34 FNCB Monte Carlo
1977 6 wheeler
P.Depailler
430 770004

Tyrrell Yamaha 021
U.Katayama Hockenheim 1993
430 750012

Tyrrell Yamaha 022
M.Blundell 1994
430 940004

The 022 competed in the 1994 season. At the San Marino Grand Prix, Ukyo Katayama finished 5th after holding second place for some time in the race, and it is for this reason that the model is well known in Japan.

Tyrrell Yamaha 023
M.Salo 1995
430 950004

Tyrrell Yamaha 024
U.Katayama 1996
430 960018

Tyrrell Ford 025
J.Verstappen with winglets
GP San Marino 1997
430 970028

Tyrrell Ford 1997
J.Verstappen Limited Edition
433 970018

Tyrrell Ford 026
1998 T.Takagi
433 980021

Tyrrell Ford
T.Tagagi 1998
with towerwings
430 980051

Tyrrell Ford 026
1998 Launch Version T.Takagi
430 980020

The team had many Japanese sponsors, including PIAA. But when Takagi was driving for the team, Tyrell was already losing momentum.

BAR 01
Supertec Testversion 1999

430 990120

BAR Honda 01
Supertec J.Villeneuve 1999

430 990022

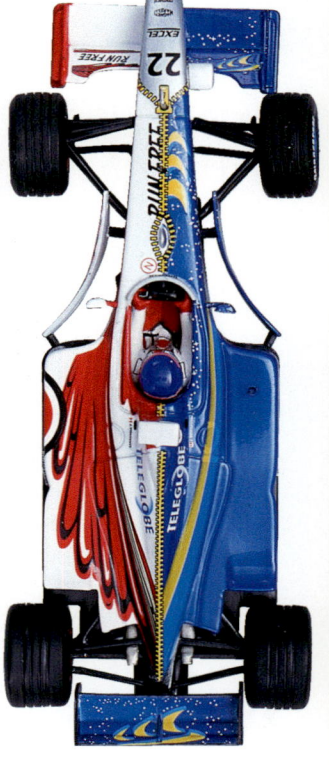

BAR Honda 02
J.Villeneuve 2000

430 000022

BAR Honda 03
O.Panis 2001

400010009

Ligier

F1 team representing France

Guy Ligier founded the Ligier team in 1976. With the support of his friend, former President Mitterrand, many state run French companies sponsored the team. Until the mid 1980's, the team was among the top performers, but the team later became Prost F1. Paul's Model Art / Minichamps make models of the recent race cars. One particularly popular model is the 1996 Monaco version, in which Panis secured the last ever victory for Ligier.

Ligier Mugen Honda
Winner GP Monaco 1996

430 960099

Ligier Mugen Honda JS43
O.Panis 1998

430 960009

Ligier Honda JS41
M.Brundle

430 950125

Ligier Honda JS41
Aguri Suzuki

430 950025

Ligier Mugen Honda JS43
1st Victory Monaco 1996
O.Panis 1996

Sauber

Sauber, renowned for endurance racing, is also doing well in F1

Sauber, who had been with the Mercedes-Benz works team for endurance races began competing in F1 from 1993. Without the backup of a major car manufacturer, Sauber is doing extremely well. In 2001, the team finished 4th, finishing above other, wealthier teams. The 2001 model, in which Raikkonen gained points in his debut year, is difficult to find.

RED BULL
Sauber Petronas Show Car 2001
K.Raikkonen

430 010087

Sauber Petronas C20
K.Raikkonen Malaysia
2001 1st Championship point

400 010117

Sauber Petronas C20
N.Heidfeld Brazil
2001

400 010216

DEUTSCHE TOURENWAGEN MEISTERSCHAFT
DTM

The machines of the German Touring Car Championship

One of the most popular motor races in Germany, the founding place of Paul's Model Art / Minichamps, is DTM. Let's now look at the machines that have strongly influenced the Japanese race scenes.

Photo cooperation/ BMW Japan/Fiat Alfa Romeo Japan

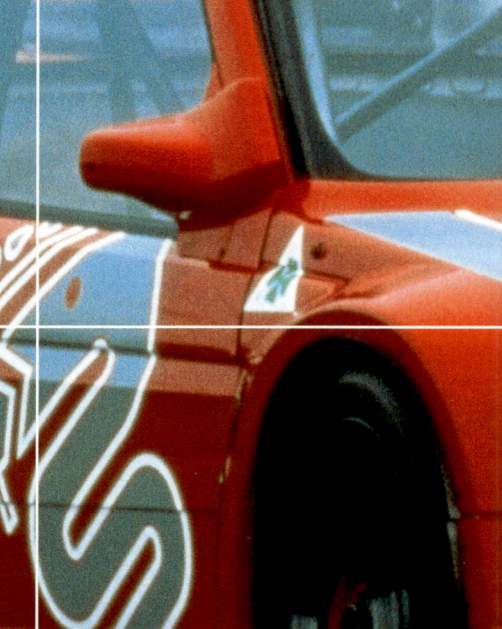

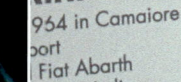

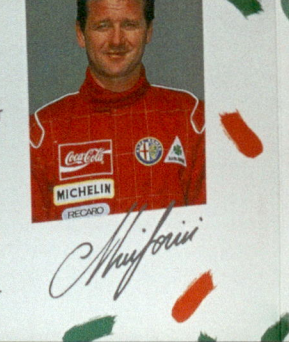

ZF-Lenkung
Wintershall
telcon
SCHNITZER
Lehto
OPEL TEAM JOEST
cliff
DEKRA
20
ITT
AlliedSignal
RECARO
Mobil 1
SONAX
BBS
DUNLOP
RECAR
BOSCH
Car Systems
SELENIA
BAUMLER
men's fashion
ERG
MICHELIN
MANNESMANN
Larini
DEKRA
8
ITT
BAUMLER
Agip

1990

DTM was becoming known in Japan for its dynamic race development. The history of Paul's Model Art / Minichamps manufacturing began with the 1990 series DTM machines. Miniaturized models produced include the Audi V8, Paul's Model Art / Minichamps very first model, the BMW M3, and the Mercedes-Benz 190E Evo 1 and Evo 2, which came out half way through the season.

All three are coloured and decorated in exactly the same way as the real cars. Beware of wear and tear to the stickers on the models. The M3 is the most popular model of the three, and is very hard to find.

Audi

Audi V8 Quattro Stuck
430 001001

H.J.Stuck drove this Audi V8, the 1990 series championship-winning machine - Paul's Model Art / Minichamps' very first production model. It is a rare model, which captures the atmosphere of the time.

Audi V8 Quattro Rohrl
430 001002

BMW

BMW M3 Schnitzer/Giroix
430 002002

BMW M3 Schnitzer/Cecotto
430 002003

BMW M3 Bigazzi/Soper
430 002010

BMW M3 Bigazzi/Winkelhock j.
430 002011

BMW M3 Bigazzi/Laffite
430 002012

BMW M3 Linder/Heger
430 002020

BMW M3 Zakspeed/Quester
430 002030

BMW M3 Valier/Grohs
430 002040

BMW M3 Isert/v.Bayern
430 002050

BMW M3 MM Diebels/Murmann
430 002060

Mercedes-Benz

Mercedes 190 E Evo1AMG Karcher/Wendlinger
430 003030

Mercedes 190 Evo1 AMG Konig Pilsener/Thiim
430 003001

Mercedes 190 Evo2 AMG Snobeck/Acsh
430 003110

Mercedes 190E Evo2 AMG MS-JET/Biela
430 003120

Mercedes 190 E Evo1 MS-JET/v.Ommen
430 003021

Mercedes 190E Evo2 AMG Pilsener/Ludwig
430 003102

1991

As the popularity of DTM grew, so did the Paul's Model Art / Minichamps range. For the 1991 series, the Opel Omega 3000 evolution was added to the previous year's range of Audi, BMW and Mercedes-Benz models. And in the DTM championships of 1991, Audi won once again.

The M3 is a popular model from the 1991 series, but so are the Mercedes-Benz West/ East models. They are hard to find. The Opel Jägermeister version is also a model that is difficult to find.

BMW

BMW M3 Sport Evolution
Schnitzer/Nissen
430 012003

BMW M3 Sport Evolution
Bigazzi/Hahne
430 012011

BMW M3 Sport Evolution
Linder/Heger
430 012021

BMW M3 Sport Evolution
Linder/Meeuvissen
430 012022

BMW M3 Sport Evolution
Unitron/Kelleners
430 012031

BMW M3 Sport Evolution
Tauber-tic tac/Berg
430 012070

Opel

Opel Omega 3000 Evolution
Schubel/Oberndorfer
430 014020

Audi

Audi V8 Quattro Evolution
AZR/Jelinski
430 011110

Mercedes-Benz

Mercedes 190 E 2.5-16
Evolution2 Snobeck/Cudini
430 013112

Mercedes 190 E 2.5-16
Evolution2 Zakspeed/Asch
430 013143

Mercedes 190 E 2.5-16
Evolution2 AMG-West/Thiim
430 013130

Mercedes 190 E 2.5-16
Evolution2 AMG-West/Lohr
430 013131

Mercedes 190 E 2.5-16
Evolution2 AMG-East/Thiim
430 013132

Mercedes 190 E 2.5-16
Evolution2 AMG-East/Lohr
430 013133

Car No.7 and Car No.78 both had West as a sponsor. But as it sometimes violates the regulations, two different designs were used accordingly, the other with the logo 'East'. Paul's Model Art / Minichamps have released all 4 models.

1992

In the 1992 season, the works teams were Audi, BMW and Mercedes-Benz. Mercedes-Benz was immensely strong, and Klaus Ludwig went on to win the championship.
Many private teams competed with M3s, and unique decorations were seen. Limited model gift versions were first released around this time. The Andorra appeared in 1991 with AMG-West. Its trendy colour and design is striking.

Mercedes-Benz

Mercedes Evo2 "Andorra"
Lohr 1991
430 013134

The very rare Andorra had two variations. If you look closely, the motif of the faces on the bonnet is different – the red is marked "red devil", and the orange is marked "black devil".

Mercedes Evo2
Laffite/Kaercher
430 023120

Mercedes Evo2
v. Ommen/Kaercher
430 023121

Mercedes Evo2
Ludwig/AMG
430 023101

Mercedes Evo2
Berlin 2000 Rosberg/AMG
430 023132

Audi

Audi V8 Jelinski
430 021102

BMW

BMW M3
Heger/Schnitzer
430 022003

BMW M3
Hahne/Jägermeister
430 022020

BMW M3
Fritz K./Katta
430 022061

The limited model with serial number was released

Mercedes Evo2 Set
Ltd. Edition Nr.4 1606
430 900004

A total of 4444 sets of Andorra were sold. It is now very difficult to find.

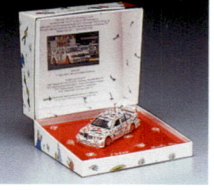

430 013134

DEUTSCHE TOURENWAGEN MEISTERSCHAFT

1993

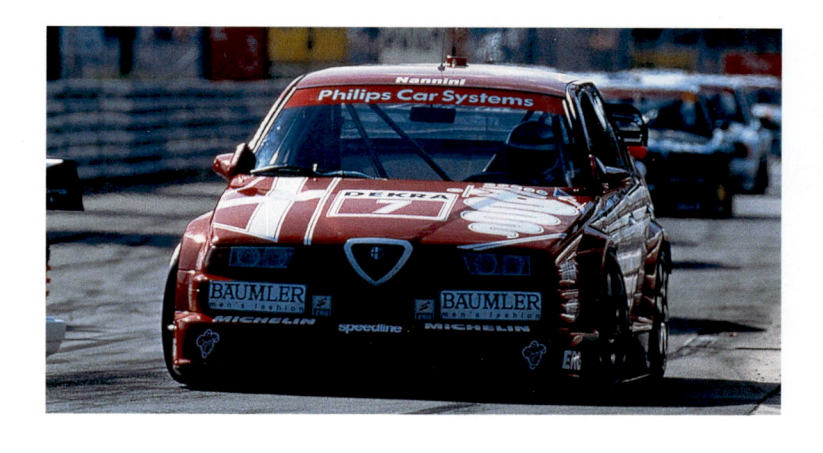

In the 1993 season, the works team were Mercedes-Benz, and from Italy, Alfa Romeo. Only private teams competed with BMW. The Alfa Romeo had a striking red-bodied exterior. It was a fast car and Nicola Larini won the championship with it.

In miniature form there are BMW, Mercedes-Benz and 4 variations of Alfa Romeo 155V6. Note the difference in wheels, antennae and so forth on the 155V6. Mercedes-Benz later released a refined version of class 1 - the Evo2.

Alfa Romeo

Alfa Romeo 155 V6 Nr.7 Nannini
430 930120

Alfa Romeo 155 V6
Nr.8 Larini
430 930121

Alfa Romeo 155 V6
Nr.14 Danner
430 930122

Alfa Romeo 155 V6
Nr.15 Francia
430 930123

Mercedes-Benz

Mercedes-Benz Evo2
AMG Berlin 2000 Ludwig
430 933130

Mercedes-Benz Evo2
AMG Berlin 2000 Lohr
430 933131

Mercedes-Benz 190E
Klasse1 Diebels Thiim
430 933240

Mercedes-Benz 190E
Klasse1 Diebels v.Ommen
430 933241

Mercedes-Benz 190E
Klasse1 TABAC SONAX Schneider
430 933202

Mercedes-Benz Evo2
AMG Junior Team Grau
430 933110

Mercedes-Benz 190E
Klasse1 TABAC SONAX Asch
430 933201

Mercedes-Benz Evo2
AMG Asch
430 933102

Mercedes-Benz 190E Klasse1 Berlin 2000 Ludwig
430 933231

BMW

BMW M3 92 DTM 93 Becker/Linder
430 932020

1994

DEUTSCHE TOURENWAGEN MEISTERSCHAFT

Mercedes-Benz introduced a new car, the C class, equipped with the all the latest technology in order to get revenge for the previous season's humbling defeat. Also, Opel Calibra competed with their works car. Mercedes-Benz's Klaus Ludwig won the championship this season.

The scale models available are of the C class, the 190 series that private teams entered, the Alfa Romeo 156V6TI, the Opel Calibra and the Ford Mustang. In this season, DTM race cars were boxed in beautifully designed original boxes.

Alfa Romeo V6 TI
N.Larini
German Touring Car Champion 1993
Limiten & individually numbered Edition 4444pcs.
431 900007

Commemorating the 1993 championship victory, the "Champion box" was released with individual serial numbers

Alfa Romeo

Alfa Romeo 155 V6 TI
N.Larini
430 940201

Alfa Romeo 155 V6 TI
A.Nannini
430 940202

Alfa Romeo 155 V6 TI
S.Modena
430 940210

Alfa Romeo 155 V6 TI
St.Buttiero
430 940233

Alfa Romeo 155 V6 TI
K.Nissen
430 940118

Alfa Romeo 155 V6 TI
K.Nissen
430 940218

Mercedes-Benz

AMG C-Class
K.Ludwig
German Touring Car Champion 1994
430 943307

C-Class Gr.A
1994 Version IAA
430 943300

AMG C-Class
E.Lohr
430 943308

AMG C-Class
R.Asch
430 943303

AMG C-Class
B.Schneider Presentation
430 953304

AMG C-Class
B.Schneider
430 943304

AMG C-Class
K.Thiim
430 943314

AMG C-Class
K.Thiim
Dealer Version 433 943314

AMG C-Class
J.v.Ommen
Dealer Version 433 943315

AMG 190E Class1
M.Gindorf / Persson
430 943220

AMG 190E Class1
S.Grau / Junior Team
430 943221

AMG 190E 2.5-16 Evo2
A.Bernhard / Bas
430 943131

minichamps
RACECARS

130 MINICHAMPS

1995

DTM was originally a competition based in Germany alone, but half way thorough the 1995 season, it went international and became the ITC, with the cooperation of FIA. Mercedes-Benz's Bernd Schneider won the title that year.

The 'King' C class Mercedes-Benz, the Martini sponsored works Alfa Romeo 156, and the Opel Calibra in its beautiful coupe body were the models from this season that were miniaturised and released. Unique to this year's range is the number of presentation models released.

Opel

Opel Calibra V6 Presentation 1995
K. Ludwig
430 954191

Opel Calibra V6
"Bye Bye Keke Rosberg"
Limited Edition 4444pcs.
430 954282

Opel Calibra V6
Team Rosberg K.Rosberg
430 954202

Opel Calibra V6
Team Joest J.J.Lehto
430 954120

Alfa Romeo

Alfa Romeo 155 V6 TI 95
Martini Racing A.Nannini
430 950207

Alfa Romeo 155 V6 TI 95
Martini Racing N.Larini
Presentation 430 950208

Alfa Romeo 155 V6 TI 95
Martini Racing N.Larini
430 950408

Alfa Romeo 155 V6 TI
Euro Team Presentation
430 950319

Alfa Romeo 155 V6 TI
Euro Team M. Bartels
430 950319

Alfa Romeo 155 V6 TI 95-2
Alfa Corse 2 G.Fisichella
430 950426

Alfa Romeo 155 V6 TI
Alfa Corse 2 G.Giudici
430 950313

Mercedes-Benz

C-Class
Team Zakspeed E.Lohr
430 953517

C-Class
Team AMG-D2 B.Schneider
German TouringCar & ITC Champion
430 953314

C-Class
Team AMG-D2 Presentation
430 953315

C-Class
Team AMG-D2 D.Franchitti
430 953515

C-Class
Team AMG-D2 B.Schneider
430 953514

C-Class
Team Zakspeed E.Lohr Presentation
430 953317

C-Class
Team Zakspeed S.Grau
430 953305

C-Class
Team Zakspeed S.Grau
430 953505

C-Class
Team Zakspeed K.Thiim Presentation
430 953306

1996

The championship became a double DTM / ITC title for the last season. However, from 1996 until then, it was competed for solely under the title of ITC. As it had become an international competition, races were also held outside of Europe, including the race at Suzuka. But as of 1996, the DTM/ITC championship was suspended.
The scale models of the Mercedes-Benz, Alfa Romeo and Opel are the same ones as those of the previous year. There were, of course, also presentation models and design study models in the range. The cars evolved with time, and by 1996 the cars had reached the pinnacle of finesse.

DEUTSCHE TOURENWAGEN MEISTERSCHAFT
minichamps RACECARS

Opel

Opel Calibra V6
Rosberg H.J.Stuck
Presentation ITC
1996 Limited Edition 4444pcs.
430 964280

Opel Calibra V6
1996 Presentation
430 954192

Opel Calibra V6
Opel Motorsport V.Strycek
430 964323

Opel Calibra V6
Zakspeed U.Alzen
430 964316

Opel Calibra V6
Zakspeed U.Alzen Presentation
430 964216

Opel Calibra V6
Joest M.Reuter ITC
Champion 1996
430 964307

Opel Calibra V6
Team Joest O.Gavin
430 964388

Opel Calibra V6
Team Joest A.Wurz
430 964325

Opel Calibra V6
Team Joest A.Wurz
430 964225

Opel Calibra V6
ITC Suzuka M.Sekiya
430 964374

Mercedes-Benz

Mercedes-Benz C 180 AMG B.Schneider
430 963601

Mercedes-Benz C 180 AMG
D.Franchitti
430 963602

Mercedes-Benz C 180 Team
Persson E.Lohr
430 963521

Mercedes-Benz C 180 AMG A.Grau
430 963604

Mercedes-Benz C 180 AMG K.Thiim
430 963612

Alfa Romeo /////

Alfa Romeo 155 V6 TI Presentation
ITC 1996
430 960405

Alfa Romeo 155 V6 TI
Alfa Corse N.Larini
430 960505

Alfa Romeo 155 V6 TI
Alfa Corse A.Nannini

Alfa Romeo 155 V6 TI Alfa JAS
J.Watt
430 960519

Alfa Romeo 155 V6 TI Alfa JAS
S.Modena
430 960509

Alfa Romeo 155 V6 TI Alfa JAS
G.Tarquini
430 960518

Alfa Romeo 155 V6 TI Alfa JAS
M.Bartels
430 960510

The Martini decoration looks beautiful on the Alfa Romeo 155V6TI. This is the 1995 model, as driven by Larini.

133

2000

DEUTSCHE TOURENWAGEN MEISTERSCHAFT

With new regulations, DTM recommenced in 2000 after the suspension of 1996. The cars looked more aggressive than ever, with the large spoilers and lowered suspension. Mercedes-Benz won the series that year, with Opel a close second.

With the return of DTM came the return of the Paul's Model Art / Minichamps models of the DTM cars. There was a full range of Mercedes-Benz CLK, Opel Astra V8 coupe and Audi TT-R models. As they are still recent models, they are not hard to find in shops. But some colours are very popular, so if you are hoping to make a complete collection, don't delay!

Audi

Audi TT-R Team Abt Sportsline Test Car
430 001890

Audi TT-R Team Abt L.Aiello
430 001809

Audi TT-R Team Abt C.Abt
430 001810

Opel

Opel V8 Coupe Team Holzer U.Alzen
430 004803

Opel V8 Coupe Team Holzer J.Winkelhock
430 004804

Opel V8 Coupe Team Phoenix M.Reuter
430 004807

Opel V8 Coupe Team Phoenix M.Bartels
430 004808

Opel V8 Coupe Team Irmscher C.Menzel
430 004812

Opel V8 Coupe S.Modena
430 004816

Mercedes-Benz

Mercedes-Benz CLK Team AMG B.Schneider
430 003701

Mercedes-Benz CLK Team AMG T.Jaeger
430 003702

Mercedes-Benz CLK Team AMG K.Ludwig
430 003705

Mercedes-Benz CLK Team Persson P.Dumbreck
430 003719

Mercedes-Benz CLK Team Rosberg D.Turner
430 003742

Mercedes-Benz CLK Team Rosberg P.Lamy
430 003724

minichamps RACECARS

2001-2002

The second year after DTM's return was even more exciting. From the 2002 series on, former F1 driver Jean Alesi drove for Mercedes-Benz.

The scale models cover the full range, including Mercedes-Benz CLK, Opel Astra V8 coupe, and Audi TT-R all in a wide variety of colours. A particularly notable limited edition range was the set that came complete with a driver figure. In order to comply with the new regulations, the rear overhang of the Audi TT-R had to be extended to meet the minimum body length. You can see by looking at the miniature model how Audi persevered in order to meet the regulation.

Audi

Audi TT-R Team Abt Sportsline L.Aiello
400 011119

Opel

Opel V8 Coupe
"Sport Bild" Team Holzer
400 014103

Opel V8 Coupe
"Service Fit" M.Reuter
400 014107

Opel V8 Coupe
B.Schneider
400 014897

Opel V8 Coupe
Opel Team Phoenix Y.Oliver
400 014808

Opel V8 Coupe
"SAT 1 JA" Opel Euro Team
400 014116

Opel V8 Coupe
S.Modena
400 014817

Mercedes-Benz

Mercedes-Benz CLK Coupe
Team Vodafone
400 023201

Mercedes-Benz CLK D2 Team AMG
DTM 2001 Champion
B.Schneider
400 013101

Mercedes-Benz CLK "Dumbreck"
Team AMG DTM 2001
400 013102

Mercedes-Benz CLK "Warsteiner"
Team AMG U.Alzen
400 013105

Mercedes-Benz CLK "Eschmann"
Team Manthey
400 013110

Mercedes-Benz CLK "Original-Teile"
Team Persson
400 013715

Mercedes-Benz CLK "Service24h"
Team Rosberg P.Lamy
400 013724

Mercedes-Benz CLK Team AMG
J.Alesi
400 023202

Mercedes-Benz CLK DTM 2001
Test Car Brueen
400 013193

The Cars that have competed in the Le Mans 24 hours

Amidst the darkness, machines speed along the race track, headlights beaming. The mechanics work hard in pursuit of the glory that could await them when 24 hours has elapsed.
The circuit shares its location with an amusement park, filled with laughing people having fun. Le Mans is not only a race, but a massive theatre of entertainment. Machines that race only once a year have many strong and endearing features which charm the spectators. Let's now look at the 1/43-scale models of the Le Mans gladiators, which exude style.

24 HEURES MANS

24 HEURES DU MANS
Porsche

The racing history of Porsche is integral to the history of Le Mans

'50s ~ '70s

Porsche has competed in the Le Mans 24 hour race since 1951, originally with the 356. The very first victory was won in 1970 with the 917K. It took Porsche 19 years to record their first Le Mans victory, despite winning many other races in different championships all around the world. Paul's Model Art / Minichamps has produced many models of Porsches that competed for private teams at the Sarthe Circuit. The models include the early 550 Spider, the famous 917 derivative – the 917L Le Mans special - which set the speed record at the Hunaudieres straight, and the 917/20, aka the "Pink Pig" with its playful design, and also the turbo models of the 936 series.

Porsche 550 A Le Mans 1956
Storez/Polenski
430 566628

Porsche 917L
Gulf 24h Le Mans 1971
Siffert/Bell
430 716717

Porsche 917/20
"Pink Pig" 1971
Joest/Kauhsen
430 716923

Porsche 917L
Le Mans 1971
Rodriguez/Oliver
430 716718

Porsche 936
Le Mans 1978
Gregg/Haywood/Joest
430 776707

Porsche 936/78
MARTINI Le Mans 78
Ickx/Pescarolo/Mass
430 786905

Porsche 936/78
MARTINI Le Mans 78
Barth/Wollek/Ickx
430 786906

Porsche 936/78
ESSEX Le Mans
Ickx/Redman
430 796912

Porsche 936/78
ESSEX Le Mans 79
Wollek/Haywood
430 796914

'80s

The 1980s was a golden era for Porsche, beginning with the 936/81's victory in 1981, and victories in 6 consecutive years in group C with the 956/962C series between 1982 and 1987. The 936/81 was sponsored by Jules, with the logos covering much of the body. The powerful 956L, ranging from the 1982 Rothmans up to the 1985 Newman are available as scale models. Because the usage of tobacco sponsorship logos was restricted, the Rothmans sticker was not put on the model, however it was included in the box. The winning machines are popular and very hard to come by. There are also other models available, in addition to the victorious ones.

WINNER
Porsche 936/81
JULES Le Mans 1981
Ickx/Bell
430 816911

Porsche 936/81
JULES Le Mans 1981
Mass/Schuppan/Haywood
430 816912

WINNER
Porsche 956L
SCHUPPAN Le Mans 1983
Holbert/Haywood
430 836503

WINNER
Porsche 956L
NEWMAN Le Mans 1984
Ludwig/Pescarolo
430 846507

WINNER
Porsche 956L
NEWMAN Le Mans 1985
Ludwig/Winter/Barilla
430 856507

Porsche 956L
BOSS Le Mans 79
Lassig/Fouche/Graham
430 846547

'90s

Porsche was surprisingly strong in a Le Mans dominated by the GT class. The 1994 winner, the Dauer Porsche 962GT, and car No. 35 with the Shell sponsorship are very hard to find. Porsche's most potent weapon, the 911GT1, is evolving and progressing every year - and you can see the changes in body sculpting between each model.

Dauer Porsche 962GT
3rd LeMans 1994

430 946435

WINNER
Dauer Porsche 962GT
1st LeMans 1994

430 946436

Porsche 911 GT1
1997
Stuck/Boutsen/Wollek
430 976825

Porsche 911 GT1
1997
Dalmas/Collard/Kelleners
430 976926

Porsche 911 GT1
1998
Alzen/Muller/Wollek
430 986925

WINNER
Porsche 911 GT1
LM 1998
Aiello/McNish/Ortelli
430 986926

WINNER
Porsche 911 GT2
Winner GT2 Class LM 97
Neugarten/Martinolle
430 976778

Porsche 911 GT2
Team Larbre 1998
430 986760

Porsche 911 GT2
Team Larbre 1999
430 996767

'00s~

With the recent abolition of the GT1 class in Le Mans racing, the LMGTP class is becoming the dominant class. For a few years, the Porsche works team did not enter, but there were many private teams competing using the 911GT3-R in the GT3 class.

The exterior is almost the same as that of the road version, but with its huge rear spoiler and low suspension, the car is an imposing sight. The paintwork has been captured beautifully, this being one of the joys of collecting these cars.

Porsche 911 GT3-R
433 006983
Dealer Version

Porsche 911 GT3-R
Repsol Racing Engineering 2000
Saldana/Lavaggi/Villaroel
430 006972

Porsche 911 GT3-R
Noel Del Bello Racing 2000
Maury-Laribiere/Zadra/Chauvin
430 006978

Porsche 911 GT3-R
Perspective Racing 2000
Perrier/Ricci
430 006979

Porsche 911 GT3-R
433 006981
Dealer Version

Porsche 911 GT3-S
Team Warmup 2001
Ligonnet/Alphand/Marques
400 016974

24 HEURES DU MANS
Audi

Clinching 1st, 2nd, and 3rd place in 2000 proved Audi's capabilities

The LM GTP class was founded in 1999, and Audi has been competing in this category ever since. They missed out on the title in the first year, but in the second year of competing, Audi amazingly took 1st, 2nd, and 3rd places! They have won the title in every year up to 2002. Paul's Model Art / Minichamps made models of all of the winning cars. There is also a special gift set consisting of all three 1st, 2nd and 3rd placed race cars.

'99

Audi R8R 1999 No.7
Alboreto/Capello/Aiello
430 990907

Audi R8C 1999
Abt/Johansson/Ortelli
430 990909

Audi R8R 1999 No.8
Biela/Pirro/Theys
430 990908

Audi R8C 1999
Weaver/Wallace/McCarthy
430 990910

'00

Audi R8R
Audi Sport Team Joest 2000
Alboreto/Abt/Capello 3rd place
430 000907

WINNER
Audi R8R
Audi Sport Team Joest 2000
Biela/Kristensen/Pirro
430 000908

Audi R8R
Audi Sport Team Joest 2000
Aiello/McNish/Ortelli 2nd place
430 000909

'01

WINNER
Audi R8S
Audi Sport Team Joest 2001
Biela/Kristensen/Pirro Winner
400 011201

Audi R8S
Team Johansson 2001
Johansson/Coronel/Lemarie
400 010904

Audi R8S
Audi Sport Team Joest 2001
Aiello/Capello/Pescatori
400 011202

Audi R8S
Team Champion 2001
Herbert/Kelleners/Theys
400 010903

MINICHAMPS

BMW

The constant progress and maturing reaped rewards at the end of the 20th century

The sound of the V12 resonates around the Sarthe circuit

BMW really committed themselves to the pursuit of victory in 1988. The V12LM was developed with Williams, and with the improved V12LMR the following year, BMW won Le Mans. There are many models of the M1, which competed in group 5.

BMW M1 "Warsteiner" 1983
Pallavicini/Winther/v.Bayern
430 832590

BMW V12 LM 1998
Kristensen/Stuck/Soper
430 982801

WINNER
BMW V12 LMR 1999
Le Mans 1999
Winkelhock/Martini/Dalmas
430 992915

Mercedes-Benz

Overcoming tragedy
The silver arrow returned to the centre stage at Le Mans

The 300SLR, a machine with beautiful spoke wheels, was involved in Le Mans' biggest tragedy. The come back was made in 1989 with the C9. Max model, the other Paul's Model Art / Minichamps brand, released many models of this.

Mercedes 300 SLR Le Mans 1955
J.M.Fangio/S.Moss
432 553000

Sauber Mercedes C9
No.61 KOUROS Le Mans 1987
Pescarolo/Thackwell/Okada
432 001007

Sauber Mercedes C9
No.62 KOUROS Le Mans 1987
Ganassi/Dumfries
432 001008

Sauber Mercedes C9
No.61 AEG Le Mans 1988
432 001005

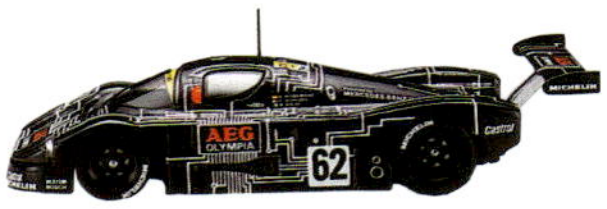

Sauber Mercedes C9
No.62 Le Mans 1988
Acheson/Niedzwiedz
432 001006

WINNER
Sauber Mercedes C9
No.63 Winner
24h Le Mans 1989
Mass/Dickens/Reuter
432 001000

24h Le Mans Winners			
1949	Ferrari 166MM	1976	Porsche 936/76
1950	Tarbot	1977	Porsche 936/77
1951	Jaguar XJ120C	1978	Alpine A442B Renault
1952	Mercedes-Benz	1979	Porsche 935/K3
1953	Jaguar Type C	1980	Londo M379B
1954	Ferrari 375MM	1981	Porsche 936/81
1955	Jaguar Type D	1982	Porsche 956L
1956	Jaguar Type D	1983	Porsche 956L
1957	Jaguar Type D	1984	Porsche 956L
1958	Ferrari TR58	1985	Porsche 956L
1959	Aston Martin DBR1	1986	Dauer Porsche 962C
1960	Ferrari TR59/60	1987	Dauer Porsche 962C
1961	Ferrari TR61	1988	Jaguar XJR9 LM
1962	Ferrari 330TR	1989	Sauber Mercedes C9
1963	Ferrari 250P	1990	Jaguar XJR12
1964	Ferrari 275P	1991	Mazda 787B
1965	Ferrari 250LM	1992	Peugeot 905
1966	Ford Mk.2	1993	Peugeot 905B
1967	Ford Mk.2	1994	Dauer Porsche 962 LM
1968	Ford GT40	1995	McLaren F1 GTR
1969	Ford GT40	1996	Joest TWR Porsche
1970	Porsche 917	1997	Joest TWR Porsche
1971	Porsche 917K	1998	Porsche 911 GT1
1972	Matra MS 670	1999	BMW V12 LMR
1973	Matra MS 670B	2000	Audi R8R
1974	Matra MS 670B	2001	Audi R8
1975	Gulf Ford GR8	2002	Audi R8

24 HEURES DU MANS
Chaparral

The white beast that dreamed of winning Le Mans

Chaparral is the constructor that had taken American racing circuits by storm. They competed in Le Mans for two years from 1966 to 67. Although they did not enjoy any victories, these classic race cars have nevertheless been miniaturized. The rear cowl panel of the 1966 model, the 2D, can be taken off, exposing the framework and impressive V8 engine. The 1967 model, the 2F, came out with a large rear wing for maximum traction. They are sold as part of the Chaparral collection.

Chaprral 2F
Le Mans 1967
Jennings/Johnson
430 671408

Chaprral 2F
Le Mans 1967
Hill/Spence
430 671407

Chaparral 2D
Le Mans 1966
Hill/Bonnier
436 661409

Renault

The French rocket that achieved the long awaited Le Mans victory

Victory at Le Mans, the biggest racing event in France, had eluded Renault for many years. But dreams of victory came to fruition in 1978 with the highly developed A442B. This model's dawn was a long time in coming. The distinctive covers over the cockpit, for better aerodynamics, and distinct wheels, have been captured superbly.

WINNER
Alpine Renault A 442B
Winner Le Mans 1978
Pironi/Jaussaud
430 781102

Matra

The French super sport that enjoyed sweeping victories at Le Mans throughout the early 1970s

The French constructor Matra won 3 consecutive titles from 1972-74. The 1973 model, the MS670B, is currently being sold decorated in the French national colours. All three of the 1973 models have been released, and we are expecting the release of the 1972 winning machine, the MS670, and the 1974 winning machine, the MS670B.

Matra MS 670B
Le Mans 1973
Beltoise/Cevert
430 731110

WINNER
Matra MS 670B
Le Mans 1973
Pescarolo/Larrousse
430 731111

Matra MS 670B
Le Mans 1973
Jabouille/Jaussaud
430 731112

Toyota

Toyota was serious about winning Le Mans in 1998-99

Toyota had long been a competitor at Le Mans, and in 1998-99, was clearly making one of their biggest pushes towards victory yet. The aerodynamic body was mounted atop a chassis that was said to be no different from the chassis of an F1 car. Toyota started in 1998, but the GT-ONE had difficulties, and were forced to retire. The following year, car No.3 - driven by Japanese drivers including Ukyo Katayama - fought well, but only made 2nd place. The basic form of the GT-ONE has not changed, but with the different colouring and detail it may appear to have. This car carried the hopes and dreams of the Japanese in Le Mans.

'98

Toyota GT-ONE
Le Mans 98
Katayama/Suzuki/Tsuchiya
430 981627

Toyota GT-ONE
Le Mans 98
Brundle/Collard/Helary
430 981628

Toyota GT-ONE
Le Mans 98
Boutsen/Kelleners/Lees
430 981629

'99

Toyota GT-ONE
Team Toyota Motor sports 24h Le Mans 1999
Brundle/Collard/Sospiri
430 991601

Toyota GT-ONE
Team Toyota Motor sports 24h Le Mans 1999
Boutsen/Mcnish/Kelleners
430 991602

Toyota GT-ONE
Team Toyota Motor sports 24h Le Mans 1999
Katayama/Tsuchiya/Suzuki
430 991603

Toyota was serious about winning Le Mans in 1998-99

The McLaren F1 was the road car designed by F1 designer, Gordon Murray. The machine consisted of a carbon Monocoque body and carried a BMW made V12 engine in the middle of the car. The structure was very similar to that of a racing car, so it was therefore an easy transition into competitive racing – manifested in the F1 GTR. In 1995, the F1 GTR won Le Mans at its first attempt, despite it being said that "time is needed for victory". The race car later competed in the Japanese GT, even after the year 2000 – when the design was considered old! The popularity of the scale model is still great, and there have been many versions released by Paul's Model Art / Minichamps.

McLaren F1 GTR Series

McLaren F1 GTR
David Price Racing
Nielsen/Bscher

530 154308

McLaren F1 GTR
Japan GT Series 1996
R.Schumacher/N.Hattori

530 164360

Short Body

1. McLaren F1 GTR Le Mans 1995 'USA' Dealer Version
2. McLaren F1 GTR Le Mans 1995 'United Kingdom' Dealer Version

The early series of the short body model has a form very similar to that of a road model. In the miniaturised versions, the Le Mans winner driven by Sekiya / Lehto / Dalmas, as well as the LARK McLaren driven by Ralf Schumacher, enjoy particular popularity.

McLaren F1 GTR
Kokusai Kaihatsu Racing 1st Le Mans
Lehto/Dalmas/Sekiya
530 154359

McLaren F1 GTR
BBA Competition 13th
Laribiere/Sourd/Poulain
530 154342

McLaren F1 GTR
Le Mans 1995 Giroix Racing 5th
Giroix/Grouillard/Deletrax
530 154350

McLaren F1 GTR
Le Mans 1995 David Price Racing
Nielsen/Bscher/Mass
530 154349

McLaren F1 GTR
Le Mans 1996 6th
Wallace/Grouillard/D.Bell
530 164329

McLaren F1 GTR
BPR Competition 1995 Giroix Racing
Giroix/Grouillard
530 154307

McLaren F1 GTR
BPR Competition 1995 Gulf Racing
Bellm/Sala
530 154301

McLaren F1 GTR
BPR Competition 1995 Gulf Racing
530 154316

McLaren F1 GTR
BPR Competition 1995 David Price Racing
Nielsen/Bscher
530 154308

McLaren F1 GTR
BPR Competition 1997
Giroix/Grouillard
530 164325

McLaren F1 GTR
Le Mans 1996 9th
Bellm/Weaver/Lehto
530 164333

McLaren F1 GTR
Le Mans 1996 5th
Owen-ones/Raphanel/Brabham
530 164334

McLaren F1 GTR
Le Mans 1996
Giroix/Deletraz/Sala
530 164353

Long Body

The glorious F1 GTR ignited the passions of other manufacturers, leading to the development of more high performance race cars. The rivals competed in the GT1 class, whereas the McLaren F1 was based on a road car. The aerodynamics became a disadvantage for the McLaren F1, so a longer bodied model was consequently developed. The LARK McLaren F1 is popular in this category, and it is now very rare.

McLaren F1 GTR
Le Mans 1997 Gulf Team Davidoff
Bellm/Gilbert-Scott
530 174339

McLaren F1 GTR
Le Mans 1997 Gulf Team Davidoff
Bscher/Nielsen
530 174340

McLaren F1 GTR
Le Mans 1997 Gulf Team Davidoff
Gounon/Raphanel
530 174341

McLaren F1 GTR
FIA-GT 1997 Team Parabolica
Ayles/Goodwin
530 174327

McLaren F1 GTR
Team Lark
Tsuchiya/Nakaya
530 174344

McLaren F1 GTR
JGTC2000 No.30 Team SOK
Yamada/Okada
533 204330

McLaren F1 GTR
JGTC2000 No.21 Hitotsuyama Racing
Hitotsuyama/Hitotsuyama/Nakaya
533 204321

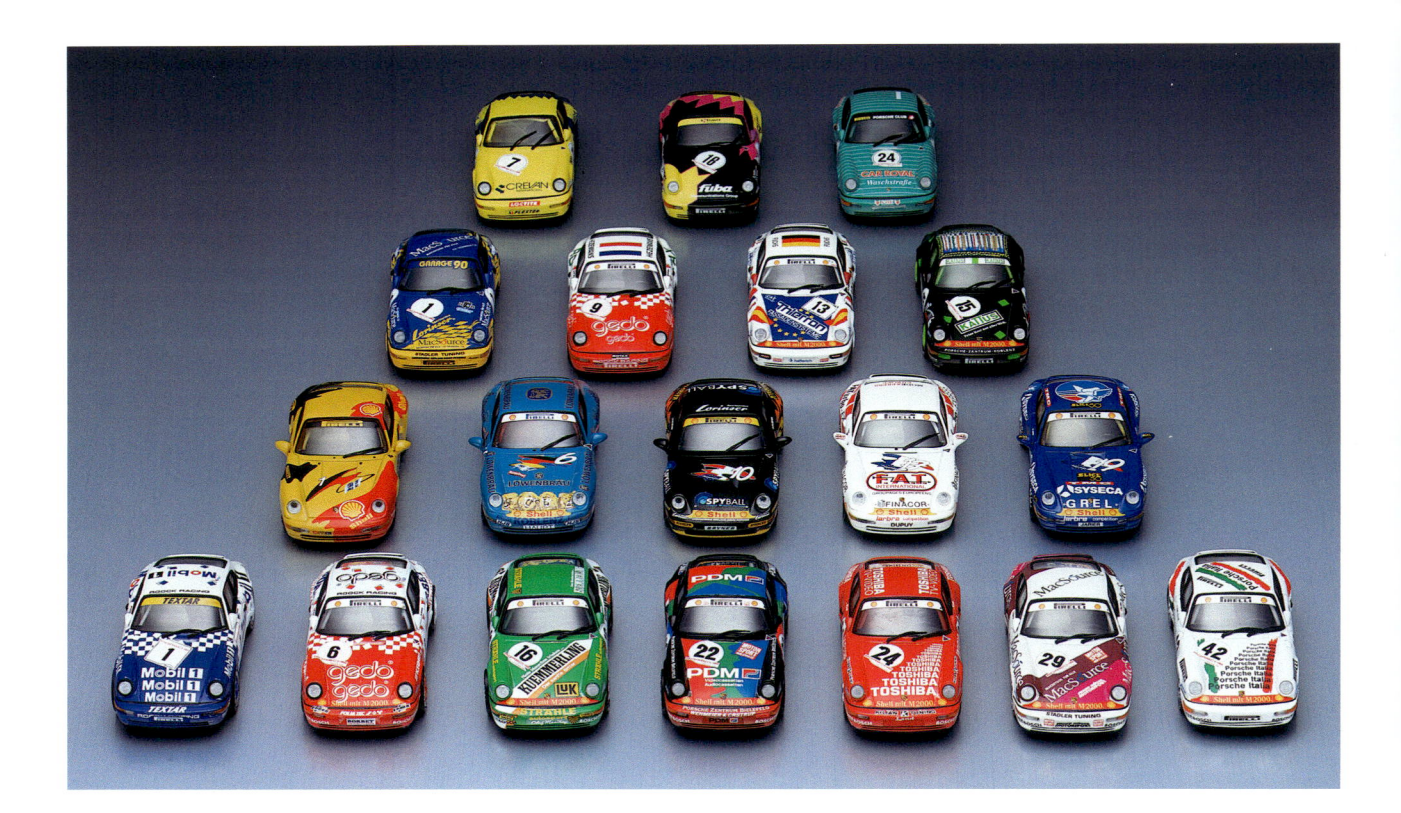

Porsche Carrera Cup Series

Porsche has always had a passion for racing. Continuously wanting to satisfy race fans, Porsche has long been holding sole manufacturer races. We will be introducing the Carrera Cup car, an example of a sole manufacturer racing car. Based on the dealership version of the 911, various parts unnecessary in racing (such as air-conditioning) were removed, and stiffer suspension was added. No modifications were permitted, so the outcome of the race was dependent on driving skill alone. This race was held in Japan. Paul's Model Art / Minichamps produce models of the 1992-94 Carrera Cup car, and the 993 Super Cup cars, which were raced in a different category. The detailed logos, colourings and the remarkable interior are particularly attractive. Just as with the real cars, the suspension is noticeably low. We will now look at them in season order.

Eight Cup cars were released from the 1992 season. There seems to be little difference in popularity between the models, however the No.1 car, sponsored by Mobil, seems to be popular because of its design. There were quite a number of models released, but it would take some time to collect them all, because they were released quite a while ago.

1992 year /////

M. Fleissner
Mobil
430 926001

B. Eichmann
Rook Racing
430 926006

O. Manthey
Stradale Autosport
430 926016

J. v. Gartzen
Castrup Racing
430 926022

W. Land
Killian Tuning
430 926024

T. Seiler
Macsource
430 926029

E. Walcher
Porsche Italia
430 926042

1993 year

Six Cup cars were released from the 1993 season. The distinctive feature of this model is that the 1-piece design wheels are the same as those used on the road version, the 964. The rear spoiler pops up when you move the rear wheels, just as the real road version does.

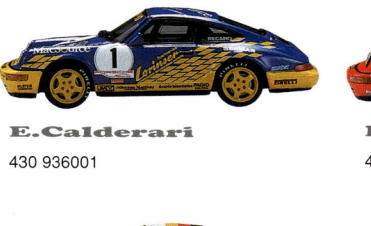

E.Calderari
430 936001

M.Hezemans
430 936009

A.Fuchs
430 936013

A.Heger
430 936015

92 Cup Car	430 926001	Nr.1 Mobil M. Fleissner
	430 926006	Nr.6 B.Eichmann Rook Racing
	430 926015	Nr.15 U.Alzen Porsche Zentrum Koblenz
	430 926016	Nr.16 O.Manthey Straehle Autosport
	430 926022	Nr.22 J.V.Gartzen Castrup Team
	430 926024	Nr.24 W.Land Kilian Tuning
	430 926029	Nr.29 T.Seiler Macsource
	430 926042	Nr.42 E.Walcher Porsche Italia
93 Cup Car	430 936001	Nr.1 E.Calderari
	430 936008	Nr.8 W.Land
	430 936009	Nr.9 M.Hezemans
	430 936010	Nr.10 H.Grohs
	430 936013	Nr.13 A.Fuchs
	430 936015	Nr.15 A.Heger
94 Cup Car	430 946300	Presentation IAA 1993
	430 946001	W.Land
	430 946003	B.Maylander
	430 946007	A.Matschull
	430 946016	H.G.Kamps
	430 946024	J.V.Gartzen
94 Super Cup	430 946305	U.Alzen
	430 946306	H.Haupt
	430 946310	L.Bryner
	430 946317	D.Dupuy
	430 946319	J.P.Jarier
	430 946324	J.P.Malcher
95 Super Cup	430 956501	V.I.P Car
	430 956502	H.Grohs Winner Porsche Cup
	430 956524	J.P.Malcher Winner Porsche Super Cup

A new Cup car based on the 993 was released for the 1994 season. To make conditions equal, the race was categorized differently from the Carrera Cup. Five models of the 964 Carrera Cup car were released. The wheels that had been changed the previous year were replaced with the original 3 piece wheels of the 1992 version. The photo on the right is of the scale model of the 993 Cup car, shown at the 1993 Frankfurt show as a prototype.

1994 year

A.Matschull
430 946007

H.G.Kamps
430 946016

J.v.Gartzen
430 946024

Porsche 911 Super Cup 1994 No.1 Presentation IAA
430 946300

1994/95 Super Cup

993 Cup cars competed in the Super Cup, and six models of the 1994 version have been released. In pursuit of lighter body weight, dual wipers became a single wiper on the Cup car.

A total of three Carrera Cup car and Super Cup car models were released from the 1995 season. Car No. 1 on the right is the 1995 season model with large rear spoiler. Other models released that are not pictured include the champion series' of both Carrera Cup and Super Cup, and a limited number of 3000 were released.

Porsche 911 Super Cup 1995 No.1
430 956501

H.Haupt
430 946306

L.Bryner
430 946310

D.Dupuy
430 946317

J.P.Jarier
430 946319

Jägermeister Collection

The individuality of the colour orange is the secret to this model's popularity

When all the machines have very intricately detailed bodies, it is striking to see a simple paintwork. The orange car with large "Jägermeister" logo has been at race tracks for quite a while now. Jägermeister, not really know in Japan, is a German herbal liqueur company. The company has a long history of supporting motor sport. This model is popular among collectors because of its design. There are some people who collect cars of all race types and disciplines that are sponsored by Jägermeister. We have collected Jägermeister sponsored cars here. Most of them are difficult to acquire. In 2002, the DTM version of the BMW M3(E30) was released. There might be more to come, so keep your eyes peeled!

Opel Omega 3000 Evo
Team Schubel

430 014020

The thick, tough body sculpting is impressive on the early Omega model.

BMW 635 CSI Monza
JÄGERMEISTER **1984**

430 842636

Because Jägermeister was sponsoring touring car races, there are many BMWs.

BMW M3 EVO DTM
1992

430 022020

This model was originally released in 1993, 2002 an '88 version was released.

BMW 320i STW
Team Isert **1998**

430 982625

The E36 that competed in Germany's touring car races. There are models with different car numbers.

Porsche 956K DRM Norisring
Jägermeister

430 846691

The 956K was released relatively recently, but is difficult to get due to its popularity.

Alfa Romeo 155
V6 TI DTM **1995**

430 950219

This is the 1995 model of the DTM version. To the right is the ITC version.

Alfa Romeo 155 V6 TI ITC
Team Alfa JAS **1996**

430 960510

The side windows and antenna are different on the 1996 model of the ITC version.

Opel V8 Coupe DTM
Team Holzer **2000**

430 004811

Opel's DTM weapon, the V8 coupe, has attractive curved wheel arches.

Other Competition Machines

We have looked at quite a number of racing models but there are more Paul's Model Art / Minichamps' racing models available. Obviously we cannot show you all the models, but we would like to give an impression of as many of our cars as possible.

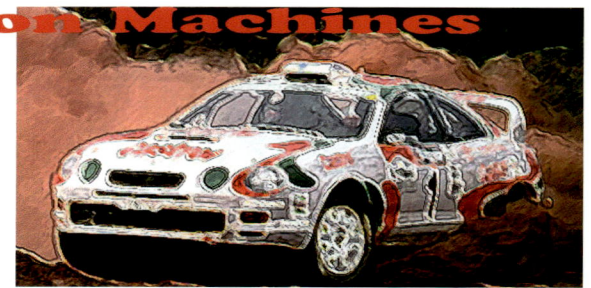

Rally Machines

Lancia Stratos

No one expected the Stratos HF to perform well because of its unconventional design. The car made its rally debut at the end of 1972, and performed extremely well the following year. After 1975, the car was improved, and subsequently won three consecutive WRC titles for the next three years. It is the most popular rally car, the most famous one being the Alitalia model. All of the models enjoy equal popularity.

Lancia Stratos
Le Point 1 TDF 1980
430 801201

Lancia Stratos
Alitalia
1st Monte Carlo 1976
430 761210

Lancia Stratos
Alitalia 1st Monte Carlo 1977
430 771201

Lancia Stratos
Pirelli 1978
430 781201

Lancia Stratos
Alitalia 1st Monte Carlo 1975
430 751214

Lancia Stratos
Chardonnet 1 TRC 1979
430 791201

Lancia Stratos
Alitalia 1st Sweden 1975
430 751204

Ford Escort

Ford, traditionally strong in rallies, confidently released the new Escort RS. Ford had all the right credentials needed to win the title, but accidents cost them the title. There are many colour variations available. The most popular variations include the debut model with Mobil 1 works colouring, and the Michelin Pilot model.

Ford Escort Cosworth
Rallye Monte Carlo 1993
430 938200

Ford Escort Cosworth
Winner Portugal 1994
430 948104

Ford Escort Cosworth
1000 Lakes Rallye 1994
430 948107

Ford Escort Cosworth
Champion of Belgian Rally
Linter 1994
430 948201

Ford Escort
C.Sainz WRC 1997
430 978705

Ford Escort
Michelin Pilot
British Rally Champion 1994
430 948291

Ford Escort
Red Bull Acropolis 1994
430 948209

Ford Escort
1st Monte Carlo
430 968203

Ford Escort Rallye
Monte Carlo 1998 2nd place
430 988707

150 MINICHAMPS

Toyota Celica

Toyota gained consecutive constructors championships with the Celica ST-185, and in 1995 released the more serious Celica ST-205. But compact cars came to dominate WRC, which ultimately saw the end of the Celica's winning ways. Toyota's next rally car was based on the Corolla, and this is the last of the "Rally Celica".

Toyota Celica
Rallye Catalunya 1995
Kankkunen/Grist

430 166502

Toyota Celica
Rally Argentina 1994
Kankkunen/Grist

430 166404

Audi

The Quattro debuted in 1981, based on the Audi Coupe GT with 4WD, and it was really fast at the Monte Carlo rally. The following year, the Quattro won the title. It is a car that will feature in any rally discussion, and the models of it are very popular.

Audi Quattro
Monte Carlo Rally winner 1984
Röhrl/Geistdörfer

430 841901

Audi Quattro
Monte Carlo Rally 1984
Mikkola/Hertz

430 841904

Audi Quattro
Monte Carlo Rally 1984
Blomquist/Cederberg

430 841907

Audi Quattro
Tour de Corse 1981
Mouton/Pons

430 811915

Audi Quattro
Rally of Portugal winner 1982
Mouton/Pons

430 821907

Audi Quattro
Swedish Rally Winners 1982
Blomquist/Cederberg

430 821904

Ford RS 200 & Focus

The Ford RS200 was made to win the Group B WRC, but just as the car was coming of age, Group B was eliminated. The Focus succeeded the Escort, and the only one still in action is featured on this page. At the beginning of the 2003 WRC, the top three places were taken by the Citroen team, but the Ford Focus achieved 4th place.

Ford RS200
Rally Sweden 1986
Grundel/Melander

430 868008

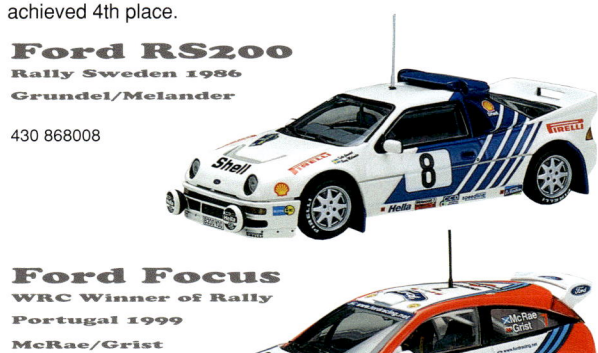

Ford Focus
WRC Winner of Rally Portugal 1999
McRae/Grist

430 998807

Mercedes-Benz

In 1963, the 230SL won the Spa-Spfia Liege Rally. The old Mercedes-Benz models that were victorious in the late 1970's, such as 450SLC5.0, are featured in the range. There aren't too many scale models of this kind produced, so this model is sure to please rally fans.

Mercedes-Benz 230SL
Rallye Spa-Sofia Liege 1963
Böhringer/Kaiser

430 032280

Mercedes-Benz 450 SLC
5.0 Rallye

B6 604 0324   (Dealer Version)

Other Competition Machines
Endurance Race Machines

Porsche

When people speak of Porsche's racing machines, they immediately think of F1 and Le Mans. But since the 1960s, endurance racing has been Porsche's main field of competition. The 917 of the 70s and the 956 of the 80s were particularly strong, enjoying unrivalled supremacy. Paul's Model Art / Minichamps produce these in miniature form, and many others from the same genre.

Porsche 718 RS 60
Sebring 12 hours 1960 Winner
Hermann/Gendebien
430 606542

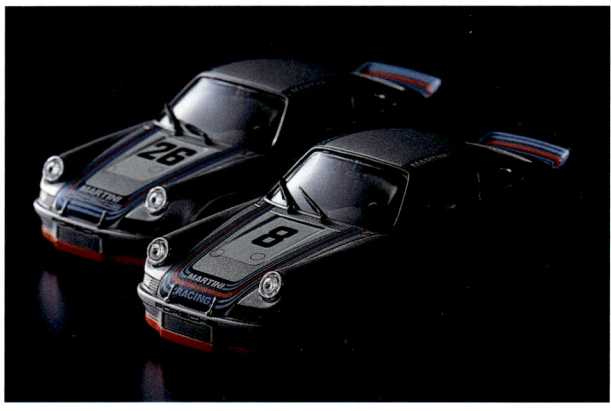

911 Carrera RSR
Porsche Le Mans set 1000km Vallelunge 1973
v.Lennep/Müller
433 736908

911 Carrera RSR Martini
1000km Dijon 1973
GT Winners Müller/v.Lennep
430 736926

Porsche 917 K GULF
DAYTONA 1970
Siffert/Redman
430 706701

Porsche 917 K GULF
DAYTONA 1970 Winners
Rodriguez/Kinnunen
430 706702

Porsche 917 KH Martini
1ST Sebring 1971
Elford/Larrousse
430 706703

Porsche 917 K
in Terserie Champion 1970
J.Neuhaus
430 706712

Porsche 917 K
24h Daytona 1970
Team Porsche Selzburg
Elford/Ahrens
430 706793

Porsche 911 Carrera RSR
Winner 24 hours Daytona 1973
Gregg/Haywood
430 736959

Porsche 911 Carrera RSR
Sebring 12 hours 1973 Winner
Gregg/Haywood/Helmick
430 736999

Porsche 956 K
1000km Nuerburgring 1983
Bell/Bellof
430 836602

Porsche 956 K
1st 1000km Nuerburgring 1983
Mass/Ickx
430 846601

Porsche 956 K
1983 Boss
K.Rosberg
430 836612

Porsche 956 K
1000km Nuerburgring 1983
Lammers/Palmer/Rosberg
430 836614

Porsche 956 k
1st 200 Miles Norisring 1984
M.Winkelhock
430 846610

Porsche 911 GT1
FIA GT 1997
Boutsen/Stuck
430 976606

Porsche 911 GT1
Daytona 24h 2001
Schumacher/Holtom/Bytzek/Brenner
400 016801

Porsche 911 GT3RS
Daytona GrandAm Final 2001
Jeannette/Bartkiw/Minkin
400 016976

BMW

The BMW M series were developed by BMW M GmbH. The M3 was victorious in DTM, and also several other races. The Paul's Model Art / Minichamps range includes the M3(E30) and the current M3(E46)GTR. The E30 had competed in the Spa 24hour Endurance race, and the M46 GTR competed in America's Petit Le Mans series.

BMW M3
Paris Mach Spa 1994
430 942045

BMW M3
1st Spa Schnitzer/Fina 1990
Cecotto/Giroix/Oestreich
430002004

BMW 3.5 CSL Winner Sebring 12hours 1975
Redman/Moffat/Stuck/Posey
430 752925

BMW M3 Bastos
1st Spa 24hours 1992
Martin/Soper/Danner
430 022013

BMW M3 Bastos
Spa 24hours 1990
430 002013

BMW M3 GTR
ALMS Petit Le Mans 2001
Lehto/Ekblom/Wendlinger
400 012142

BMW M3 GTR
ALMS Petit Le Mans 2001
J. Müller/D. Müller
400 012143

Audi

The Audi R8, which has been racing strongly in Le Mans, competes in America's Petit Le Mans Series. There are many beautifully decorated R8 models, and it would be appealing to make a collection of these attractive miniature models.

Audi R8
Petit Le Mans Rood Atlanta 2001
Herbert/Wallace
400 010938

Audi R8
ALMS Adelaide 2000 Winner
Capello/McNish
430 000977

The magnificent design on this car is one of a swimming crocodile, which led to the car being nicknamed "the crocodile". The model replicates the design of the original with stunning accuracy and authenticity.

Mercedes-Benz

Mercedes-Benz led the racing scene in the 50's. After the dreadful 1955 crash at Le Mans, Mercedes-Benz withdrew from the race, but they have since become involved once again. The classic car series' are popular models among fans.

Mercedes 300 SLR
1955 Mille Miglia
Moss/Jenkinson
432 553100

Mercedes W196
1954 1st GP France
J.M.Fangio
432 543018

Mercedes W196
1954 GP France
K. Kling
432 543020

Mercedes W196
1954 GP France
H. Lang
432 543022

McLaren is also renowned for endurance races, and the miniature model enjoys popularity proportionate to the car's success.

The McLaren F1 GTR not only competed in Le Mans, but also in BPR and various other races. The Mc Laren in the photo is the model that won the Japanese GT with Ralf Schumacher and Naoki Hattori driving. They are popular drivers, and many collectors desperately want to get this model.

153

Other Competition Machines

Chaparral & McLaren

Chaparral

Chaparral was founded by the American Jim Hall. The cars did not have a striking appearance, however they were fitted with innovative technology, such as the Venturi machine, adjustable rear high wing, and 3 speed automatic transmission. In the 60's Chaparral faced the McLaren Can-am, and later achieved success in Europe's endurance races. Other than the models shown here, the 'Fan Car' using the Venturi suction duct effect was miniaturized.

Chaparral 2H Can am Edmonton 1969 J. Surtees
436 691407

Chaparral 2D
1000km Nuerburgring 1966 Winner
P.Hill/Bonnier
436 661407

The 2F with high rear wing was the race car challenging for Le Mans 24 hours honours.

McLaren

Bruce McLaren started the team and dominated with the Can-am series in the late 60's to early 70's. Bruce became a champion in 1969, but sadly died in 1970 whilst developing a new race car. But the team continued winning. After merging with Ron Dennis' English 'Project Four' team, it became the McLaren of today. The models shown below are the race cars that competed in America.

McLaren M8A
B.McLaren Can-am 1968
530 684304

McLaren M8B
B.McLaren Can-am Champion 1969
530 694304

McLaren M8D
D.Gurney Can-am 1970
530 704307

McLaren M8A
D.Hulme Can-am Champion 1968
530 684305

McLaren M8F
D.Hulme Can-am 1971
530 714305

McLaren M8B
D.Hulme Can-am 1969
530 694305

McLaren Chevrolet M8D
D.Hulme Can-am Champion 1970
530 704305

McLaren M8D
P.Gethin Can-am 1970
530 704397

McLaren M8F
P.Revson Can-am Champion 1971
530 714307

154 MINICHAMPS

ITEM-No	ITEM	YEAR
430120000	ALFA ROMEO 147 2001 RED	
430120001	ALFA ROMEO 147 2001 BLUE MET.	
430120090	ALFA ROMEO 147 IAA 2001 SILVER	
430120400	ALFA ROMEO 155 SALOON BLUE MET.	1992
430120401	ALFA ROMEO 155 SALOON BLACK	1992
430120402	ALFA ROMEO 155 SALOON RED	1992
430930120	ALFA ROMEO 155 V6 NANNINI NR7 1993	1993
430930121	ALFA ROMEO 155 V6 LARINI NR 8 1993	1993
430930122	ALFA ROMEO 155 V6 DANNER NR 14 1993	1993
430930123	ALFA ROMEO 155 V6 FRANCIA NR15 1993	1993
430940111	ALFA ROMEO 155 V6 TI DANNER/S.94 OLD BODY	1994
430940112	ALFA ROMEO 155 V6 TI FRANCIA 94 OLD BODY	1994
430940118	ALFA ROMEO 155 V6 TI NISSEN/S.94 OLD BODY	1994
430940125	ALFA ROMEO 155 V6 TI ENGSTLER 94 OLD BODY	1994
430940126	ALFA ROMEO 155 V6 TI STRUWE/E.94 OLD BODY	1994
430940127	ALFA ROMEO 155 V6 TI BARTELS 94 OLD BODY	1994
430940130	ALFA ROMEO 155 V6 TI GIUDICI 94 OLD BODY	1994
430940201	ALFA ROMEO 155 V6 TI LARINI 94 NEW BODY	1994
430940202	ALFA ROMEO 155 V6 TI NANNINI 94 NEW BODY	1994
430940210	ALFA ROMEO 155 V6 TI/94 MODENA AVUS DTM94	1994
430940211	ALFA ROMEO 155 V6 TI DANNER/S.94 NEW BODY	1994
430940212	ALFA ROMEO 155 V6 TI FRANCIA 94 NEW BODY	1994
430940218	ALFA ROMEO 155 V6 TI NISSEN/S.94 NEW BODY	1994
430940233	ALFA ROMEO 155 V6 TI BUTTIERO 94 NEW BODY	1994
430941206	ALFA ROMEO 155 A.TAMBURINI SUP.T.94	1994
430941209	ALFA ROMEO 155 S.MODENA SUP.T.94	1994
430941255	ALFA ROMEO 155 G.TARQUINI BR.CH. 94	1994
430941256	ALFA ROMEO 155 G.SIMONI BTCC CL2 94	1994
430950207	ALFA ROMEO 155 94 PRES. NANNINI DTM95	1995
430950208	ALFA ROMEO 155 94 PRES. LARINI DTM 95	1995
430950212	ALFA ROMEO 155 94 PRES. ALBORETO DTM 95	1995
430950218	ALFA ROMEO 155 94 PRES. S.MODENA DTM 95	1995
430950219	ALFA ROMEO 155 94 PRES. M.BARTELS DTM95	1995
430950227	ALFA ROMEO 155 94 PRES. M.ALEN DTM95	1995
430950311	ALFA ROMEO 155 SCHUEBEL C.DANNER DTM 95	1995
430950312	ALFA ROMEO 155 SCHUEBEL ALBORETO DTM 95	1995
430950313	ALFA ROMEO 155 A.CORSE2 G.GIUDICI DTM95	1995
430950318	ALFA ROMEO 155 EUROTEAM S.MODENA DTM 95	1995
430950319	ALFA ROMEO 155 EUROTEAM M.BARTELS DTM95	1995
430950407	ALFA ROMEO 155 BODY 95-2 NANNINI DTM95	1995
430950408	ALFA ROMEO 155 BODY 95-2 LARINI DTM 95	1995
430950426	ALFA ROMEO 155 A.CORSE2 FISICHELLA 95	1995
430960313	ALFA ROMEO 155 GIUDICI GIUDICI ITC 96	1996
430960405	ALFA ROMEO 155 LARINI PRESENTATION	1996
430960505	ALFA ROMEO 155 ALFA CORSE LARINI ITC 96	1996
430960506	ALFA ROMEO 155 A. CORSE NANNINI ITC 96	1996
430960509	ALFA ROMEO 155 ALFA JAS MODENA ITC 96	1996
430960510	ALFA ROMEO 155 ALFA JAS BARTELS ITC 96	1996
430960514	ALFA ROMEO 155 A.CORSE FISICHELLA ITC96	1996
430960515	ALFA ROMEO 155 A. CORSE DANNER ITC 96	1996
430960518	ALFA ROMEO 155 ALFA JAS TARQUINI ITC 96	1996
430960519	ALFA ROMEO 155 ALFA JAS WATT ITC 96	1996
431900007	ALFA ROMEO 155TI LARINI CHAMPION DTM 93	1990
433930123	ALFA ROMEO 155 V6 FRANCIA NR15 1993	1993
430120700	ALFA ROMEO 156 SALOON SILVER	
430120701	ALFA ROMEO 156 SALOON RED	
430120702	ALFA ROMEO 156 SALOON NUVOLA BLUE	
430120704	ALFA ROMEO 156 SALOON ACHILLE BLUE	
430120710	ALFA ROMEO 156 SPORTWAGON '01 BLACK	
430120711	ALFA ROMEO 156 SPORTWG.'01 GREY MET	
430982010	ALFA ROMEO 156 EUROTEAM/MODENA STW 98	1998
430982020	ALFA ROMEO 156 ALFA/LARINI STW 98	1998
430992011	ALFA ROMEO 156 S.MODENA/EUROTEAM STW'99	1999
430992012	ALFA ROMEO 156 A.SCHELD/EUROTEAM STW'99	1999
430992027	ALFA ROMEO 156 N.LARINI/ALFA STW'99	1999
430992028	ALFA ROMEO 156 F.GIOVANARDI/ALFA STW'99	1999
433002002	ALFA ROMEO 156 KERSEBOOM 2000	
400120100	ALFA ROMEO ALFASUD 1972 BLUE	1972
400120101	ALFA ROMEO ALFASUD 1972 GREEN	1972
400120120	ALFA ROMEO ALFETTA GT COUPE '76 RED	1976
400120121	ALFA ROMEO ALFETTA GTV '76 GREEN MT	1976
436120920	ALFA ROMEO TIPO 33 STRADALE	
433970101	ARROWS FA 18 D.HILL 6TH GP GB 1997	1997
430970001	ARROWS FA 18 YAMAHA D.HILL 1997	1997
430970002	ARROWS FA 18 YAMAHA P.DINIZ 1997	1997
430980016	ARROWS A 19 P.DINIZ 1998	1998
430980017	ARROWS A 19 M.SALO 1998	1998
430980086	ARROWS FA 19 TWR P.DINIZ PRES.98	1998
430980087	ARROWS FA 19 TWR M.SALO PRES.98	1998
430990014	ARROWS A 20 P. DE LA ROSA 1999	1999
430990015	ARROWS A 20 T. TAKAGI 1999	1999
430990084	ARROWS F1 T.TAKAGI PRES. 1999	1999
430990085	ARROWS F1 P. DE LA ROSA PRES. 1999	1999
430990184	ARROWS F1 T.TAKAGI BLACK PRES. 1999	1999
430000018	ARROWS ASIATECH A21 P.DE LA ROSA 2000	2000
430000019	ARROWS ASIATECH A21 J.VERSTAPPEN 2000	2000
430000088	ARROWS ASIATECH DE LA ROSA PRES. 2000	2000
430000089	ARROWS ASIATECH J. VERSTAPPEN PRES. 2000	2000
430000119	ARROWS ASIATECH A21 J.VERSTAPPEN '00 FOR SET	2000
430010084	ARROWS ASIATECH J.VERSTAPPEN PRES. 2001	2001
430010085	ARROWS ASIATECH E. BERNOLDI PRES. 2001	2001
400010014	ARROWS ASIATECH A22 J.VERSTAPPEN 01	2001
400010015	ARROWS ASIATECH A22 E.BERNOLDI 2001	2001
400010114	ARROWS ASIATECH A22 J.V. NOSEWING 2001	2001
400010115	ARROWS ASIATECH A22 NOSEWING BERN. 01	2001
400020020	ARROWS COSWORTH A23 H.H. FRENTZEN 2002	2002
400020021	ARROWS COSWORTH A23 E. BERNOLDI 2002	2002
400020070	ARROWS COSWORTH H.H.FRENTZEN LAUNCH 2002	2002
400020071	ARROWS COSWORTH E.BERNOLDI LAUNCH 2002	2002
400137220	ASTON MARTIN VANQUISH J.B. 2002	
430010400	AUDI 50 1975 GREEN	1975
430010401	AUDI 50 1975 BLUE	1975
433010403	AUDI 50 1976 PHOENIX RED	
400011310	AUDI 60 BREAK 1970 BEIGE	1970
400011311	AUDI 60 BREAK 1970 GREEN	1970
403011303	AUDI 60 SALOON 1970 JAVA GREEN	
400011300	AUDI 60 SALOON 1970 RED	1970
400011301	AUDI 60 SALOON 1970 ORANGE	1970
403011313	AUDI 60 VARIANT 1970 BLUE	
433019103	AUDI 100 SALOON GREEN	
430019100	AUDI 100 SALOON 1969-75 RED	
430019101	AUDI 100 SALOON 1969-75 BROWN MET.	
430019102	AUDI 100 SALOON 1969-75 SILVER	
433019123	AUDI 100 COUPE S 1969-75 BLUE MET.	
430019120	AUDI 100 COUPE S 1969-75 BLUE MET.	
430019121	AUDI 100 COUPE S 1969-75 ORANGE	
430019122	AUDI 100 COUPE S 1969-75 RED	
433019003	AUDI A2 LIGHT SILVER EXCL.	
433019004	AUDI A2 PINE GREEN EXCL.	
433019005	AUDI A2 ICELAND GREEN EXCL.	
433019006	AUDI A2 JAIPUR RED EXCL.	
433019007	AUDI A2 ATLANTIC BLUE EXCL.	
433019008	AUDI A2 PINE GREEN EXCL.	
433019009	AUDI A2 SILVER POLISHED	
430019000	AUDI A2 SALOON 2000 BLACK MET.	
430019001	AUDI A2 SALOON 2000 BLUE MET.	2000
430019002	AUDI A2 SALOON 2000 BLACK	
430019004	AUDI A2 SALOON 2000 DARK BLUE	
430015100	AUDI A3 LIMOUSINE 1995 BLUE MET	1996
430015101	AUDI A3 LIMOUSINE 1995 SILVER MET	1996
430015102	AUDI A3 LIMOUSINE 1995 RED MET	1996
433015103	AUDI A3 LIMOUSINE 1995 MAJA YELLOW EXCL.	1996
433015104	AUDI A3 LIMOUSINE 1995 BLUE EXCL.	1996
433015105	AUDI A3 LIMOUSINE 1995 RED EXCL.	1996
433015106	AUDI A3 LIMOUSINE 1995 GREEN MET. EXCL.	1996
433015107	AUDI A3 LIMOUSINE 1995 BLACK EXCL.	1996
430010300	AUDI A3 4-DOOR 2000 BLACK	
430010301	AUDI A3 4-DOOR 2000 GREEN MET.	
430010302	AUDI A3 4-DOOR 2000 BLUE MET.	
433010303	AUDI A3 4-DOOR 2000 SANTORIN BLUE	
433010304	AUDI A3 4-DOOR 2000 LASER RED	
433010305	AUDI A3 4-DOOR 2000 ALU SILVER MET.	
430018300	AUDI A3 5-DOOR 1998 GREEN MET.	
430018301	AUDI A3 5-DOOR 1998 BLACK MET.	
430018302	AUDI A3 5-DOOR 1998 DARK BLUE	1998
433018303	AUDI A3 5-DOOR 1998 SANTORIN	
433018304	AUDI A3 5-DOOR 1998 LASER RED	
433018305	AUDI A3 5-DOOR 1998 ALU SILVER	
430018400	AUDI A4 SALOON FACEL.98 GREEN MET.	
430018401	AUDI A4 FACELIFT DARK GREY MET.	1999
433018403	AUDI A4 FACELIFT 98 JASPIS GREEN EXCL	
433018404	AUDI A4 FACELIFT 98 LIGHT SILVER EXCL	
433018405	AUDI A4 FACELIFT 98 JAIPU RED EXCL	
433018406	AUDI A4 FACELIFT 98 CACTUS GREEN EXCL	
433018407	AUDI A4 FACELIFT 98 SANTORIN BLUE EXCL	
430010100	AUDI A4 2000 GREEN METALLIC	
430010101	AUDI A4 2000 BLUE METALLIC	
433010103	AUDI A4 2000 LIGHT SILVER MET.EXCL	
433010104	AUDI A4 2000 DOLPHIN GREY MET.EXCL	
433010105	AUDI A4 2000 EBONY BLACK MET.EXCL.	
433010106	AUDI A4 2000 DENIM BLUE MET. EXCL.	
430015000	AUDI A4 LIMOUSINE SILVER	1994
430015001	AUDI A4 LIMOUSINE BLUE MET	1994
430015002	AUDI A4 LIMOUSINE RED MET.	1994
433015004	AUDI A4 LIMOUSINE BLUE MET.	1995
433015005	AUDI A4 LIMOUSINE SILVER MET	1995
433015006	AUDI A4 LIMOUSINE GREEN MET.	1995
433015007	AUDI A4 LIMOUSINE BLACK	1995
430015008	AUDI A4 SALOON 1995 BLACK MET.	1995
430015009	AUDI A4 SALOON 1995 RED	
433015001	AUDI A4 SALOON PELICAN BLUEMET EXCL	
433015003	AUDI A4 SALOON EXCL. LASER RED	1995
433015008	AUDI A4 SALOON 1995 EXCL BLACK MET.	1995
430018410	AUDI A4 AVANT FACELIFT 1998	
430018411	AUDI A4 AVANT FACELIFT BLUE MET.	1999
430015010	AUDI A4 AVANT 1995 GREY METALLIC	1995
430015011	AUDI A4 AVANT 1995 GREEN METALLIC	1995
430015012	AUDI A4 AVANT 1995 RED METALLIC	1995
430010110	AUDI A4 AVANT 2001 GREY	
430010111	AUDI A4 AVANT 2002 BLUE METALLIC	
433010113	AUDI A4 AVANT 2000 AMULETT RED	
433010114	AUDI A4 AVANT 2000 MING BLUE	
433010115	AUDI A4 AVANT 2000 SILVER GREY	
433010116	AUDI A4 AVANT 2000 SILVER GREY	
433010117	AUDI A4 AVANT 2000 SILVER GREY	
433010118	AUDI A4 AVANT 2000 SILVER GREY	
433015011	AUDI A4 AVANT 1995 GREEN METALLIC	1995
433015013	AUDI A4 AVANT 1995 EXCL. GREEN MET	1995
433015014	AUDI A4 AVANT EXCL. MANDARIN MET.	1995
433015015	AUDI A4 AVANT 1995 EXCL. COLOUR 3	1995
433015016	AUDI A4 AVANT 1995 EXCL. BLUE MET	1995
433015017	AUDI A4 AVANT 1995 EXCL. RED	1995
433015018	AUDI A4 AVANT 1995 EXCL. SILVER	
433015019	AUDI A4 AVANT 1995 EXCL. BLACK	
433018413	AUDI A4 AVANT FACELIFT 98 LASER RED EX	
433018414	AUDI A4 AVANT 98 BRILLIANT BLACK EX	
433018415	AUDI A4 AVANT 98 LAUREL GREEN EXCL.	
433018416	AUDI A4 AVANT 98 LIGHT SILVER EXCL.	
433018417	AUDI A4 AVANT FACEL.98 MING BLUE EX	
433951504	AUDI A4 COURSE/T.VIDALI EXCL.	1995
433951511	AUDI A4 CLASS2 SCHNEIDER/HEGER EXCL	1995
433951544	AUDI A4 CLASS2 SCHNEIDER/STUCK EXCL	1995
433951545	AUDI A4 CLASS2 COURSE/F.BIELA EXCL.	1995
433961500	AUDI A4 PRESENTATION 1996	1996
433961501	AUDI A4 CAPELLO ITALY 1996	1996
433961503	AUDI A4 ORIX AUSTRALIA CL 2	1996
433961504	AUDI A4 VIDALI STW CUP 1996	1996
433961505	AUDI A4 PIRRO STW CUP 1996	1996
433961506	AUDI A4 WENDLINGER STW CUP 1996	1996
433961507	AUDI A4 PETER STW CUP 1996	1996
433961508	AUDI A4 MOSS RSA 1996	1996
433961514	AUDI A4 HEMROULLE BELGIUM 1996	1996
433961545	AUDI A4 BIELA GB 1996	1996
433961594	AUDI A4 GENE SPAIN 1996	1996
433971501	AUDI A4 E.PIRRO STW CUP GERMANY 97	1997
433971504	AUDI A4 T.VIDALI STW CUP GERMANY 97	1997
433971521	AUDI A4 R.CAPELLO STW CUP ITALY 97	1997
433971522	AUDI A4 WENDLINGER STW CUP ITALY 97	1997
433971590	AUDI A4 PRESENTATION STW 1997	1997
433971591	AUDI A4 SUPERTOURING PRES. BIELA 97	1997
430991909	AUDI A4 K.NISSEN/ABT STW'99	1999
430991910	AUDI A4 CH.ABT/ABT STW'99	1999
430991914	AUDI A4 M.BARTELS/PHOENIX STW'99	1999
430991915	AUDI A4 A.MEIER/PHOENIX STW'99	1999
430951501	AUDI A4 E.PIRRO ITALIAN CHAMPION 95	1995
430951503	AUDI A4 F.BIELA WORLD CHAMPION 1995	1995
430951504	AUDI A4 COURSE/VIDALI STW95	1995
430951511	AUDI A4 SCHNEIDER/HEGER STW95	1995
430951544	AUDI A4 SCHNEIDER/STUCK STW95	1995
430951545	AUDI A4 COURSE/BIELA STW95	1995
430961503	AUDI A4 ORIX AUSTRALIA CL 2	1996
430961504	AUDI A4 VIDALI STW CUP 1996	1996
430961505	AUDI A4 PIRRO STW CUP 1996	1996
430961506	AUDI A4 WENDLINGER STW CUP 1996	1996
430961507	AUDI A4 PETER STW CUP 1996	1996
430971501	AUDI A4 QU. AZK/ROC E.PIRRO STW 97	1997
430971502	AUDI A4 QU. AZK/ROC P.PETER STW 97	1997
430971503	AUDI A4 AZK/ROC Y.MULLER STW 97	1997
430971504	AUDI A4 QU. AZK/ROC T.VIDALI STW 97	1997
430971511	AUDI A4 QUATTRO ORIX NO. 11 1997	1997
430971518	AUDI A4 QUATTRO ABT/CH.ABT STW 97	1997
430971519	AUDI A4 QUATTRO ABT/K.NISSEN STW 97	1997
430971544	AUDI A4 QU. MIG/K.NIEDZWIEDZ STW 97	1997
430971545	AUDI A4 QUATTRO MIG/D.MUELLER STW97	1997
430971561	AUDI A4 QUATTRO ORIX B.JONES 1997	1997
430981805	AUDI A4 ABT/PIRRO STW 98	1998
430981818	AUDI A4 ABT/ABT STW 98	1998
430981845	AUDI A4 ABT/BIELA STW 98	1998
433017103	AUDI A6 SALOON 1997 PEARL BLUE EXCL	1997
433017104	AUDI A6 SALOON 97 RACING GREEN EXCL	1997
433017105	AUDI A6 97 JASPIS GREEN PEARL EXCL	1997
433017106	AUDI A6 SALOON 97 YELLOW EXCL	1997
433017107	AUDI A6 SALOON 97 ALU SILVER EXCL	1997
433017113	AUDI A6 AVANT 1997 BLUE MET.	1997
433017114	AUDI A6 AVANT 1997 RACING GREEN	
433017115	AUDI A6 AVANT 1997 SILVER	
433017116	AUDI A6 AVANT 1997 TURMALIN	
433010013	AUDI A6 ALLROAD HIGHLAND GREEN	
433010014	AUDI A6 ALLROAD ATLAS GREY	
433010203	AUDI A6 SALOON 2001 SILVER EXCL.	
433010213	AUDI A6 AVANT 2001 RACING GREEN MET	
430010210	AUDI A6 AVANT 2001 BLUE METALLIC	
430010211	AUDI A6 AVANT 2001 GREY METALLIC	
430010200	AUDI A6 SALOON 2001 BLACK	
430010201	AUDI A6 SALOON 2001 BLUE METALLIC	
430017100	AUDI A6 SALOON 1997 BLUE METALLIC	1997
430017101	AUDI A6 SALOON 1997 BLACK	1997
430017110	AUDI A6 AVANT 1997 BLUE METALLIC	
433013001	AUDI A8 BLACK/ANTHRACITE EXCLUSIV	1994
433013002	AUDI A8 CERISE/IVORY EXCLUSIV	1994
433013003	AUDI A8 1994 EXCLUSIV	1994
433013004	AUDI A8 1994 EXCLUSIV	1994
433013005	AUDI A8 1994 ISISRED/BEIGE EXCL.	1994
433013006	AUDI A8 1994 SILVER/BLACK EXCL.	1994
433013007	AUDI A8 1994 GREEN MET. EXCL.	1994
430013000	AUDI A8 1994 BLACK	1994
430013001	AUDI A8 1994 CASHMERE	1994
430013002	AUDI A8 1994 RUBIN RED	1994
433013008	AUDI A8 SILVER/BLACK EXCLUSIV	1994
433013009	AUDI A8 BLUE/GREY EXCLUSIV	1994
403011803	AUDI A8 SALOON EBONY BLACK PEARL	
403011804	AUDI A8 SALOON LIGHT SILVER	
403011805	AUDI A8 SALOON NIGHT BLUE PEARL	
430018800	AUDI A8 SALOON 1999 BLACK	
433018803	AUDI A8 FACELIFT 98 LIGHT SILVER EXCL.	
433018804	AUDI A8 FACELIFT 98 SANTORIN BLUE EXCL	
433018805	AUDI A8 FACELIFT 98 RACING GREEN EXCL.	
433018806	AUDI A8 '98 BLUE/GREEN MET. EXCL.	
433019423	AUDI QUATTRO SILVER EXCL.	
433019424	AUDI QUATTRO RED EXCL.	
433019425	AUDI QUATTRO WHITE EXCL.	
433811915	AUDI QUATTRO MOUTON/P. CORSICA 1981	
433821904	AUDI QUATTRO BLOMQUIST SWEDEN 1982	
433821907	AUDI QUATTRO RALLYE PORTUGAL 1982	
433841901	AUDI QUATTRO ROEHRL/G. MONTE C 1984	
433841904	AUDI QUATTRO MIKKOLA/H MONTE C 1984	
433841907	AUDI QUATTRO BLOMQUIST MONTE C 1984	
430010010	AUDI ALLROAD QUATTRO BLACK	
430010011	AUDI ALLROAD QUATTRO SILVER MET.	
430010012	AUDI ALLROAD QUATTRO DARK BLUE	
430010014	AUDI ALLROAD QUATTRO BLUE MET.	
430019420	AUDI QUATTRO ROAD CAR 1981 RED	
430019421	AUDI QUATTRO ROAD CAR 1981 BLACK	
430841904	AUDI QUATTRO MIKKOLA/H MONTE C 1984	
430841907	AUDI QUATTRO BLOMQUIST MONTE C 1984	
430811915	AUDI QUATTRO MOUTON/P. CORSICA 1981	
430821904	AUDI QUATTRO BLOMQUIST SWEDEN 1982	
430821907	AUDI QUATTRO RALLYE PORTUGAL 1982	
430841901	AUDI QUATTRO ROEHRL/G. MONTE C 1984	
400010918	AUDI R8 ROAD ATLANTA PETIT LM 2001	2001
400010938	AUDI R8 ROAD ATLANTA PETIT LM 2001	
400021301	AUDI R8 NO.1 1ST LE MANS 2002	
400021302	AUDI R8 NO.2 2ND LE MANS 2002	
400021303	AUDI R8 JOEST KRUMM 3RD LE MANS '02	
400021391	AUDI R8 2002 SEBRING 12H	2002
400021392	AUDI R8 2002 WINNER SEBRING 12H	2002
403021391	AUDI R8 2002 SEBRING 12H	
403021392	AUDI R8 2002 WINNER SEBRING 12H	
403021301	AUDI R8 INFINEON NO.1 LE MANS 2002	2002
403021302	AUDI R8 INFINEON NO.2 LE MANS 2002	2002
403021303	AUDI R8 INFINEON NO.3 LE MANS 2002	2002
403011201	AUDI R8 TEAM JOEST 1ST LE MANS '01	
403011202	AUDI R8 TEAM N.AMERICA LE MANS '01	
430990909	AUDI R8C ABT/JOHANSSON/OR. LM 1999	
430990910	AUDI R8C WEAVER/WALLACE/MC. LM 1999	
433990909	AUDI R8C START NO. 9 LE MANS 1999	
433990910	AUDI R8C START NO. 10 LE MANS 1999	
430000907	AUDI R8R JOEST ALBORETO 3RD LM 2000	2000
430000908	AUDI R8R JOEST BIELA 1ST LE MANS 00	2000
430000909	AUDI R8R JOEST AIELLO 2ND LM 2000	2000
430990907	AUDI R8R ALBORETO/CAP./AIE. LM 1999	
430990908	AUDI R8R BIELA/PIRRO/THEYS LM 1999	
433000907	AUDI R8R JOEST ALBORETO 3RD LM 2000	
433000908	AUDI R8R JOEST BIELA 1ST LE MANS 00	
433000909	AUDI R8R JOEST AIELLO 2ND LM 2000	
433990907	AUDI R8R START NO. 7 LE MANS 1999	
433990908	AUDI R8R START NO. 8 LE MANS 1999	
430000977	AUDI R8S ALMS WINNER ADELAIDE 2000	2000
400010903	AUDI R8S HERBERT/.. LE MANS 2001	
400010904	AUDI R8S CORONEL/.. LE MANS 2001	
400011201	AUDI R8S TEAM JOEST 1ST LE MANS '01	
400011202	AUDI R8S TEAM N.AMERICA LE MANS '01	
433000977	AUDI R8S ALMS WINNER ADELAIDE 2000	
430019310	AUDI RS4 BRILLIANT BLACK	
430019311	AUDI RS4 2000 YELLOW	
433019313	AUDI RS4 AVUS SILVER	
433019314	AUDI RS4 MISANO RED	
433019315	AUDI RS4 BRILLIANT BLACK	
403011703	AUDI RS6 2001 DAYTONA GREY	
400011700	AUDI RS6 2002 RED	
400011701	AUDI RS6 2002 BLACK METALLIC	
400011710	AUDI RS6 AVANT 2002 SILVER	
400011711	AUDI RS6 AVANT 2002 GREY METALLIC	
403011713	AUDI RS6 AVANT 2001 MISANO RED	
403011714	AUDI RS6 AVANT 2001 MUGELLO BLUE	
403011715	AUDI RS6 AVANT 2001 MUGELLO BLUE	
400011118	AUDI TT-R ABT SPORTSL. C.ABT DTM 01	2001
400011119	AUDI TT-R ABT SPORTSL.AIELLO DTM 01	2001
400011122	AUDI TT-R ABT JUNIOR EKSTROEM DTM01	2001
400011123	AUDI TT-R ABT JUNIOR TOMCZYK DTM 01	2001
430001809	AUDI TT-R ABT L.AIELLO DTM 2000	2000
430001810	AUDI TT-R ABT C.ABT DTM 2000	2000
430001820	AUDI TT-R ABT K.NISSEN DTM 2000	2000
430001821	AUDI TT-R ABT J.THOMPSON DTM 2000	2000
430001890	AUDI TT-R ABT TESTCAR BLACK DTM '00	2000
433017223	AUDI TT COUPE SILVER	1997
433017224	AUDI TT COUPE 1997 BRILLIANT BLACK	
433017225	AUDI TT COUPE 1997 DENIM BLUE	
433017226	AUDI TT COUPE 1997 TALISMAN GREEN	
433017227	AUDI TT COUPE 1997 SPEC. DENIM BLUE	
433017228	AUDI TT COUPE 1997 AMULETT RED	
430017220	AUDI TT COUPE 1998 LIGHT YELLOW	1998
430017221	AUDI TT COUPE 1998 RED	1998
430017222	AUDI TT COUPE 1998 BLACK	1998
430017224	AUDI TT COUPE 1998 WHITE	
430017229	AUDI TT COUPE 1998 BLUE METALLIC	
430017250	AUDI TT COUPE 2000 RED	
433017233	AUDI TT ROADSTER 99 SILVER SEA EXCL	1997
433017234	AUDI TT ROADSTER 99 NIMBUS GREY EXCL	
433017235	AUDI TT ROADSTER TALISMAN GREEN EXCL	
433017236	AUDI TT ROADSTER LIGHT GREY SEMPERIT	
430017230	AUDI TT ROADSTER 1999 BLACK	1996
430017231	AUDI TT ROADSTER 1999 GREEN MET.	
430017232	AUDI TT ROADSTER 1999 RED	
430017234	AUDI TT ROADSTER 2000 BLACK	
430001001	AUDI V8 DTM 90 STUCK NR.44	1990
430001002	AUDI V8 DTM 90 ROEHRL NR.45	1990
430011101	AUDI V8 DTM 91 SMS/STUCK NO. 1	1991
430011102	AUDI V8 DTM 91 SMS/HAUPT NO. 2	1991
430011110	AUDI V8 DTM 91 AZR/JELINSKI NO.44	1991
430011111	AUDI V8 DTM 91 AZR/BIELA NO.45	1991
430001010	AUDI V8 TEAM BELGA	1990
43001000C	AUDI V8 STREET CAYENNE METALLIC	1990
43001000I	AUDI V8 STREET INDIGO METALLIC	1990
430021101	AUDI V8 EVOLUTION BIELA DTM 92	1992
430021102	AUDI V8 EVOLUTION JELINSKI DTM 92	1992
430021110	AUDI V8 EVOLUTION STUCK DTM 92	1992
430021111	AUDI V8 EVOLUTION HAUPT DTM 92	1992
430021120	AUDI V8 1992 BELGA PROCAR 1992	1992
430931120	AUDI V8 PROCAR THIBAUT/BELGA	1993
430931121	AUDI V8 PROCAR HEMROULLE/JUNIOR T.	1993
433901044	AUDI V8 H.J. STUCK NO. 44 1990	
430T01000	AUDI V8 STREET 1991 TITAN METALLIC	1990
400011020	AUTO UNION 1000 SP COUPE '58 CREAM	1958
400011021	AUTO UNION 1000 SP COUPE DARK GREEN	1958
400011030	AUTO UNION 1000 SP ROADSTER '58 RED	1958
400011031	AUTO UNION 1000 SP ROADSTER 1958 BLUE	1958
403011023	AUTO UNION 1000 SP COUPE '58 BLUE	
403011033	AUTO UNION 1000 SP ROADSTER 58 WHITE	
400121100	AUTOBIANCHI A 112 1974 GREEN	1974
400121101	AUTOBIANCHI A 112 1974 DARK BLUE	1974
430990022	BAR 01 SUPERTEC J.VILLENEUVE 1999	1999
430990023	BAR 01 SUPERTEC R.ZONTA 1999	1999
430990120	BAR 01 SUPERTEC TESTCAR BLUE 1999	1999
430990223	BAR 01 SUPERTEC M.SALO 1999	1999
430000022	BAR 02 HONDA J.VILLENEUVE 2000	2000
430000023	BAR 02 HONDA R.ZONTA 2000	2000
400010009	BAR 03 HONDA O.PANIS 2001	2001
400010010	BAR 03 HONDA J.VILLENEUVE 2001	2001
403010109	BAR 03 HONDA TESTCAR T.SATO 2001	2001
430000072	BAR J.VILLENEUVE PRES. 2000	2000
430010079	BAR J. VILLENEUVE PRES. 2001	2001
430000073	BAR R. ZONTA PRES. 2000	2000
430010080	BAR O.PANIS PRES. 2001	2001
431952701	BENETTON ALESI RIDING ON	1995
430000081	BENETTON G.FISICHELLA PRES. 2000	2000
430000082	BENETTON A.WURZ PRES. 2000	2000
430010097	BENETTON G.FISICHELLA PRES. 2001	2001
430010098	BENETTON J.BUTTON PRES. 2001	2001
430980075	BENETTON FISICHELLA LTD SILVERST.98	1998
430980076	BENETTON A.WURZ LTD ED. SILVERST.98	1998
430860019	BENETTON 186 F1 T. FABI 1986	1986
430860020	BENETTON 186 F1 G. BERGER 1986	1986
433860020	BENETTON 186 G. BERGER F1 1986	1986
433930006	BENETTON B193B PATRESE HOCKENH. 93	1993
510430009	BENETTON B193B SIEGER PORTUGAL 93	1993
430941106	BENETTON B193 J.VERSTAPPEN 1994	1994
430950092	BENETTON B194/B195 SHOWCAR J.H. 95	1995
510954391	BENETTON B194/B195 SHOWCAR M.S. 95	1995
510954301	BENETTON B195 M.SCHUMACHER 1995	1995
510954311	BENETTON B195/1 M.S. GP FRANCE 1995	1995
510954312	BENETTON B195 M.S. GP ENGLAND 1995	1995
510954313	BENETTON B195 M.S. GP GERMANY 1995	1995
510954314	BENETTON B195 M.S. GP BELGIUM 1995	1995
510954315	BENETTON B195 M.S. GP ITALY 1995	1995
510954316	BENETTON B195 M.S. GP EUROPE 1995	1995
510954317	BENETTON B195 M.S. GP AUSTRALIA 95	1995
510954318	BENETTON B195 M.S. GP FRANCE 95	1995
513954311	BENETTON B195 M.S. GP FRANCE 1995	1995
510954322	BENETTON B195/2 M.S. GP ENGLAND 95	1995
430950002	BENETTON B195 J.HERBERT 1995	1995
433950012	BENETTON B195 J. HERBERT G.P.FRANCE	1995
430970097	BENETTON B197 PRESENT. J.ALESI 97	1997
430970098	BENETTON B197 PRESENT. G.BERGER 97	1997
430980005	BENETTON B198 G.FISICHELLA 1998	1998
430980006	BENETTON B198 A.WURZ 1998	1998
430980095	BENETTON B198 G.FISICHELLA PRES.98	1998
430980096	BENETTON B198 A.WURZ PRES.98	1998
430990009	BENETTON B199 PLAYLIFE G.FISICHELLA	1999
430990010	BENETTON B199 PLAYLIFE A.WURZ 1999	1999
430000011	BENETTON B200 PLAY. G.FISICHELLA 00	2000
430000012	BENETTON B200 PLAY. A.WURZ 2000	2000
433000111	BENETTON B200 TESTCAR J.BUTTON 2000	2000
510430000	BENETTON FORD M.SCHUMACHER SPA 1992	1992
433930005	BENETTON FORD SCHUMACHER HOCKENH 93	1993
430920020	BENETTON FORD B192 M.BRUNDLE 1992	1992
430930006	BENETTON FORD B193 B PATRESE 1993	1993
430941006	BENETTON FORD B193 PRES. J.LEHTO	1994
510430010	BENETTON FORD B193 M.S. PRES.1994	1994
510430011	BENETTON FORD B193/4 GB PRES.	1994
430940006	BENETTON FORD B194 J.J.LEHTO 1994	1994
430940206	BENETTON FORD B194 J.VERSTAPPEN 94	1994
430940306	BENETTON FORD B194 J.HERBERT 94	1994
430940906	BENETTON FORD B194 VERSTAPPEN GER94	1994
510944305	BENETTON FORD B194 BENETTON 1994	1994
510944325	BENETTON FORD B194 MINICHAMPS 1994	1994
510944335	BENETTON FORD B194 BITBURGER 1994	1994
430960093	BENETTON F1 ALESI PRESENTATION 1996	1996
430960094	BENETTON F1 BERGER PRESENTATION '96	1996
430990079	BENETTON F1 G.FISICHELLA PRES. 1999	1999
430990080	BENETTON F1 A.WURZ PRES. 1999	1999
515954301	BENETTON RENAULT M.SCHUMACHER 1995	1995
445960094	BENETTON RENAULT G. BERGER 1996	1996
445960093	BENETTON RENAULT J. ALESI 1996	1996
512954302	BENETTON RENAULT B195 J.HERBERT 95	1995
430960003	BENETTON RENAULT B196 J. ALESI 96	1996
430960004	BENETTON RENAULT B196 G.BERGER 96	1996
430960023	BENETTON RENAULT B196 J.ALESI GP BELG.	1996
430960033	BENETTON RENAULT B196 J.ALESI GP FRANCE	1996
430960034	BENETTON RENAULT B196 BERGER GP FRANCE	1996
430960043	BENETTON RENAULT B196 J.ALESI GP ITALY	1996
430960053	BENETTON RENAULT B196 J.ALESI BRIT. GP	1996
430960054	BENETTON RENAULT B196 B.BERGER BRIT. GP	1996
430960063	BENETTON RENAULT B196 J.ALESI GP MONACO	1996
430960064	BENETTON RENAULT B196 BERGER GP MONACO	1996
433960003	BENETTON RENAULT B196 J. ALESI 96	1996
433960004	BENETTON RENAULT B196 G.BERGER 96	1996
433970007	BENETTON RENAULT B197 J.ALESI 1997	1997
433970008	BENETTON RENAULT B197 G.BERGER 1997	1997
430970007	BENETTON RENAULT B197 J.ALESI 1997	1997
430970008	BENETTON RENAULT B197 G.BERGER 1997	1997
430970058	BENETTON RENAULT B197 A.WURZ 1997	1997
400010108	BENETTON RENAULT B201 J.BUTTON INDIAN.'01	2001
400010007	BENETTON RENAULT B201 G.FISICH. '01	2001
400010008	BENETTON RENAULT B201 J.BUTTON 2001	2001
400010107	BENETTON RENAULT B201 G.FISICH.INDIAN.'01	2001
433022103	BMW 1600 SALOON BAIKAL METALLIC EXC	
433022104	BMW 1600 SALOON 1966 INKA ORANGE	
403021114	BMW 1600 TOURING CHAMONIX WHITE	
403021134	BMW 1600 CABRIOLET GRANADA RED	
430022100	BMW 1600/2 LIM 1966-75 ORANGE	1966
430022101	BMW 1600/2 LIM 1966-75 YELLOW	1966
430022102	BMW 1600/2 LIM 1966-75 LIGHT GREEN	1966
430022104	BMW 1600/2 LIM 1966-75 WHITE	1966
430022103	BMW 1602 LIMOUSINE EXCL. BMW SILVER	1966
400021110	BMW 2000 TII TOURING 1972 ORANGE	
400021111	BMW 2000 TII TOURING 1972 BLUE MET.	
400021130	BMW 2002 CABRIOLET 1971 BLUE MET.	
400021131	BMW 2002 CABRIOLET 1971 RED	
403021113	BMW 2002 TII TOURING VERONA RED	
403021133	BMW 2002 CABRIO '71 POLARIS SILVER	
430022200	BMW 2002 TURBO 1973/4 CREAM	1973
430022201	BMW 2002 TURBO 1973/4 SILVER	1973
433022203	BMW 2002 TURBO CHAMONIX WHITE EXCL.	
433022204	BMW 2002 TURBO SILVER POLISHED EXCL	
433023333	BMW 3-SERIES CABRIO SAFRAN EXCLUSIV	1992
433023334	BMW 3-SERIES CABRIOLET EXCLUSIV	1992
430025400	BMW 3-SERIES SALOON 1975-83 ORANGE	1975
430025401	BMW 3-SERIES 1975-83 LIGHT BLUE MET	1975
430025402	BMW 3-SERIES 1975-83 COPPER MET	1975
430025409	BMW 3-SERIES SALOON 75/83 DARK BLUE	
430023300	BMW 3-SERIES LIMOUSINE SILVER	1992
430023301	BMW 3-SERIES LIMOUSINE BLACK	1992
430023302	BMW 3-SERIES LIMOUSINE RED	1992
430023320	BMW 3-SERIES COUPE BLUE	1992
430023321	BMW 3-SERIES COUPE YELLOW	1992
430023322	BMW 3-SERIES COUPE RED	1992
430023330	BMW 3-SERIES CABRIOLET GREEN MET.	1992
430023331	BMW 3-SERIES CABRIOLET BLACK MET.	1992
430023332	BMW 3-SERIES CABRIOLET RED MET.	1992
431020070	BMW 3-SERIES COMPACT 2000 RED	
431020071	BMW 3-SERIES COMPACT 2000 BLACK	
431028030	BMW 3-SERIES CABRIO SIENA RED MET.	
431028031	BMW 3-SERIES CABRIO TOPAS BLUE MET.	
433028033	BMW 3-SERIES CABRIO '99 LIGHT YELLOW	
433028034	BMW 3-SERIES CABRIO '99 COSM BLACK MT	
4434932304	BMW 318I FINA/W. NO.4 DUEZ MONZA93	1993
434932307	BMW 318I FINA/WARST. NO.7 TASSIN	1993
434942007	BMW 318I TASSIN BELGIUM PRO-CAR 94	1994
434942303	BMW 318I CASTROL NO.3 MARTIN PRC94	1994
434942308	BMW 318I FINA/B. NO.8 DUEZ PROC.94	1994
434942309	BMW 318I ECHO NO.9 SLAUS PROCAR 94	1994
434942403	BMW 318IS BASTOS/FINA NO.3 DUEZ	1994
434942405	BMW 318IS BASTOS/FINA NO.5 MARTIN	1994
430024300	BMW 318IS/4 EVO 1994 YELLOW	1994
430024302	BMW 318IS/4 EVO 1994 RED	1994
433024303	BMW 318IS/4 EXCL	1994
433028313	BMW 318I TOURING 4-CYL SIENA RED	
430942002	BMW 318I J.CECOTTO/BMW MOTORSP. TW	1994
430942003	BMW 318I A.BURGSTALLER/BMW MOTORSP.	1994
430942008	BMW 318I Y.SURER/BMW TEAM ISERT	1994
430942011	BMW 318I A.HEGER/BMW TEAM SCHNEIDER	1994
430942031	BMW 318I M.DUEZ/VALIER MOTORSPORT	1994
430942032	BMW 318I T.TASSIN/VALIER MOTORSP.	1994

ITEM-No	ITEM	YEAR
430942301	BMW 318 IS/4 J.WINKELHOCK BTCC 94	1994
430942302	BMW 318 IS/4 S.SOPER BTCC CL. 2 94	1994
430942401	BMW 318 IS/4 R.RAVAGLIA SUP.T.94	1994
430942402	BMW 318 IS/4 BMW MOTORSP. ADAC CECO	1994
430942410	BMW 318 IS/4 BMW SCHNITZER J SOPER	1994
430942493	BMW 318 IS/4 BMW MOTORSP. RSA LINDE	1994
433942402	BMW 318 IS/4 BMW MOTORSP. ADAC CECO	1994
433942410	BMW 318 IS/4 BMW SCHNITZER J SOPER	1994
433942493	BMW 318 IS/4 BMW MOTORSP. RSA LINDE	1994
431028320	BMW 318 CI E46 COUPE 99 SIENNA RED	
431028321	BMW 318 CI COUPE 1999 SILVER	1999
433952501	BMW 318I SIEGER 24H NUERBURGR. EXCL	1995
433952508	BMW 318I SCHNITZER/J.WINKELH.95EXCL	1995
433952516	BMW 318I CLASS 2 GB CECOTTO EXCL.	1995
433952598	BMW 318I SIEGER SPA FRANCORCH EXCL.	1995
430952503	BMW 318I BIGAZZI/BURGSTALLER STW95	1995
430952507	BMW 318I T.TASSIN BELGIAN CHAMPION	1995
430952508	BMW 318I SCHNITZER/WINKELHOCK STW95	1995
430952513	BMW 318I Y.MULLER FRENCH CHAMPION	1995
430952521	BMW 318I ISERT/MUELLER STW95	1995
433028324	BMW 318I COUPE '99 4-CYL LIGHT RED	
433982610	BMW 320D 24H NUERBURGRING 1998	
430962602	BMW 320I STW S. SOPER 1996	1996
430972625	BMW 320I ISERT/L.V.BAYERN STW 1997	1997
430972633	BMW 320I PMC/M.GINDORF STW 97	1997
430972705	BMW 320I BIGAZZI/J.CECOTTO STW 97	1997
430972706	BMW 320I BIGAZZI/J.WINKELHOCK STW97	1997
433992601	BMW 320I STCC 1999	
433982608	BMW 320I BMW/WINKELHOCK STW 98	1998
433982609	BMW 320I BMW/CECOTTO STW 98	1998
433982611	BMW 320I STCC 1998	
433982625	BMW 320I ISERT/V.BAYERN STW 98	1998
433982626	BMW 320I ISERT/MENZEL STW 98	1998
430982608	BMW 320I BMW/WINKELHOCK STW 98	1998
430982609	BMW 320I BMW/CECOTTO STW 98	1998
430982625	BMW 320I ISERT/V.BAYERN STW 98	1998
430982626	BMW 320I ISERT/MENZEL STW 98	1998
433962603	BMW 320I STW BURGSTALLER SOPER 96	1996
433962622	BMW 320I BTCC SCHNITZER WINKELH.96	1996
433972705	BMW 320I BIGAZZI/J.CECOTTO STW 97	1997
433972706	BMW 320I BIGAZZI/J.WINKELHOCK STW97	1997
433972726	BMW 320I MENZEL STW 97	1997
433028314	BMW 323I TOURING 6-CYL ORIENTAL BL.	
433028315	BMW 323I TOURING 6-CYL TITAN SILVER	
433025473	BMW 323I 1975-83 CORAL RED EXCL.	
433025474	BMW 323I 1975-83 YELLOW EXCL.	
430025470	BMW 323I SALOON 1975-83 SILVER	1975
430025471	BMW 323I SALOON 1975-83 RED	1975
430025472	BMW 323I SALOON 1975-83 GREY MET.	
430025474	BMW 323I SALOON 1975-83 GREEN MET.	
430025475	BMW 323I 1975 BLACK	
431028310	BMW 323I TOURING 1999 GREEN MET.	
430942223	BMW 325I COUPE GOEPEL/SCHNEIDER MOT	1994
430942225	BMW 325I COUPE GEDLICH	1994
430942227	BMW 325I COUPE D. SCHIELEIN	1994
433020073	BMW 325 TI COMPACT '00 FLAMENCO RED	
433020074	BMW 325 TI COMPACT '00 TITAN SILVER	
433020075	BMW 325 TI COMPACT ORIENTAL BLUE MT	
433020076	BMW 325 TI COMPACT 00 BLACK SAPHIRE	
433028323	BMW 328I COUPE '99 6-CYL TOPAS BLUE	
431028311	BMW 328I TOURING 1999 STEEL GREY	1999
431028312	BMW 328I TOURING 1999 LIGHT RED	
431028322	BMW 328 CI COUPE 1999 LIGHT YELLOW	
431028324	BMW 328 CI COUPE 1999 GREEN	
430022400	BMW 501/502 LIM. WHITE	1954
430022401	BMW 501/502 LIM. BLACK	1954
430022402	BMW 501/502 LIM. DARK RED	1954
433022403	BMW 502 SALOON VELOURS RED EXCL.	
433022503	BMW 507 CABRIO	1956
433022504	BMW 507 CABRIOLET ULTRAMARIN BLUE	
433022523	BMW 507 SOFTTOP EXCLUSIV	1956
433022533	BMW 507 HARDTOP'BERGMEISTER' NO.140	1956
430022507	BMW 507 CABRIO RED	1956
430022508	BMW 507 CABRIO SILVER	1956
430022509	BMW 507 CABRIO CREAM	1956
430022520	BMW 507 SOFTTOP RED	1956
430022521	BMW 507 SOFTTOP BLACK	1956
430022522	BMW 507 SOFTTOP GREEN	1956
430022530	BMW 507 HARDTOP RED/BLACK	1956
430022531	BMW 507 HARDTOP SILVER/DARK BLUE	1956
430022532	BMW 507 HARDTOP CREAM/DARK RED	1956
430882613	BMW 635 CSI SCHNITZER GOES. DTM '88	
430832611	BMW 635 CSI BOUTSEN/GIACOM.MONZA 83	1983
430842623	BMW 635 STRYCEK GERMAN CHAMPION 84	1984
430842636	BMW 635 CSI JAEGERM.BRUN/GR MONZA 84	1984
430842805	BMW 635 CSI SURER/R./B. SPA 1984	1984
433025124	BMW 635 CSI LIGHT BLUE METALLIC	
433852610	BMW 635 CSI GR.A PIRRO/RAVAGLIA '85	
433020203	BMW 7 SERIES 2001 RED MET. EXCL.	
433020204	BMW 7 SERIES 2001 GREY MET. EXCL.	
433020205	BMW 7 SERIES 2001 TOMALIN VIOLET	
433020206	BMW 7 SERIES 2001 DARK BLUE MET EX.	
433020207	BMW 7 SERIES 2001 BLACK	
433020208	BMW 7 SERIES 2001 GREY MET. EXCL.	
433020209	BMW 7 SERIES 2001 TOLEDO BLUE MET.	
433020210	BMW 7 SERIES V8 GREEN METALLIC	
431020200	BMW 7 SERIES 2001 SILVER	
431020201	BMW 7 SERIES 2001 GREEN	
433023704	BMW 700 SAL. 60/61 CAPRI GREEN EXCL	
430023700	BMW 700 LIM 1960/61 ANTHRACITE MET.	1960
430023701	BMW 700 LIM 1960/61 CREAM	1960
430023702	BMW 700 LIM 1960/61 SILVER	1960
430023703	BMW 700 LIM 1960/61 EXCLUSIV .	1960
430752925	BMW CSL 3,5 12H SEBRING 1975	
433932383	BMW CECOTTO/NISSEN 932380/1 GIFTSET	1993
430023000	BMW E1 1993 YELLOW/GREY	1993
430023001	BMW E1 1993 AVUSBLUE/GREY	1993
430023002	BMW E1 1993 RED/GREY	1993
430023003	BMW E1 1993 GREEN	1993
433023005	BMW E1 1993 FROSTY YELLOW IND.	1993
433023006	BMW E1 1993 MYSTIC GREY IND.	1993
433023007	BMW E1 VIOLET METALLIC	1993
433932311	BMW E36-4 RACING EXCLUSIV	1993
433932322	BMW E36-4 RACING EXCLUSIV	1993
430932306	BMW E36-4 BTCC 93 S.SOPER	1993
430932322	BMW E36-4 BTCC 93 WINKELHOCK GB	1993
433024363	BMW M ROADSTER ESTORIL BLUE	1997
433024364	BMW M ROADSTER IMOLA RED	1997
433024365	BMW M ROADSTER ESTORIL BLUE EXCL.	1997
433024366	BMW M ROADSTER EVERGREEN EXCL.	
430024360	BMW M ROADSTER 1997 ORANGE	1997
433025023	BMW M1 STREET 1978/81 ORANGE	1978
430025020	BMW M1 STREET 1978/81 WHITE	1978
430025022	BMW M1 STREET 1978/81 RED	1978
430792505	BMW M1 PROCAR D.PIRONI 1979	1979
430802501	BMW M1 NUERBURGRING H.J.STUCK 1980	1980
430802505	BMW M1 PROCAR N.PIQUET 1980	1980
430802580	BMW M1 PROCAR BASF H.G.BUERGER 80	1980
430802581	BMW M1 PROCAR DENIM H.HEYER 1980	1980
430802583	BMW M1 CARTE DE FRANCE LE MANS 1980	1980
430812571	BMW M1 SPATENBRAEU LE MANS 1981	1981
430812572	BMW M1 VSD LOIS LE MANS 1981	1981
430832590	BMW M1 WARSTEINER LE MANS 1983	1983
433792506	BMW M1 PROCAR N. PIQUET 1979	1979
433792528	BMW M1 PROCAR C. REGAZZONI 1979	1979
433020023	BMW M3 2000 TOPAS BLUE MET. EXCL.	
433020024	BMW M3 2000 CARBON BLACK MET. EXCL.	
433020025	BMW M3 2000 PHOENIX YELLOW MET.	
433020026	BMW M3 2000 PHOENIX YELLOW MET.	
433020027	BMW M3 2000 DRIVER TRAIN. YELLOW MT	
433020028	BMW M3 COUPE SAFETY CAR M-BIKE GP	

ITEM-No	ITEM	YEAR
433020033	BMW M3 CABRIO 2000 LAGUNA SECA BLUE	
433020034	BMW M3 CABRIO 2000 TITAN SILVER MET	
400012142	BMW M3 GTR 2001 WENDLINGER	
400012143	BMW M3 GTR 2001 MUELLER	
403012103	BMW M3 GTR 2001 BLACK EXCL.	
403012104	BMW M3 GTR 2001 CARBON BLACK EXCL.	
403012142	BMW M3 GTR J.MUELLER/LETHO 2001	
433023383	BMW M3 GTR WHITE MOTORSPORT	1993
403012143	BMW M3 GTR EKBLOM/D.MUELLER 2001	
430002001	BMW M3 DTM 90 SCHNITZER/RAVAGLIA	1990
430002002	BMW M3 DTM 90 SCHNITZER/GIROIX NR 2	1990
430002003	BMW M3 DTM 90 SCHNITZER/CECOTTO 3	1990
430002004	BMW M3 SPA/FRC SCHNITZER/FINA NR 25	1990
430002010	BMW M3 DTM 90 BIGAZZI/SOPER NR. 8	1990
430002011	BMW M3 DTM 90 BIGAZZI/WINKELHOCK 9	1990
430002012	BMW M3 DTM 90 BIGAZZI/LAFITTE NR.10	1990
430002013	BMW M3 SPA/FRC BIGAZZI/BASTOS NR 27	1990
430002020	BMW M3 DTM 90 LINDER/HEGER NR.11	1990
430002030	BMW M3 DTM 90 ZAKSP./QUESTER NR.18	1990
430002031	BMW M3 DTM 90 ZAKSP./HAHNE NR.19	1990
430002040	BMW M3 DTM 90 VALIER/GROHS NR.22	1990
430002050	BMW M3 DTM 90 ISERT/PRINZ V. BAYERN	1990
430002060	BMW M3 DTM 90 MM DIEBELS/MURMANN 30	1990
430012001	BMW M3 DTM 91 SCHNITZER/CECOTTO	1991
430012002	BMW M3 DTM 91 SCHNITZER/WINKELHOCK	1991
430012003	BMW M3 DTM 91 SCHNITZER/NISSEN	1991
430012004	BMW M3 WATSON PIRRO 1. MACAU 1991	1991
430012010	BMW M3 DTM 91 BIGAZZI/SOPER NR.11	1991
433942208	BMW M3 WOLLGARTEN/SCHNITZER DTT94	1994
433952203	BMW M3 QUESTER RED BULL EXCL.	1995
433952206	BMW M3 AC SCHNITZER KATTUS EXCL.	1995
433952384	BMW M3 GTR BRASIL EXCL.	1995
433982030	BMW M3 WHITE BMW CLUB OF AMERICA	
433982031	BMW M3 WHITE	
430012011	BMW M3 DTM 91 BIGAZZI/HAHNE NR.12	1991
430012020	BMW M3 DTM 91 LINDER/QUESTER NR.15	1991
430012021	BMW M3 DTM 91 LINDER/HEGER NR.16	1991
430012022	BMW M3 DTM 91 LINDER/MEEUVISSEN N17	1991
430012030	BMW M3 DTM 91 UNITRON/ZAKOWSKI NR13	1991
430012031	BMW M3 DTM 91 UNITRON/KELLENERS N14	1991
430012050	BMW M3 DTM 91 ISERT/PRINZ V. BAYERN	1991
430012060	BMW M3 DTM 91 MM DIEBELS/DANNER N31	1991
430012061	BMW M3 DTM 91 MM DIEBELS/RENSING 32	1991
430012062	BMW M3 DTM 91 MM DIEBELS/MURMANN 33	1991
430012070	BMW M3 DTM 91 TAUBER TICTAC/BERG 43	1991
430012080	BMW M3 DTM 91 MAASS/KOENIG NR.28	1991
430012090	BMW M3 DTM 91 BMW HOLLAND/EUSER N42	1991
43002000B	BMW M3 1990 STREET SCHWARZ METALLIC	1990
43002000R	BMW M3 1990 STREET ROT	1990
43002000W	BMW M3 1990 STREET WEISS	1990
430020300	BMW M3 STREET 1987 BLACK	1987
430020301	BMW M3 STREET 1987 ROYAL BLUE	1987
430022003	BMW M3 HEGER/SCHNITZER DTM 92	1992
430022004	BMW M3 WINNER MACAU 92 PIRRO-MOBIL	1992
430022013	BMW M3 BASTOS 1. 24H SPA 1992	1992
430022020	BMW M3 HAHNE/JAEGERMEISTER DTM 92	1992
430022030	BMW M3 NISSEN/UNITRON DTM 92	1992
430022040	BMW M3 ENGSTLER/TIC TAC DTM 92	1992
430022061	BMW M3 FRITZ K./LAETTA DTM 92	1992
430022090	BMW M3 CECOTTO/FINA DTM 92	1992
430022095	BMW M3 1991 -SONY SPANIEN- BMW EXCL	1992
430022096	BMW M3 B&H AUSTRALIEN PROCAR 1992	1992
430022300	BMW M3 COUPE 1992 MUGELLO RED	1992
430022301	BMW M3 COUPE 1992 SCHWARZ MET.	1992
430022302	BMW M3 COUPE 1992 DAYTONA VIOLETT	1992
430022303	BMW M3 COUPE 1992 EXCL. AVUSBLAU	1992
430022304	BMW M3 COUPE 1992 EXCL. DAKKARGELB	1992
430022305	BMW M3 COUPE 1992 AVUSBLUE/GREY	1992
430023380	BMW M3 GTR 1993 STREET VERS. WHITE	1993
430023381	BMW M3 GTR 1993 STREET VERS. BLACK	1993
430023382	BMW M3 GTR 1993 STREET VERS. RED	1993
430872024	BMW M3 O.MANTHEY DTM 1987	1987
430882039	BMW M3 AVUS M.KETTERER DTM 1988	1988
430932020	BMW M3 92 DTM93 BECKER/LINDER	1993
430932030	BMW M3 92 DTM93 LACKINGER/DELTA RAC	1993
430932040	BMW M3 92 DTM93 SEVERICH/RAC.DYN.	1993
430932380	BMW M3 GTR J.CECOTTO ADAC CUP 1993	1993
430932381	BMW M3 GTR K.NISSEN ADAC CUP 1993	1993
430942045	BMW M3 PARIS MATCH SPA 1994	1994
430942208	BMW M3 WOLLGARTEN/SCHNITZER DTT94	1994
430942210	BMW M3 STROTMANN/MENTON DTT94	1994
430942211	BMW M3 SCHMITZ/MENTON DTT94	1994
430942215	BMW M3 M.VOLK/TEC MELKUS TEAM DTT94	1994
430962306	BMW M3 GTR VALVOLINE DONOHUE IMSA96	1996
430962307	BMW M3 GTR VALVOLINE QUESTER IMSA96	1996
431020020	BMW M3 COUPE 2000 BLACK	
431020021	BMW M3 COUPE 2000 YELLOW	
431020030	BMW M3 CABRIOLET 2001 RED	
431020031	BMW M3 CABRIOLET 2001 BLUE MET	
430982310	BMW M3 GTR 1. GT3 24H DAYTONA 98	1998
433020303	BMW M3 1987 RED	
433022306	BMW M3 COUPE 1992 YELLOW	1992
434932006	BMW M3 CASTROL/LEASE NO.6 MARTIN	1993
434932007	BMW M3 FINA/B.NO.7 TASSIN PROCAR 93	1993
434932013	BMW M3 CASTROL/LEASE NO.13 V.D.POEL	1993
434932014	BMW M3 FINA/B. NO.14 DUEZ PROCAR 93	1993
434952043	BMW M3 E-30 24H SPA '95 MINICHAMPS	1995
430025120	BMW M635 CSI 1982-87 SILVER	1982
430025121	BMW M635 CSI 1982-87 BLACK	1982
433025123	BMW M635 CSI DARK BLUE EXCLUSIVE	1982
433025125	BMW M635 CSI SILVER MET.	
433842608	BMW M635 CSI GENUINE PARTS EXCL.	1984
433982801	BMW V12 LE MANS 1998	
433982802	BMW V12 LE MANS 1998	
430982801	BMW V12 LE MANS 1998	1998
430982802	BMW V12 LE MANS 1998	1998
430992818	BMW V12 PRICE BSCHER/BSCHER LM99	
430992819	BMW V12 GOH MATSUSHITA/KATO LM99	
433002942	BMW V12 LMR ALMS 2000 MUELLER	
433002943	BMW V12 LMR ALMS 2000 J.M.GOUNON	
430002815	BMW V12 LE MANS 2000	2000
430992915	BMW V12 LMR BMW WINKELHOCK 1999	
430992917	BMW V12 LMR BMW KRISTENSEN 1999	
430992942	BMW V12 LMR SEBRING 1999	1999
433992818	BMW V12 LM98 LEMANS'99 PRICE+BSCHER	
433992819	BMW V12 LM98 LE MANS'99 TEAM GOH	
433992915	BMW V12 LMR LE MANS 1999	
433992916	BMW V12 LMR ART CAR	
433992917	BMW V12 LMR LE MANS 1999	
433992942	BMW V12 LMR SEBRING 1999	
431028470	BMW X5 8 CYLINDER SILVER	
431028471	BMW X5 LIGHT YELLOW	2000
431028472	BMW X5 BLACK	
431028474	BMW X5 GREEN MET.	
431028475	BMW X5 1999 PURPLE MET.	
433028473	BMW X5 4.4I 8 CYLINDER COSMOS BLACK	
433028474	BMW X5 3.0 D 6-CYL DIESEL MAHAGONY	
433028475	BMW X5 4.4I 8-CYL TOPAS BLUE	
433028476	BMW X5 4.4I 8-CYL TOPAS BLUE MET.	
433024333	BMW Z3 ROADSTER 2.8 SILVER EXCLUSIV	1997
433024334	BMW Z3 ROADSTER 2.8 GREEN EXCLUSIV	1997
430024330	BMW Z3 CABRIOLET 2.8 1997 RED	1996
430024331	BMW Z3 CABRIOLET 2.8 1994 BLACK	1994
430024341	BMW Z3 CABRIOLET 1.9 SILVER	
430028230	BMW Z3 ROADSTER 1998 BLACK MET.	
430028231	BMW Z3 ROADSTER 1998 SILVER	1998
430028232	BMW Z3 ROADSTER 1999 GREEN	
430028234	BMW Z3 ROADSTER 1999 YELLOW	
433028233	BMW Z3 FACELIFT 98 PACIFIC BLUE EXC	
433028234	BMW Z3 FACELIFT 98 ORANGINA EXCL.	
403021037	BMW Z4 AFTER SALES CUP TOL.BLUE MET	

ITEM-No	ITEM	YEAR
403021034	BMW Z4 ROADSTER 2002 STERLING GREY	
403021035	BMW Z4 ROADSTER 2002 MALEDIVE BLUE	
403021036	BMW Z4 ROADSTER 2002 SAPHIRE BLACK	
403021033	BMW Z4 ROADSTER 2002 TITAN SILVER	
431028730	BMW Z8 CABRIOLET 1999 BLACK	
431028731	BMW Z8 CABRIO 99 MORENA RED MET.	1999
431028736	BMW Z8 CABRIO 1999 TITAN SILVER	
431028739	BMW Z8 CABRIO 99 CREMA DARK MET.	
431028740	BMW Z8 CABRIO 99 TOPAS BLUE	
431028750	BMW Z8 HARDTOP 2000 TITAN SILVER	1999
433028733	BMW Z8 CABRIO 1999 JAPAN RED	
433028734	BMW Z8 CABRIO 1999 TOPAS BLUE MET	
433028735	BMW Z8 CABRIO 1999 BLACK	
433028736	BMW Z8 CABRIO J.BOND TITAN SILVER	
433028737	BMW Z8 CABRIOLET VIOLET	
433028738	BMW Z8 CABRIOLET BLACK	
433028739	BMW Z8 CABRIO VELVETBLUE METALLIC	
433028740	BMW Z8 CABRIO 99 TOPAS BLUE	
433028753	BMW Z8 HARDTOP 99 CREMA DARK MET.	1999
433028754	BMW Z8 HARDTOP 99 MORENO MET.	
433028755	BMW Z8 HARDTOP PACE CAR M.BIKE G.P.	
433028756	BMW Z8 HARDTOP 1999 BLACK EXCL.	
433029023	BMW Z9 COLD CAST CHROMED	
430780001	BRABHAM BT 46 N.LAUDA 1978	1978
430780002	BRABHAM BT 46 J.WATSON 1978	1978
430780101	BRABHAM BT 46 FANCAR N.LAUDA 1978	1978
430780102	BRABHAM BT 46 FANCAR J.WATSON 1978	1978
430830005	BRABHAM BT 52 GP BRAZIL N.PIQUET 83	1983
430830006	BRABHAM BT 52 R.PATRESE 1983	1983
433830005	BRABHAM BT 52 F1 1983	1983
430102110	BUGATTI EB 110 BLUE	
430102111	BUGATTI EB 110 RED	
430102112	BUGATTI EB 110 BLACK	
430102115	BUGATTI EB 110 RACING SILVER	
510430012	BUGATTI EB 110 YELLOW	
436661407	CHAPARRAL 2D NUERBURGRING 1966	
436661409	CHAPARRAL 2D HILL/BONNIER LE MANS66	
430671407	CHAPARRAL 2F HILL/SPENCE LE MANS'67	
430671408	CHAPARRAL 2F JENNINGS/J. LE MANS'67	
436691407	CHAPARRAL 2H J.SURTEES EDMONTON '69	
430142620	CHEVROLET CORVETTE 1997 RED	1997
430142621	CHEVROLET CORVETTE 1997 BLUE MET	1997
AC4001403	CHEVROLET CORVETTE C5R NO3 DAYTONA 2000	
AC4001404	CHEVROLET CORVETTE C5R NO4 DAYTONA 2000	
AC4001463	CHEVROLET CORVETTE C5R 11TH LM 2000	2000
AC4001464	CHEVROLET CORVETTE C5R 10TH LM 2000	
AC4011402	CHEVROLET CORVETTE C5R NO2 DAYTONA 2001	2001
AC4011403	CHEVROLET CORVETTE C5R NO3 DAYTONA 2001	2001
AC4011404	CHEVROLET CORVETTE C5R PETIT LE MANS 01	
AC4011463	CHEVROLET CORVETTE C5R FELLOWS LM 2001	
AC4011464	CHEVROLET CORVETTE C5R PILGRIM LM 2001	
AC4991402	CHEVROLET CORVETTE C5R DAYTONA 1999	
AC4991404	CHEVROLET CORVETTE C5R DAYTONA 1999	
400011457	CHRYSLER VIPER GTS-R TOTAL/. LM '01	
400011458	CHRYSLER VIPER GTS-R CHEREAU/. LM01	
430001451	CHRYSLER VIPER GTS-R BERETTA/. LM 2000	2000
430001457	CHRYSLER VIPER GTS-R HEZEMANS/. LM '00	2000
400111020	CITROEN SM 1970 GOLD METALLIC	1970
400111021	CITROEN SM 1970 GREEN METALLIC	1970
430943001	DALLARA OPEL F3 TEAM WTS MAASEN	1994
430943002	DALLARA OPEL F3 WTS R.SCHUMACHER	1994
430943009	DALLARA FIAT J.MUELLER DT.MEISTR 94	1994
430953105	DALLARA OPEL TEAM R.SCHUMACHER 1995	1995
430953107	DALLARA OPEL TEAM KMS N.FONTANA '95	1995
430953119	DALLARA FIAT A.COUTO MACAU 1995	1995
400011500	DKW JUNIOR DE LUXE 1961 DARK RED	1961
400011501	DKW JUNIOR DE LUXE 1961 GREY	1961
403011503	DKW JUNIOR DE LUXE 1961 TURQUOISE	
436140020	DE LOREAN DMC 12	
400011414	DODGE VIPER GTS-R ZONCA/.. DAYT.'01	2001
430001446	DODGE VIPER GTS-R SEILER/. DAYT.'00	
430001491	DODGE VIPER GTS-R WENDLINGER/. DAYT.'00	
430144021	DODGE VIPER COUPE 1993 BLUE MET.	1993
430144022	DODGE VIPER COUPE 1993 RED	1993
430144023	DODGE VIPER INDY PACE CAR 1996	1996
430144030	DODGE VIPER CABRIO 93 YELLOW	1993
430144031	DODGE VIPER CABRIO 93 BLUE	1993
430144032	DODGE VIPER CABRIO 93 RED	1993
430941440	DODGE VIPER R.ARNOUX LE MANS 94	1994
430941441	DODGE VIPER F.MIGAULT LE MANS 94	1994
430961449	DODGE VIPER GTS-R CANASKA CUDINI LM 96	
430961450	DODGE VIPER GTS-R OREKA HELARY LM 96	
430961498	DODGE VIPER GTS-R CANASKA ARCHER DAY96	
430971461	DODGE VIPER GTS-R ORECA AYARI LM 97	1997
430971462	DODGE VIPER GTS-R ORECA DUPUY LM 97	1997
430971463	DODGE VIPER GTS-R ORECA BELL LM 97	1997
430971464	DODGE VIPER GTS-R CHAMBERLAIN LM 97	1997
430981453	DODGE VIPER GTS-R 1.GT2 LM 1998	
430981455	DODGE VIPER GTS-R AMORIM LM 1998	
430981456	DODGE VIPER GTS-R AYLES LM 1998	
430991451	DODGE VIPER GTS-R DUPUY/.. LM 1999	
430991454	DODGE VIPER GTS-R MONTEIRO/. LM '99	
430991455	DODGE VIPER GTS-R CLERICO/. LM '99	
430820027	FERRARI 126 C2 G.VILLENEUVE 1982	1982
430820028	FERRARI 126 C2 D.PIRONI 1982	1982
430750011	FERRARI 312 T C.REGAZZONI 1975	1975
430750012	FERRARI 312 T N.LAUDA WORLDCH. 1975	1975
430797311	FERRARI 312 T4 J.SCHECKTER 1979	1979
430797312	FERRARI 312 T4 G.VILLENEUVE 1979	1979
430947400	FERRARI 333 SP 1994 PRESENTATION	1994
430947405	FERRARI 333 SP 1994 BALDI/SIGALA	1994
430947430	FERRARI 333 SP 1994 MORETTI/SALAZAR	1994
430947450	FERRARI 333 SP 1994 J. COCHRAN	1994
430967430	FERRARI 333 SP 2ND PL. DAYTONA 1996	1996
430967627	FERRARI 333 SP LISTA DESIGN 1996	1996
430977603	FERRARI 333 SP SEBRING WINNER 1997	1997
430977604	FERRARI 333 SP FERTE/CAMPOS LM 1997	1997
430977643	FERRARI 333 SP SEBRING VELEZ/. 1997	1997
430977693	FERRARI 333 SP MORETTI/THEYS LM 97	1997
430987603	FERRARI 333 SP MORETTI LE MANS 1998	
430987605	FERRARI 333 SP J.B.GIESSE LM 1998	
430987612	FERRARI 333 SP PROTOTYPE LM 1998	
430940027	FERRARI 412 T1 J. ALESI 1994	1994
430940028	FERRARI 412 T1 G. BERGER 1994	1994
430941027	FERRARI 412 T1 N. LARINI 1994	1994
430950027	FERRARI 412 T2 J.ALESI 1995	1995
430950028	FERRARI 412 T2 G.BERGER 1995	1995
510964391	FERRARI 412 T2 PRESENTATION M.S. 96	1996
430072400	FERRARI 456 GT 2+2 1992 RED	1992
430072401	FERRARI 456 GT 2+2 1992 YELLOW	1992
430072402	FERRARI 456 GT 2+2 1992 DARK BLUE	1992
510430014	FERRARI 456 GT 2+2 1992 BLUE MET.	1996
430074120	FERRARI 512 M SILVER	1994
430074121	FERRARI 512 M YELLOW	1994
430074122	FERRARI 512 M RED	1994
430072500	FERRARI 512 TR 1992 RED	1992
430072501	FERRARI 512 TR 1992 YELLOW	1992
430072502	FERRARI 512 TR 1992 BLACK	1992
430076020	FERRARI 550 MARANELLO 1996 RED	1996
430076021	FERRARI 550 MARANELLO 96 SILVER	1996
430076022	FERRARI 550 MARANELLO 1996 YELLOW	1996
430960092	FERRARI F1 IRVINE PRESENTATION 1996	1996
515964391	FERRARI F1 M.SCHUMACHER 1996	1996
445950027	FERRARI F1 J. ALESI 1995	1995
445960092	FERRARI F1 E. IRVINE 1996	1996
430980004	FERRARI F300 V10 E.IRVINE 1998	1998
430980034	FERRARI F300 E.IRVINE TOWER WING 98	1998
430980094	FERRARI F300 E.IRVINE PRES.98	1998
510984300	FERRARI F300 FIORANO TEST VERS 1998	1998
510984303	FERRARI F300 V10 M.SCHUMACHER 1998	1998
510984333	FERRARI F300 M.SCHUMACHER TOWER W98	1998

ITEM-No	ITEM	YEAR
510984393	FERRARI F300 M.SCHUMACHER PRES.98	1998
430960002	FERRARI F310 E.IRVINE 1996	1996
430960022	FERRARI F310 NEW NOSE E.IRVINE 96	1996
433960002	FERRARI F310 E.IRVINE 1996	1996
510964301	FERRARI F310 M.SCHUMACHER 1996	1996
510964311	FERRARI F310 WINNER GP SPAIN 1996	1996
510964321	FERRARI F310/2 M.SCHUMACHER 1996	1996
430970096	FERRARI F310/2 E.IRVINE PRESENT. 97	1997
510974395	FERRARI F310/2 PRESENTATION M.S. 97	1997
513964321	FERRARI F310/2 M.SCHUMACHER 1996	1996
430970006	FERRARI F310B E.IRVINE 1997	1997
510974305	FERRARI F310B M.SCHUMACHER 1997	1997
510974315	FERRARI F310B M.S. MAGNY COURS 1997	1997
430074020	FERRARI F355 1994 YELLOW	1994
430074021	FERRARI F355 1994 BLACK	1994
430074022	FERRARI F355 1994 RED	1994
430074030	FERRARI F355 SPIDER BLACK	1994
430074031	FERRARI F355 SPIDER YELLOW	1994
430074032	FERRARI F355 SPIDER RED	1994
430074033	FERRARI F355 SPIDER BLUE MET.	1994
430074040	FERRARI F355 SOFTTOP BLACK	1994
430074042	FERRARI F355 SOFTTOP RED	1994
430074050	FERRARI F355 TARGA BLACK	1994
430074051	FERRARI F355 TARGA YELLOW	1994
430074052	FERRARI F355 TARGA RED	1994
510430013	FERRARI F355 1994 BLUE METALLIC	1994
430075150	FERRARI F50 1995 SILVER	1995
430075151	FERRARI F50 1995 YELLOW	1995
430075152	FERRARI F50 1995 RED	1995
430075160	FERRARI F50 SPIDER 1995 BLACK	1995
430075161	FERRARI F50 SPIDER 1995 YELLOW	1995
430075162	FERRARI F50 SPIDER 1995 RED	1995
430920027	FERRARI F92A J. ALESI 1992	1992
430920028	FERRARI F92A I. CAPELLI 1992	1992
430930027	FERRARI F93A ALESI 1993	1993
430930028	FERRARI F93A BERGER 1993	1993
433930027	FERRARI F93A ALESI HOCKENHEIM 1993	1993
433930028	FERRARI F93A BERGER HOCKENHEIM 1993	1993
430121660	FIAT X 1/9 1972-78 RED	
430121661	FIAT X 1/9 1972-78 RED METALLIC	
430121930	FIAT BARCHETTA CABRIOLET RED	
430121931	FIAT BARCHETTA CABRIOLET YELLOW	
430121932	FIAT BARCHETTA CABRIO LUXOR BLACK	
430121934	FIAT BARCHETTA CABRIOLET ORANGE	
430085500	FORD CAPRI 1969 SILVER	1969
430085501	FORD CAPRI 1969 GOLD	1969
430085502	FORD CAPRI 1969 DARK BLUE	1969
430085504	FORD CAPRI 1969 LIGHT GREEN MET.	
430085505	FORD CAPRI 1969 DARK VIOLET	
430085506	FORD CAPRI 1969 RED	
430085507	FORD CAPRI 1969 BROWN MET.	
400081200	FORD CAPRI II 1974 YELLOW	1974
400081201	FORD CAPRI II 1974 ORANGE	1974
430085800	FORD CAPRI RS 2600 1972-73 BLUE MET	1972
430085801	FORD CAPRI RS 2600 1972-73 YELLOW	1972
430085802	FORD CAPRI RS 2600 1972-73 RED	1972
430085804	FORD CAPRI RS 2600 1972-73 WHITE	
430798501	FORD CAPRI GR.5 SACHS H.ERTL 1979	1979
430798552	FORD CAPRI GR.5 MAMPE H.HEYER 1979	1979
430808501	FORD CAPRI GR.5 KRAUS K.LUDWIG 1980	1980
430818502	FORD CAPRI GR.5 WUERTH K.LUDWIG 81	1981
430818521	FORD CAPRI GR.5 D&W K.NIEDZWIEDZ 81	1981
430818555	FORD CAPRI GR.5 NIGRIN WINKELH. 81	1981
430088020	FORD COUGAR 1998 RED METALLIC	1998
430088021	FORD COUGAR 1998 GREEN METALLIC	
430088022	FORD COUGAR 1998 BLACK	1998
433088023	FORD COUGAR 1998	
400081000	FORD ESCORT I 1968 LHD YELLOW	1968
400081001	FORD ESCORT I 1968 LHD LIGHT BLUE	1968
430082100	FORD ESCORT COSWORTH 92 SCHW.MET	1992
430082101	FORD ESCORT COSWORTH 1992 WEISS	1992
430082102	FORD ESCORT COSWORTH 92 GRUEN MET.	1992
430082104	FORD ESCORT RS COSWORTH 1992 RED	1992
430938200	FORD ESCORT COSWORTH RALLYE MC 1993	1993
430938204	FORD ESCORT COSWORTH NIEDZWIEDZ 1993	1993
430938205	FORD ESCORT COSWORTH SCHMIDT ADAC 1993	1993
430938217	FORD ESCORT COSWORTH KELLENERS 1993	1993
430938218	FORD ESCORT COSWORTH BERMEL ADAC 1993	1993
30948104	FORD ESCORT RS 2. PORTUGAL BIASON	1994
430948106	FORD ESCORT COSWORTH Monte Carlo 94	1994
430948107	FORD ESCORT 1000 SEEN RALLYE FINNLAND	1994
430948108	FORD ESCORT RS 6. MC THIRY/PREVOT	1994
430948119	FORD ESCORT RS 8. MC JENOT/SLO F	1994
430948123	FORD ESCORT RS 9. MC PURAS/ROMANI E	1994
430948201	FORD ESCORT C.HUERTGEN WOLF-RACING	1994
430948202	FORD ESCORT W.KRANKEMANN WOLF-RCG.	1994
430948204	FORD ESCORT H.DREXLER WOLF-RACING	1994
430948206	FORD ESCORT W.UTRECHT AMC DIEPHOLZ	1994
430948207	FORD ESCORT F.HUBER WOLF-RACING	1994
430948209	FORD ESCORT VATANEN-PONS ACR. 1994	1994
430948291	FORD ESCORT MICHELIN CHAMPION 1994	1994
430958203	FORD ESCORT MARTINI 1.MM 1995	1995
430968203	FORD ESCORT 1ST MC 96 BERNARDINI/OC	1996
430968204	FORD ESCORT 2ND SWEDEN 96 REPSOL/SA	1996
430978705	FORD ESCORT C.SAINZ WRC 1997	1997
430978711	FORD ESCORT A.VATANEN RAC RALLYE WRC97	1997
430988707	FORD ESCORT WRC 2ND MONTE CARLO 98	1998
433082103	FORD ESCORT COSWORTH 1992 EXCL. RED	1992
433082105	FORD ESCORT RS COSWORTH 92 BLUE MET	1992
433082106	FORD ESCORT RS COSWORTH 1992	1992
434938202	FORD ESCORT COSWORTH BOXYS NO.2 Droogmans	1993
434948201	FORD ESCORT COSWORTH BASTOS NO.1 SNISERS	1994
434948205	FORD ESCORT COSWORTH CRACK NO.5 LIETAER	1994
434948206	FORD ESCORT COSWORTH RIZLAT NO.6 VERREYDT	1994
510430005	FORD ESCORT COSWORTH	1992
430085000	FORD FIESTA 1995 BLUE	1995
430085001	FORD FIESTA 1995 WHITE	1995
430085002	FORD FIESTA 1995 RED	1995
400081100	FORD FIESTA 2001 BLACK	
400081101	FORD FIESTA 2001 RED METALLIC	
403081103	FORD FIESTA 2001 SILVER MET. EXCL.	
403081104	FORD FIESTA 2001 PANTHER BLACK MET.	
403081105	FORD FIESTA 2001 NEPTUNE GREEN MET.	
403081106	FORD FIESTA 2001 METROPOLIS BLUE MT	
403081107	FORD FIESTA 2001 RED	
403081108	FORD FIESTA 2001 5-DOOR BLACK	
403081109	FORD FIESTA 2001 LUGANO BLUE MET.	
433085003	FORD FIESTA 1995 RED METALLIC EXCL	1995
430008905	FORD FOCUS MCRAE CATALUNYA WRC 2000	2000
430008906	FORD FOCUS SAINZ MONTE C. WRC 2000	2000
430008907	FORD FOCUS RED BULL BAUMS. WRC 2000	
430008916	FORD FOCUS SOLBERG ARGENT. WRC 2000	2000
430008996	FORD FOCUS SOLBERG FINLAND WRC 2000	
430018903	FORD FOCUS RS WRC C.SAINZ MONTE '01	2001
430018904	FORD FOCUS RS WRC C.MCRAE MONTE '01	2001
430018917	FORD FOCUS RS WRC DELECOUR M.C. '01	2001
430028934	FORD FOCUS RS WRC RALLY CATAL. 2002	2002
430087000	FORD FOCUS 3-DOOR SALOON 1998 RED	1998
430087001	FORD FOCUS 3-DOOR SALOON '98 BLACK	
430087010	FORD FOCUS BREAK 1998 BLUE METALLIC	1998
430087011	FORD FOCUS BREAK 1998 RED METALLIC	
430087020	FORD FOCUS 5-DOOR 1998 GREEN MET.	1998
430087021	FORD FOCUS 5-DOOR 98 LIGHT BLUE MET	
430998807	FORD FOCUS WRC C.MCRAE 1999	1999
430998900	FORD FOCUS TEST CAR WRC 1999	
431968293	FORD ESCORT MINICHAMPS B.THIRY 96	1996
433008904	FORD FOCUS P.BERNHARDT NO.4 DTC'00	
433008905	FORD FOCUS T.KLENKE NO.5 DTC'00	
433008907	FORD FOCUS M.FUNKE NO.7 DTC'00	
433008908	FORD FOCUS M.GEDLICH NO.44 DTC'00	
433008995	FORD FOCUS MCRAE WRC 2000	2000

ITEM-No	ITEM	YEAR
433028934	FORD FOCUS RS WRC RALLY CATAL. 2002	
433087003	FORD FOCUS SALOON 98 SALSA RED MET.	1998
433087004	FORD FOCUS SALOON 1998 SILVER MET.	
433087013	FORD FOCUS BREAK 98 PACIFIC GREEN M	1998
433087014	FORD FOCUS BREAK 1998 SILVER MET.	
433087023	FORD FOCUS 5-DOOR SALOON 1998	
433087090	FORD FOCUS BREAK POLICE CAR	
433998907	FORD FOCUS DTC BLUE	
403082203	FORD FUSION SILVER METALLIC EXCL.	
403082204	FORD FUSION SALSA RED MET. EXCL.	
403082205	FORD FUSION LUGANO BLUE MET. EXCL.	
430089500	FORD GALAXY 2000 GREEN MET.	
430089501	FORD GALAXY 2000 BLACK	
430084160	FORD GALAXY VAN 95 BLACK	1995
430084161	FORD GALAXY VAN 95 BLUE METALLIC	1995
430084162	FORD GALAXY VAN 95 RED METALLIC	1995
433084163	FORD GALAXY VAN 95 EXCL.	1995
433089503	FORD GALAXY SILVER EXCL.	
433089504	FORD GALAXY LOGANO BLUE MET. EXCL.	
430086400	FORD KA 1997 RED	1997
430086401	FORD KA 1997 PURPLE	1997
430086402	FORD KA 1997 BLACK	1997
433086403	FORD KA 1997	1997
433086404	FORD KA 1997 RADIANT RED EXCL.	
433086405	FORD KA 1997 AMPARO BLUE EXCL.	
433086406	FORD KA 1997 RED EXCL.	
430080000	FORD MONDEO 2001 COLORADO RED	
430080001	FORD MONDEO 2001 PANTHER BLACK MET.	
430080010	FORD MONDEO BREAK 2001 SILVER MET.	
430080011	FORD MONDEO BREAK 01 SALSA RED MET.	
430080070	FORD MONDEO 5-DOOR 2001 BLACK MET.	
430080071	FORD MONDEO 5-DOOR 2001 SILVER MET.	
430082000	FORD MONDEO LIMOUSINE 4T RED	1993
430082001	FORD MONDEO LIMOUSINE 4T YELLOW	1993
430082002	FORD MONDEO LIMOUSINE 4T BLUE	1993
430082010	FORD MONDEO TURNIER 1993 RED	1993
430082011	FORD MONDEO TURNIER 1993 GREEN MET	1993
430082012	FORD MONDEO TURNIER 1993 BLACK	1993
430082070	FORD MONDEO LIMOUSINE 5T RED	1993
430082071	FORD MONDEO LIMOUSINE 5T YELLOW	1993
430082072	FORD MONDEO LIMOUSINE 5T BLUE	1993
430082073	FORD MONDEO LIMOUSINE 5T EXCL.	1993
430082090	FORD MONDEO 4-DOOR POLIZEI	1993
433080003	FORD MONDEO 2000 SILVER MET. EXCL.	
433080004	FORD MONDEO 2000 BLUE MET. EXCL.	
433080013	FORD MONDEO TURNIER 2000 BLUE MET.	
433080073	FORD MONDEO 5-DOOR 2000 BLACK EXCL.	
433082000	FORD MONDEO LIMOUSINE 4T ROT	1993
433082001	FORD MONDEO LIMOUSINE 4T GELB	1993
433082002	FORD MONDEO LIMOUSINE 4T BLAU	1993
433082003	FORD MONDEO LIMOUSINE 4-DOOR EXCL.	1993
433082073	FORD MONDEO LIMOUSINE 5T EXCL.	1993
433082091	FORD MONDEO 4-DOOR POLICE NL	1993
430086300	FORD MONDEO 4-DOOR SALOON 97 SILVER	1997
430086301	FORD MONDEO 4-DOOR SALOON 97 RED	1997
430086310	FORD MONDEO BREAK 1997 RED	1997
430086311	FORD MONDEO BREAK 1997 BLACK	1997
430938005	FORD MONDEO N.MANSELL BTCC CL.2 93	1993
430948001	FORD MONDEO RACING WHITE UNDECORATED	1994
430948003	FORD MONDEO 1994 R.RADISICH	1994
430948006	FORD MONDEO B.Eichmann/Eggenberger	1994
430948007	FORD MONDEO T.BOUTSEN/EGGENBERGER	1994
430948009	FORD MONDEO M.OESTREICH/Wolf-Racing	1994
430948013	FORD MONDEO 94 P.RADISICH TCWCUP CH	1994
430948033	FORD MONDEO 1994 A.ROUSE	1994
430958516	FORD MONDEO WOLF/HUERTGEN STW95	1995
430958517	FORD MONDEO Eggenberger/Asch STW95	1995
433086303	FORD MONDEO 4-DOOR SALOON 1997	1997
433086313	FORD MONDEO BREAK 1997	1997
430085631	FORD MUSTANG 1994 CABRIOLET BLUE M.	1994
430085632	FORD MUSTANG 1994 CABRIOLET RED	1994
430938313	FORD MUSTANG CHALL./J.FEUCHT DTM 93	1993
430938333	FORD MUSTANG RUCH/G.RUCH DTM 93	1993
430948323	FORD MUSTANG RUCH/J.RUCH DTM 94	1994
430086520	FORD PUMA COUPE 1997 BLACK METALLIC	1997
430086521	FORD PUMA COUPE 1997 RED	1997
430086522	FORD PUMA COUPE 1997 BLUE MET	1997
430086524	FORD PUMA COUPE 1997 GREEN MET	1997
433086523	FORD PUMA COUPE 1997 EXCL. COLOUR 1	1997
433086524	FORD PUMA POLARIS GREY MET. EXCL.	
433998600	FORD PUMA CUP MODEL WHITE 1999	
430080200	FORD RS 200 ROAD CAR WHITE	
430080201	FORD RS 200 ROAD CAR 1986 RED	
430868008	FORD RS 200 RALLY SWEDEN 1986	
430084000	FORD SCORPIO 1995 BLACK	1995
430084001	FORD SCORPIO 1995 BLUE	1995
430084002	FORD SCORPIO 1995 GREEN MET.	1995
430084010	FORD SCORPIO BREAK 1995 BLACK/GREY	1995
430084011	FORD SCORPIO BREAK 1995 BLUE/GREY	1995
430084012	FORD SCORPIO BREAK 1995 GREEN METAL	1995
433084003	FORD SCORPIO SALOON 1995 EXCL.	1995
433084013	FORD SCORPIO BREAK 95 BLUE MET EXCL	1995
430878067	FORD SIERRA RS COSW. 1ST NUERBRG'87	
430888018	FORD SIERRA COSW. SPEEDWARE DTM'88	1988
430888025	FORD SIERRA RS COSW. HAHNE DTM '88	
400082130	FORD THUNDERBIRD 03 J.B.CONVERTIBLE	
430085100	FORD TAUNUS SALOON 1960 WHITE	1960
430085101	FORD TAUNUS SALOON 1960 GREY	1960
430085102	FORD TAUNUS SALOON 1960 DARK RED	1960
430085104	FORD TAUNUS SALOON 1960 BLUE	
430085105	FORD TAUNUS SALOON 1960 YELLOW	
430085106	FORD TAUNUS SALOON 1960 TURQUOISE	
430085107	FORD TAUNUS 1960 TURQUOISE METALLIC	
400081210	FORD TRANSIT TOURNEO 2001 RED	
403081213	FORD TRANSIT TOURNEO 2001	
403081263	FORD TRANSIT EUROLINE 2001	
430089000	FORD TRANSIT SINGLE CABINE PLATFORM	
430089100	FORD TRANSIT DOUBLE CABINE PLATFORM	
430089300	FORD TRANSIT BOX VAN HIGH ROOF	
430089400	FORD TRANSIT BASE VAN MEDIUM ROOF	
433089003	FORD TRANSIT SINGLE CABINE PLATFORM	
433089103	FORD TRANSIT DOUBLE CABINE PLATFORM	
433089303	FORD TRANSIT BOX VAN HIGH ROOF	
433089304	FORD TRANSIT BOXVAN HIGH ROOF WHITE	
433089403	FORD TRANSIT BREAK MEDIUM ROOF	
AC4010300	FORMULA 1 AGP EVENT CAR 2001	
AC4010301	FORMULA 1 BGP EVENT CAR 2001 ACTION	
AC4010302	FORMULA 1 BGP EVENT CAR '01 OCTAGON	
AC4020300	FORMULA 1 CANADIAN GP EVENT CAR '02	
AC4000300	FORMULA 1 IMS EVENT CAR	
AC4010303	FORMULA 1 US GP EVENT CAR 2001	
AC4010304	FORMULA 1 US GP EVENT CAR 2001 SAP	
AC4020301	FORMULA 1 USA GP EVENT CAR '02	2002
430161520	HONDA CR-X COUPE 1989 BLACK	1989
430161521	HONDA CR-X COUPE 1989 SILVER	1989
430161522	HONDA CR-X COUPE 1989 RED	1989
430161524	HONDA CR-X COUPE 1989 GREY MET.	
430161525	HONDA CR-X COUPE 1989 YELLOW	
430161526	HONDA CR-X COUPE 1989 SILVER	
436990099	HONDA RA 099 PROTO. J.VERSTAPPEN 99	1999
433130603	JAGUAR MARK 2 SALOON BLACK EXCL	1959
430130600	JAGUAR MK 2 SALOON 1959-67 GREEN	1959
430130602	JAGUAR MK 2 SALOON 1959-67 DARK RED	1959
430102220	JAGUAR XJ 220 BLUE	1992
430102221	JAGUAR XJ 220 YELLOW	1992
430102222	JAGUAR XJ 220 SILVER	1992
430931300	JAGUAR XJ 220 G.GIUDICI NO.11 MART.	1993
430931312	JAGUAR XJ 220 G.CUTRERA NO.12 ERG	1993
400130230	JAGUAR XKR CONVERTIBLE J.B. 2002	
430149660	JEEP GRAND CHEROKEE BLACK	1993
430149661	JEEP GRAND CHEROKEE GREEN MET.	1993

ITEM-No	ITEM	YEAR
430149662	JEEP GRAND CHEROKEE RED	1993
430910031	JORDAN 191 A. DE CESARIS 1991	1991
430910032	JORDAN 191 B.GACHOT F1 1991	1991
430910132	JORDAN 191 A.ZANARDI F1 1991	1991
4309300JD	JORDAN 193 NO. 14/15 1993	
4309400JD	JORDAN 194 NO. 14/15 1994	
4309500JD	JORDAN 195 1995	1995
4309600JD	JORDAN 196 1996	1996
4309700JD	JORDAN 197 1997	1997
4309800JD	JORDAN 198 1998	1998
433960011	JORDAN BARRICHELLO 1996	1996
433960012	JORDAN BRUNDLE 1996	1996
514964380	JORDAN 196 TESTCAR R.SCHUMACHER 96	1996
430970012	JORDAN 197 PEUGEOT G.FISICHELLA 97	1997
430970082	JORDAN 197 PRESENT. G.FISICHELLA 97	1997
514974311	JORDAN 197 PEUGEOT R.SCHUMACHER 97	1997
514974381	JORDAN 197 PRESENT. R.SCHUMACHER 97	1997
430980009	JORDAN 198 MUGEN HONDA D.HILL 1998	1998
430980039	JORDAN 198 D.HILL TOWER WING 1998	1998
433980109	JORDAN 198 D.HILL 4TH GP D 1998	1998
514984310	JORDAN 198 M.HONDA R.SCHUMACHER 98	1998
514984340	JORDAN 198 R.SCHUMACHER TOWER W. 98	1998
430960081	JORDAN F1 BARICHELLO PRES. 1996	1996
430960082	JORDAN F1 BRUNDLE PRESENTATION 1996	1996
510914332	JORDAN F1 M.SCHUMACHER 1991	1991
511984310	JORDAN MUGEN HONDA H.H.F TESTCAR 98	1998
430950014	JORDAN PEUGEOT R.BARRICHELLO 1995	1995
430950015	JORDAN PEUGEOT E.IRVINE 1995	1995
430960011	JORDAN PEUGEOT 196 R.BARRICHELLO 96	1996
430960012	JORDAN PEUGEOT 196 M.BRUNDLE 96	1996
433950014	JORDAN PEUGEOT R.BARRICHELLO 1995	1995
433950015	JORDAN PEUGEOT E.IRVINE 1995	1995
510430006	KART M. SCHUMACHER 1987	1987
540094300	KART MODELL 1993 AYRTON SENNA	1993
540095300	KART MODELL 1980 AYRTON SENNA	1980
510954396	KART SET M. SCHUMACHER	1995
510964304	KART TONY M.SCHUMACHER 1996	
430090000	KART WHITE	
430090001	KART RED	
430103200	LAMBORGHINI 350 GT BLUE METALLIC	
430103201	LAMBORGHINI 350 GT RED	
430103300	LAMBORGHINI 400 GT 2+2 SILVER	
430103301	LAMBORGHINI 400 GT 2+2 GREEN	
430103100	LAMBORGHINI COUNTACH LP 400 GOLD	
430103101	LAMBORGHINI COUNTACH LP 400 YELLOW	
430103102	LAMBORGHINI COUNTACH LP 400 BLACK	
433103103	LAMBORGHINI COUNTACH LP 400 YELLOW	
430103000	LAMBORGHINI MIURA BLACK	1966
430103001	LAMBORGHINI MIURA GOLD	1966
430103002	LAMBORGHINI MIURA RED	1966
430103004	LAMBORGHINI MIURA VIPER GREEN	
430103005	LAMBORGHINI MIURA YELLOW	
430103006	LAMBORGHINI MIURA ORANGE	
433103004	LAMBORGHINI MIURA VIPER GREEN	
403125103	LANCIA NEA SALOON 2001	
430125020	LANCIA STRATOS 1972-78 YELLOW	1972
430125022	LANCIA STRATOS 1972-78 RED	1972
430751204	LANCIA STRATOS ALITALIA 1.SWE 1975	1975
430751214	LANCIA STRATOS ALITALIA 1.MC 1975	1975
430761210	LANCIA STRATOS ALITALIA 1.MC 1976	1976
430771201	LANCIA STRATOS ALITALIA 1.MC '77	1977
430781201	LANCIA STRATOS PIRELLI 1978	1978
430791201	LANCIA STRATOS CHARDONNET 1.TDC '79	1979
430801201	LANCIA STRATOS LE POINT 1.TDF 1980	1980
400166130	LEXUS SC 430 CABRIOLET 2001 BLACK	
400166131	LEXUS SC 430 CABRIOLET 01 GREEN MET	
403166123	LEXUS SC 430 HARDTOP 2001 SILVER MT	
403166133	LEXUS SC 430 OPEN CABRIO. SILVER MT	
430950025	LIGIER HONDA JS 41 A.SUZUKI 1995	1995
430950026	LIGIER HONDA JS 41 O. PANIS 1995	1995
430950125	LIGIER HONDA JS 41 M.BRUNDLE 1995	1995
430960009	LIGIER MUGEN HONDA JS43 O.PANIS 96	1996
430960010	LIGIER MUGEN HONDA JS43 P.DINIZ 96	1996
430960099	LIGIER O.PANIS WINNER GP MONACO 96	1996
430086100	LINCOLN CONTINENTAL KENNEDY W.FIGS.	1965
436086101	LINCOLN CONTINENTAL JOHNSON	
520934303	LOLA 93 CHEVY GALLES R. NO.3 UNSER	1993
520934305	LOLA 93 ROADTR. NEWM.HAAS MANSELL	1993
520934306	LOLA 93 ROADTR. NEWM.HAAS ANDRETTI	1993
520934309	LOLA 93 FORD D.SIMON NR.9 R.BOESEL	1993
520934403	LOLA 93 CHEVY GALLES R. NO.3 UNSER	1993
520934405	LOLA 93 SPEEDW. NEWM.HAAS MANSELL	1993
520934406	LOLA 93 SPEEDW. NEWM.HAAS ANDRETTI	1993
520934409	LOLA 93 FORD D.SIMON NR.9 R.BOESEL	1993
520944306	LOLA 94 FORD N.HAAS NO.6 ARR. MARIO	1994
521964320	LOLA 95 GOODYEAR T.STEWART 96	1996
523934390	LOLA HONDA PROMOTIONAL	1997
520944319	LOLA T93/06 DALE CONE NO.19 ZAMPEDR	1994
520944324	LOLA T93/06 WALKER NO.24 W.T.RIBBS	1994
520944419	LOLA T93/06 DALE CONE NO.19 ZAMPEDR	1994
520944422	LOLA T93/06 D.SIMON NO.22 MATSUSHI.	1994
520944323	LOLA T93/07 LEADER NO.23 B.LAZIER .	1994
520944355	LOLA T93/07 EURO-MS NO.55 J.ANDRETT	1994
520944301	LOLA T94/00 NEWMAN/H NO.1 N.MANSELL	1994
520944304	LOLA T94/00 RAHAL-HOG. NO.4 B.RAHAL	1994
520944309	LOLA T94/00 WALKER NO.9 R.GORDON	1994
520944328	LOLA T94/00 INDY.R. NO.28 A.LUYEND.	1994
520944446	LOLA T94/00 NEWMAN/H. NO.6 M.ANDRET	1994
430700005	LOTUS 72 J. RINDT 1970	1970
430700024	LOTUS 72 E.FITTIPALDI 1ST GP WIN 70	1970
430720008	LOTUS 72 E. FITTIPALDI 1972	1972
430780005	LOTUS 79 M.ANDRETTI WORLDCHAMP. '78	1978
430780006	LOTUS 79 R.PETERSON 1978	1978
430790001	LOTUS 79 MARTINI M. ANDRETTI 1979	1979
430790002	LOTUS 79 MARTINI C. REUTEMANN 1979	1979
430850011	LOTUS 97T E. DE ANGELIS 1985	1985
540854312	LOTUS 97T 1985 AYRTON SENNA	1985
430860011	LOTUS 98T J. DUMFRIES 1986	1986
540864312	LOTUS 98T 1986 AYRTON SENNA	1986
430870011	LOTUS 99T S.NAKAJIMA 1987	1987
540874312	LOTUS 99T 1987 AYRTON SENNA	1987
430135630	LOTUS SUPER 7 1968 GREEN	1968
430135632	LOTUS SUPER 7 1968 RED	1968
400790004	MARCH 792 BMW F2 SCAINI T.FABI 1979	1979
433790001	MARCH BMW 792 MARC SURER 1979	1979
430731110	MATRA MS 670B BELTOISE/CEVERT LM 73	1973
430731111	MATRA MS 670B PESCAROLO/LAR. LM '73	1973
430731112	MATRA MS 670B JABOUILLE/JAUS. LM 73	1973
433039403	MAYBACH ZEPPELIN 1932 BEIGE	1932
436039400	MAYBACH ZEPPELIN 1932 BLACK	
436039401	MAYBACH ZEPPELIN 1932 2-TONE GREY	
433930008	McLAREN AYRTON SENNA HOCKENHEIM 93	1993
530164325	McLAREN BMW '96 BBA COMP. FIA 1997	1997
530154301	McLAREN F1 GTR GULF NUERBURGRING	1995
530154305	McLAREN F1 GTR DAVIDOFF MONZA	1995
530154307	McLAREN F1 GTR JACADI NUERBURGRING	1995
530154308	McLAREN F1 GTR D.PRICE-R. NUERBGRG.	1995
530154309	McLAREN F1 GTR MACH ONE NUERBGRG.	1995
530154316	McLAREN F1 GTR GULF NUERBURGRING	1995
530154324	McLAREN F1 GTR GULF 4TH LE MANS	1995
530154325	McLAREN F1 GTR GULF LE MANS	1995
530154342	McLAREN F1 GTR BBA COMP. 13.LE MANS	1995
530154349	McLAREN F1 GTR WEST FM LE MANS	1995
530154350	McLAREN F1 GTR JACADI 5TH LE MANS	1995
530154351	McLAREN F1 GTR MACH ONE 3RD LE MANS	1995
530154359	McLAREN F1 GTR KOKUSAI 1ST LE MANS	1995
530164329	McLAREN F1 GTR HARRODS 1996	1996
530164330	McLAREN F1 GTR WEST COMPETITION 96	1996
530164333	McLAREN F1 GTR GULF RACING 1996	1996
530164334	McLAREN F1 GTR GULF RAC OWEN 1996	1996
530174339	McLAREN F1 GTR GULF BELLM/G. LM 97	1997

ITEM-No	ITEM	YEAR
530174340	McLAREN F1 GTR GULF BSCHER/N. LM 97	1997
530174341	McLAREN F1 GTR GULF GOUNON/R. LM 97	1997
530164353	McLAREN F1 GTR GIROIX/GIROIX 1996	1996
530164360	McLAREN F1 GTR R.S. JAPAN SERIES 96	1996
530174342	McLAREN F1 GTR BMW LEHTO/S. LM 97	1997
530174343	McLAREN F1 GTR BMW KOX/R. LM 97	1997
530174344	McLAREN F1 GTR LARK TSUCHIYA LM 97	1997
530184340	McLAREN F1 GTR 4TH LE MANS 1998	
530184341	McLAREN F1 GTR LOCTITE 1998	
533154308	McLAREN F1 GTR WEST CIGARETTES LM	1995
533154390	McLAREN F1 GTR FLAGGENDESIGN 1996	1996
533164338	McLAREN F1 GTR F/GB LM 1996	1996
533164339	McLAREN F1 GTR USA LM 1996	1996
533174308	McLAREN F1 GTR BMW LEHTO/S. GT 97	1997
533174309	McLAREN F1 GTR BMW KOX/R. GT 97	1997
533174343	McLAREN F1 GTR BMW KOX/R. LM 97	1997
533204321	McLAREN F1 GTR HITOTSUYAMA JGTC '00	2000
533204330	McLAREN F1 GTR TAKE ONE JGTC 2000	2000
530133434	McLAREN F1 ROADCAR 1993 RED MET.	1993
530133430	McLAREN F1 ROADCAR 1993 GREEN MET.	1993
530133431	McLAREN F1 ROADCAR 1993 SILVER	1993
530133432	McLAREN F1 ROADCAR 1993 RED	1993
530133433	McLAREN F1 STREET CAR TAG-HEUER	1993
530774340	McLAREN FORD M23 G.V.BRITISH GP'77	1977
530155359	McLAREN GTR SIEGER LE MANS	1995
530174327	McLAREN GTR PARABOLICA FIA GT 1997	
533155359	McLAREN GTR SIEGER LE MANS EXCL.	1995
530684304	McLAREN M8A CAN AM B. McLAREN 1968	
530684305	McLAREN M8A CAN AM D. HULME	1968
530694304	McLAREN M8B CAN AM B. McLAREN 1969	
530694305	McLAREN M8B CAN AM D. HULME 1969	
530704305	McLAREN M8D CAN AM D.HULME 1970	
530704307	McLAREN M8D CANAM D.GURNEY NO.48'70	1970
530704397	McLAREN M8D CAN AM P. GETHIN 1970	1970
530714305	McLAREN M8F CAN AM D. HULME 1971	1971
530714307	McLAREN M8F CAN AM P. REVSON 1971	1971
530764311	McLAREN M23 J.HUNT	1976
530764312	McLAREN M23 J.MASS 1976	1976
530954307	McLAREN MERCEDES MP 4/10 N.MANSELL 1995	1995
530954308	McLAREN MERCEDES MP 4/10 M.HAKKINEN 1995	1995
530954317	McLAREN MERCEDES MP 4/10 M.BLUNDELL 1995	1995
533954307	McLAREN MERCEDES MP 4/10 N.MANSELL 1995	1995
533954308	McLAREN MERCEDES MP 4/10 M.HAKKINEN 1995	1995
533954317	McLAREN MERCEDES MP 4/10 M.BLUNDELL 1995	1995
533964307	McLAREN MERCEDES MP4/11 M.HAKKINEN 96	1996
533964308	McLAREN MERCEDES MP4/11 D.COULTHARD 96	1996
530964307	McLAREN MERCEDES MP4/11 M.HAKKINEN 96	1996
530964308	McLAREN MERCEDES MP4/11 D.COULTHARD 96	1996
533974309	McLAREN MERCEDES MP4/12 M.HAKKINEN 97	1997
533974310	McLAREN MERCEDES MP4/12 D.COULTHARD 97	1997
530974309	McLAREN MERCEDES MP4/12 M.HAKKINEN 97	1997
530974310	McLAREN MERCEDES MP4/12 D.COULTHARD 97	1997
433970009	McLAREN MERCEDES MP4/12 M.HAKKINEN 97	1997
433970010	McLAREN MERCEDES MP4/12 D.COULTHARD 97	1997
403010003	McLAREN MERCEDES MP4/16 WEST HAKK. '01	2001
403010004	McLAREN MERCEDES MP4/16 WEST COULT.'01	2001
530014303	McLAREN MERCEDES MP4/16 HAKKINEN 01	2001
530014304	McLAREN MERCEDES MP4/16 COULTH. '01	2001
533014303	McLAREN MERCEDES MP4/16 HAKKINEN 01	2001
533014304	McLAREN MERCEDES MP4/16 COULTH. '01	2001
530024303	McLAREN MERCEDES MP4/17 D.COULTHARD 02	2002
530024304	McLAREN MERCEDES MP4/17 RAIKKONEN 02	2002
403020103	McLAREN MERCEDES MP4/17 WEST COULTH.'02	2002
403020104	McLAREN MERCEDES MP4/17 WEST RAIKK.'02	2002
503024303	McLAREN MERCEDES MP4/17 D.COULTHARD 02	2002
503024304	McLAREN MERCEDES MP4/17 RAIKKONEN 02	2002
538024303	McLAREN MERCEDES MP4/17 D.COULTHARD 02	2002
538024304	McLAREN MERCEDES MP4/17 RAIKKONEN 02	2002
530844307	McLAREN MP4/2 A.PROST 1984	1984
530844308	McLAREN MP4/2 N.LAUDA WORLDCH.1984	1984
530854301	McLAREN MP4/2B N.LAUDA 1985	1985
530854302	McLAREN MP4/2B A.PROST WORLDCH 1985	1985
430850002	McLAREN MP4/2B A.PROST WORLDCH 1985	1985
430860001	McLAREN MP4/2C A.PROST 1986	1986
530864301	McLAREN MP4/2C A.PROST 1986	1986
530864302	McLAREN MP4/2C K.ROSBERG 1986	1986
430880012	McLAREN MP4/4 HONDA TURBO A. SENNA	1988
530884311	McLAREN MP4/4 A. PROST VIZECH.1988	1988
540884312	McLAREN MP4/4 HONDA TURBO A. SENNA	1988
540894301	McLAREN MP4/5 HONDA V10 A. SENNA	1989
430890002	McLAREN MP4/5 A.PROST WORLDCHAMP 89	1989
530894302	McLAREN MP4/5 A.PROST WORLDCHAMP 89	1989
530904328	McLAREN MP4/5B G.BERGER 1990	1990
430900027	McLAREN MP4/5B 1990 AYRTON SENNA	1990
540904327	McLAREN MP4/5B 1990 AYRTON SENNA	1990
430910001	McLAREN MP4/6 1991 AYRTON SENNA	1991
530914302	McLAREN MP4/6 G.BERGER 1991	1991
540914301	McLAREN MP4/6 1991 AYRTON SENNA	1991
540924301	McLAREN MP4/7 1992 AYRTON SENNA	1992
530924302	McLAREN MP4/7 G.BERGER 1992	1992
433930007	McLAREN MP4/8 ANDRETTI HOCKENH. 93	1993
530934307	McLAREN MP4/8 FORD M.ANDRETTI 1993	1993
530934308	McLAREN MP4/8 FORD A.SENNA 1993	1993
530934317	McLAREN MP4/8 FORD M.HAKKINEN 1993	1993
540414341	McLAREN MP4/8 FORD A.S.ADELAIDE'93	1993
540934308	McLAREN MP4/8 1993 AYRTON SENNA	1993
530974389	McLAREN MP4/12 TESTC ORANGE HAKKIN.	1997
530974390	McLAREN MP4/12 TESTC ORANGE COULTH.	1997
430980008	McLAREN MP4/13 M.HAKKINEN 1998	1998
433980007	McLAREN MP4/13 D.COULTHARD 1998	1998
433980008	McLAREN MP4/13 M.HAKKINEN 1998	1998
530984307	McLAREN MP4/13 D.COULTHARD 1998	1998
530984308	McLAREN MP4/13 M.HAKKINEN 1998	1998
530994399	McLAREN MP4/13 N.HEIDFELD F.O.S 99	1999
533984307	McLAREN MP4/13 D.COULTHARD 1998	1998
533984308	McLAREN MP4/13 M.HAKKINEN 1998	1998
533994301	McLAREN MP4/14 M.HAKKINEN 1999	1999
533994302	McLAREN MP4/14 D.COULTHARD 1999	1999
530994301	McLAREN MP4/14 M.HAKKINEN 1999	1999
530994302	McLAREN MP4/14 D.COULTHARD 1999	1999
433990001	McLAREN MP4/14 M.HAKKINEN 1999	1999
433990002	McLAREN MP4/14 D.COULTHARD 1999	1999
430990001	McLAREN MP4/14 M.HAKKINEN 1999	1999
433000001	McLAREN MP4/15 M.HAKKINEN 2000	2000
433000002	McLAREN MP4/15 D.COULTHARD 2000	2000
530004301	McLAREN MP4/15 M.HAKKINEN 2000	2000
530004302	McLAREN MP4/15 D.COULTHARD 2000	2000
533004301	McLAREN MP4/15 M.HAKKINEN 2000	2000
533004302	McLAREN MP4/15 D.COULTHARD 2000	2000
530944307	McLAREN PEUGEOT MP4/9 HAKKINEN 94	1994
530944308	McLAREN PEUGEOT MP4/9 M.BRUNDLE 94	1994
533944367	McLAREN PEUGEOT MP 4/9 M.H.CODE BAR	1994
533944377	McLAREN PEUGEOT MP 4/9 M.H.MCL-DECO	1994
533944387	McLAREN PEUGEOT MP 4/9 M.H.CODE BAR	1994
533944397	McLAREN PEUGEOT MP 4/9 M.H.MCL-DECO	1994
430010120	MELKUS RS 1000 RED	
430010121	MELKUS RS 1000 WHITE	
430033100	MERCEDES 180 LIMOUSINE 1953 GREY	1953
430033101	MERCEDES 180 LIMOUSINE 1953 BLACK	1953
430033102	MERCEDES 180 SALOON '53 PASTEL BLUE	1953
430033104	MERCEDES 180 SALOON '53 RED	
430033105	MERCEDES 180 SALOON '53 IVORY	
433033103	MERCEDES 180 BLACK	
430B03000	MERCEDES 190 EVO1 BLACK METALLIC	1990
430G03000	MERCEDES 190 EVO1 PEARLGREY MET	1990
430R03000	MERCEDES 190 EVO1 RED	1990
430B03100	MERCEDES 190 EVO2 BLACK METALLIC	1991
430G03100	MERCEDES 190 EVO2 PEARLGREY MET	1991
430R03100	MERCEDES 190 EVO2 RED	1991
510430002	MERCEDES 190E EVO2	1990
540844311	MERCEDES 190E 1984 AYRTON SENNA	1984

ITEM-No	ITEM	YEAR
430013101	MERCEDES 190E EVO2 AMG KOENIG P LUDWIG	1991
430013102	MERCEDES 190E EVO2 AMG KOEPI KREUTZP.	1991
430013103	MERCEDES 190E EVO2 ZUNG FU LUDW MAC.91	1991
430013104	MERCEDES 190E EVO2 ZUNG FU THIIM MAC91	1991
430013105	MERCEDES 190E EVO2 MERIDIAN SCHNEIDER	1991
430023101	MERCEDES 190E EVO2 LUDWIG/AMG DTM 92	1992
430023102	MERCEDES 190E EVO2 SCHNEIDER/AMG DTM 92	1992
430035600	MERCEDES 190E 2.3-16 '84 BLUE BLACK MET	1984
430843518	MERCEDES 190E 2.3-16 N. LAUDA 1984	1984
430033131	MERCEDES 190 SL CABRIO 55/62 SILVER	1955
430033132	MERCEDES 190 SL CABRIO 55/62 RED	1955
430033134	MERCEDES 190 SL CABRIO 55/62 BLACK	
430033135	MERCEDES 190 SL CABRIO 55/62 IVORY	
430033136	MERCEDES 190 SL CABRIO 55/62 BLUE	
430033137	MERCEDES 190 SL CABRIO 55/62 DK.BLUE	
430033138	MERCEDES 190 SL CABRIO 55/62 GREY	
433033133	MERCEDES 190 SL CABRIOLET RED	
430003302	MERCEDES 200 TD KOMBI CR-GRUEN/SCHW	
430003201	MERCEDES 200 E LIM D.BLAU/BEIGE	
430003202	MERCEDES 200 D LIM ROT/GRAU	
430032224	MERCEDES 200 T 1980-85 GREEN	
430033000	MERCEDES 220 SALOON 1956-59 BLACK	1954
430033002	MERCEDES 220 SALOON 1956-59 RED	1954
433033003	MERCEDES 220 S LIGHT BLUE	
430003203	MERCEDES 230 E LIM ZIRCON SILVER	1992
430003303	MERCEDES 230 TE KOMBI BLAU/D.BLAU	
430003403	MERCEDES 230 CE COUPE CR-GREEN/BL.	
430032204	MERCEDES 230 E 1976-85 GREEN	
430032214	MERCEDES 230 CE 1977-85 GREEN	
430032280	MERCEDES 230 SL RALLYE E.BOEHRINGER 1963	1963
433032243	MERCEDES 230 SL SOFTTOP SILVER/BLUE EXCL.	1968
433032253	MERCEDES 230 SL HARDTOP BLUE	
433032283	MERCEDES 230 SL RACING NO. 39 RED	
433032284	MERCEDES 230 SL RACING NO. 90 BLUE	
430003204	MERCEDES 250 D LIM BLAU/SCHWARZ	
430003820	MERCEDES 250 TD KOMBI TAXI	
430003900	MERCEDES 250 D DEUTSCHE POLIZEI	
430003920	MERCEDES 250 TD KOMBI D. POLIZEI	
430003304	MERCEDES 250 TD KOMBI ROT/GRAU	
430003206	MERCEDES 260 E LIM BLAU/GRAU	
433032233	MERCEDES 280 SL CABRIO 68/71 WHITE EXCL.	1968
430032230	MERCEDES 280 SL CABRIO 1968/71 SILVER	1968
430032231	MERCEDES 280 SL CABRIO 1968/71 RED	1968
430032232	MERCEDES 280 SL CABRIO 1968/71 DARK BLUE	1968
430032234	MERCEDES 280 SL CABRIO 1968/71 LIGHT BLUE	
430032240	MERCEDES 280 SL SOFTTOP 1968/71 WHITE	1968
430032241	MERCEDES 280 SL SOFTTOP 1968/71 RED	1968
430032242	MERCEDES 280 SL SOFTTOP 1968/71 BLACK	1968
430032250	MERCEDES 280 SL HARDTOP 1968/71 GOLD	1968
430032251	MERCEDES 280 SL HARDTOP 1968/71 WHITE	1968
430032252	MERCEDES 280 SL HARDTOP 1968/71 RED	1968
430003208	MERCEDES 300 E LIM SCHWARZBLAU	
430003209	MERCEDES 300 D LIM ALMANDINE RED	1992
430003210	MERCEDES 300 D TURBO LIM ROT/SCHW.	
430003214	MERCEDES 300 E-24 LIM BLAU/SCHW.	
430003514	MERCEDES 300 CE-24 CABR BLUE/CREAM	1992
430003515	MERCEDES 300 CE-24 CABRIO RED MET.	
430003550	MERCEDES 300 CE-24 CABR RED/GREY	1992
430003551	MERCEDES 300 CE-24 CABR SILV/BLACK	1992
430032320	MERCEDES 300 S COUPE 1954 BLACK	1951
430032321	MERCEDES 300 S COUPE 1954 DARK BLUE	1951
430032322	MERCEDES 300 S COUPE 1954 WHITE	1951
430032324	MERCEDES 300 S COUPE 1951/58 SILVER	1951
430032330	MERCEDES 300 S CABRIO 1951/58 BLACK	1951
430032331	MERCEDES 300 S CABRIO 1951/58 BLUE/GREY	1951
430032332	MERCEDES 300 S CABRIO 1951/58 DARK RED	1951
430032340	MERCEDES 300 S SOFTTOP 1951/58 GREEN	1951
430032341	MERCEDES 300 S SOFTTOP 1951/58 WHITE	1951
430032342	MERCEDES 300 S SOFTTOP 1951/58 BLACK	1951
433032323	MERCEDES 300 S COUPE 1954 EXCLUSIV	1951
433032333	MERCEDES 300 S CABRIOLET WHITE EXCL. MERC	1951
433032334	MERCEDES 300 S CABRIOLET WHITE EXCL. MERC	
433032343	MERCEDES 300 S SOFTTOP 1951/58 EXCLUSIV	1951
430003308	MERCEDES 300 TE KOMBI BERYLL/CREME	
430003408	MERCEDES 300 CE COUPE ALMANDINE/RED	
430003414	MERCEDES 300 CE COUPE BORN/BEIGE	1992
430003309	MERCEDES 300 TD KOMBI SILBER/SCHW	
430003310	MERCEDES 300 TD TURBO KOMBI BL/BEIG	1992
430039100	MERCEDES 300 SEL 6.3 68-72 GOLD MET	
430039101	MERCEDES 300 SEL 6.3 68-72 BLACK	
430039102	MERCEDES 300 SEL 6.3 68-72 RED	
430039104	MERCEDES 300 SEL 6.3 68-72 BEIGE MT	
430039105	MERCEDES 300 SEL 6.3 1968-72 GREY	
433553103	MERCEDES 300 SLR MOSS/JENK. MM 1955	
433553203	MERCEDES 300 SLR SILVER	
430300000	MERCEDES 300 SL ZINNMODELL	
432553000	MERCEDES 300 SLR LM 55 J.M. FANGIO	1955
432553100	MERCEDES 300 SLR MOSS/JENK. MM 1955	1955
432553200	MERCEDES 300 SLR COUPE M.FANGIO	1955
432003300	MERCEDES 300 SL 1.ED. WITHOUT DOOR	1952
432003301	MERCEDES 300 SL 1952 UR SL	1952
432003310	MERCEDES 300 SL LE MANS 1952 NO 21 LANG/R	1952
432003311	MERCEDES 300 SL LE MANS 1952 NO 20 LTD.ED	1952
432003312	MERCEDES 300 SL LM 1952 NO 22 LTD.ED	1952
432003313	MERCEDES 300 SL GP BERN 52 WINNER K.KLING	1952
432003314	MERCEDES 300 SL GP BERN 52 2.PL. H.LANG	1952
432003315	MERCEDES 300 SL GP BERN 52 R.CARACCIOLA	1952
432003320	MERCEDES 300 SL PANAM. H.LANG/GRUPP 2.PL.	1952
432003330	MERCEDES 300 SL SPIDER NUERBG.RG LANG 21	1952
432003331	MERCEDES 300 SL SPIDER NUERBGRG 52 RIESS	1952
432003350	MERCEDES 300 SL SPIDER PANAMERICANA NO 6	1952
433003301	MERCEDES 300 SL PROTOTYP VERSION 2	
433003323	MERCEDES 300 SL MILLE MIGLIA NO 300	1952
433003324	MERCEDES 300 SL PANAMERICANA NO. 4	
433523313	MERCEDES 300 SL CARACCIOLA/. NO.613	
433523323	MERCEDES 300 SL KLING/KLENK NO.623	
433523326	MERCEDES 300 SL LANG/GRUPP NO.626	
433039103	MERCEDES 300 SEL 6.3 W109 BLUE MET.	
433039104	MERCEDES 300 SEL 6.3 W109 SILVER	
430003215	MERCEDES 320 CE RAUCHSILBER EXCLUSIV	
430003415	MERCEDES 320 CE B66005703 BL.MET GR	
430003315	MERCEDES 320 TE BORNITE	
430033430	MERCEDES 350 SL CABRIO 1971/80 SILVER	1971
430033431	MERCEDES 350 SL CABRIO 1971/80 DARK BLUE	1971
430033432	MERCEDES 350 SL CABRIO 1971/80 RED	1971
430033440	MERCEDES 350 SL SOFTTOP WHITE	1971
430033441	MERCEDES 350 SL SOFTTOP GREEN MET.	1971
430033442	MERCEDES 350 SL SOFTTOP RED	1971
430033450	MERCEDES 350 SL HARDTOP SILVER	1971
430033451	MERCEDES 350 SL HARDTOP DARK GREEN	1971
430033452	MERCEDES 350 SL HARDTOP RED	1971
433033433	MERCEDES 350 SL CABRIO EXCL.	1971
433033434	MERCEDES 350 SL CABRIO 71/80 SILVER EXCL	
433033443	MERCEDES 350 SL SOFTTOP EXCL.	1971
433033444	MERCEDES 350 SL SOFTTOP BLUE MET.EX	
433033453	MERCEDES 350 SL HARDTOP BROWN MET.	1971
430003230	MERCEDES 400 E V8 LIM. BORNITE/GRAU	
430003231	MERCEDES 400 E V8 LIM IMPALA D.ROT	
430033420	MERCEDES 450 SLC 1972/80 SILVER	1972
430033421	MERCEDES 450 SLC 1972/80 GREEN MET.	1972
430033422	MERCEDES 450 SLC 1972/80 GOLD	1972
430039200	MERCEDES 450 SEL 6.9 72-79 SILVER	
430039201	MERCEDES 450 SEL 6.9 72-79 SMOKE SILVER	
430039202	MERCEDES 450 SEL 6.9 72-79 GREEN MET.	
430039204	MERCEDES 450 SEL 6.9 72-79 DARK ORANGE	
430039205	MERCEDES 450 SEL 6.9 1972-79 GREEN	
433033423	MERCEDES 450 SLC 1972/80 EXCL.	1972
433033424	MERCEDES 450 SLC 1972/80 SILVER EXCL.	1972
433039203	MERCEDES 450 SEL W116 72-79 BLACK	
433039204	MERCEDES 450 SEL W116 GOLD MET.	
433793900	MERCEDES 450 SLC RALLY SILVER UNDEC.	

ITEM-No	ITEM	YEAR
433793910	MERCEDES 450 SLC EAST AFRICA NO. 10	
430003240	MERCEDES 500 E V8 LIM BLACK	1992
430003241	MERCEDES 500 E V8 LIM ANTRACITE	1992
430039300	MERCEDES 560 SEL 89-91 ANTRACITE	
430039301	MERCEDES 560 SEL 89-91 PETROL MET.	
430039302	MERCEDES 560 SEL 89-91 BLUE MET.	
430039304	MERCEDES 560 SEL 89-91 BLACK	
430039305	MERCEDES 560 SEL 1989-91 RED	
433039303	MERCEDES 560 SEL W126 89-91 SILVER	
433039304	MERCEDES 560 SEL W126 DARK BLUE	
430032600	MERCEDES 600 SEC COUPE 1992 BLACK/GREY	1992
430032601	MERCEDES 600 SEC COUPE 1992 GREEN/CREAM	1992
430032602	MERCEDES 600 SEC COUPE 1992 SILVER/RED	1992
430032603	MERCEDES 600 SEC SILBER METALLIC	1992
430943219	MERCEDES AMG 190E EVO 3 ALZEN/PERS.DTM 94	1994
430943220	MERCEDES AMG 190E EVO 3 GINDORF/P. DTM 94	1994
430943221	MERCEDES AMG 190E EVO 3 GRAU/JUN. DTM 94	1994
430943224	MERCEDES AMG 190E EVO 3 AMTHOR/JUN.DTM 94	1994
433963501	MERCEDES AMG AFFALTERBACH SCHNEIDER	1996
510430003	MERCEDES C11 1991	1991
433001101	MERCEDES C11 1990 NO.1	
436030060	MERCEDES C111/II 1970 ORANGE MET.	1970
430953303	MERCEDES C180 94 PRES. V.OMMEN DTM 95	1995
430953304	MERCEDES C180 94 PRES.MAGNUSSEN DTM 95	1995
430953305	MERCEDES C180 94 PRES. S.GRAU DTM 95	1995
430953306	MERCEDES C180 94 PRES. K.THIIM DTM 95	1995
430953314	MERCEDES C180 94 PRES.SCHNEIDER DTM 95	1995
430953315	MERCEDES C180 94 PRES.FRANCHITTI DTM95	1995
430953317	MERCEDES C180 94 PRES. E.LOHR DTM 95	1995
430953503	MERCEDES C180 AMG V.OMMEN 95-2 DTM 95	1995
430953504	MERCEDES C180 AMG MAGNUSSEN 95-2 DTM 95	1995
430953505	MERCEDES C180 ZAKSPEED GRAU 95-2 DTM 95	1995
430953506	MERCEDES C180 ZAKSP. THIIM 95-2 DTM 95	1995
430953514	MERCEDES C180 B.SCHNEIDER 95-2 DTM 95	1995
430953515	MERCEDES C180 AMG FRANCHITTI 95-2 DTM95	1995
430953517	MERCEDES C180 ZAKSPEED LOHR 95-2 DTM 95	1995
430963521	MERCEDES C180 PERSSON E.LOHR ITC 96	1996
430963522	MERCEDES C180 PERSSON MAYLAENDER ITC 96	1996
430963601	MERCEDES C180 AMG SCHNEIDER ITC 96	1996
430963602	MERCEDES C180 AMG FRANCHITTI ITC 96	1996
430963603	MERCEDES C180 AMG MAGNUSSEN ITC 96	1996
430963604	MERCEDES C180 AMG GRAU ITC 96	1996
430963611	MERCEDES C180 AMG V. OMMEN ITC 96	1996
430963612	MERCEDES C180 AMG THIIM ITC 96	1996
430963682	MERCEDES C180 CH.FITTIPALDI ITC 96	1996
433953303	MERCEDES C180 94 PRES. V.OMMEN DTM 95	1995
433953306	MERCEDES C180 94 PRES. K.THIIM DTM 95	1995
433953314	MERCEDES C180 94 PRES.SCHNEIDER DTM 95	1995
433953317	MERCEDES C180 94 PRES. E.LOHR DTM 95	1995
433953503	MERCEDES C180 AMG V.OMMEN 95/2 DTM 1995	1995
433953506	MERCEDES C180 K.THIIM 95-2 DTM 1995	1995
433953514	MERCEDES C180 B.SCHNEIDER 95-2 DTM 1995	1995
433953517	MERCEDES C180 E.LOHR 95-2 DTM 1995	1995
433963521	MERCEDES C180 PERSSON E.LOHR ITC 96	1996
433963522	MERCEDES C180 PERSSON MAYLAENDER ITC 96	1996
433963601	MERCEDES C180 AMG SCHNEIDER ITC 96	1996
433963602	MERCEDES C180 AMG FRANCHITTI ITC 96	1996
433963603	MERCEDES C180 AMG MAGNUSSEN ITC 96	1996
433963604	MERCEDES C180 AMG GRAU ITC 96	1996
433963611	MERCEDES C180 AMG V. OMMEN ITC 96	1996
433963612	MERCEDES C180 AMG THIIM ITC 96	1996
433030003	MERCEDES C200 JAPIS BLUE MET EXCL.	
433030004	MERCEDES C200 BRILLIANT SILVER EXC	
433030005	MERCEDES C200 OBSIDIAN BLACK MET.	
433030006	MERCEDES C200 ADVENTURIN ORANGE MET	
433030007	MERCEDES C200 EVOLUTION SILVER	
433030008	MERCEDES C200 EVOLUTION BLUE MET.	
433030113	MERCEDES C200 T MODEL '00 SILVER	
433030114	MERCEDES C200 T MODEL '00 BLUE MET	
430032108	MERCEDES C220 1998 BLUE BLACK MET.	1998
432001291	MERCEDES C291 1991 START NR. 1	1991
433001291	MERCEDES C291 1991 START NR. 1	
433001292	MERCEDES C291 1991 START NR. 2	
510430001	MERCEDES C291	1991
433001003	MERCEDES C9 NO. 61	
433001004	MERCEDES C9 NO. 62	
430943303	MERCEDES C-CLASS ASCH DTM 94	1994
430943304	MERCEDES C-CLASS SCHNEIDER DTM 94	1994
430943307	MERCEDES C-CLASS LUDWIG DTM 94	1994
430943308	MERCEDES C-CLASS LOHR DTM 94	1994
430943314	MERCEDES C-CLASS THIIM DTM 94	1994
430943315	MERCEDES C-CLASS V. OMMEN DTM 94	1994
430032104	MERCEDES C CLASS 1993 GREEN MET.	1993
430030110	MERCEDES C-CLASS T-MODEL 2001 BLACK	
430030111	MERCEDES C-CLASS T-MOD JASPIS BLUE	
430032165	MERCEDES C-CLASS AMG SAFETY CAR F1	1997
430032166	MERCEDES C-CLASS AMG DOCTORS CAR F1 97	1997
430032195	MERCEDES C-CLASS 1994 TAXI	1993
430953416	MERCEDES C-CLASS ZAKSPEED KRAGES DTM 95	1995
430953422	MERCEDES C-CLASS PERSSON U.ALZEN DTM 95	1995
430953423	MERCEDES C-CLASS PERSSON MAYLAENDER 95	1995
430953424	MERCEDES C-CLASS RUCH G.RUCH DTM 95	1995
433032190	MERCEDES C-CLASS POLICE NL	1993
433037003	MERCEDES C-CLASS SAL. 1997 ORANGE EXCL.	1997
433037004	MERCEDES C-CLASS SAL. 97 VARIOCOL EXCL.	1997
433037013	MERCEDES C-CLASS BREAK 97 SP.-RED EXCL.	1997
433037014	MERCEDES C-CLASS BREAK 97 GREEN EXCL.	1997
433037015	MERCEDES C-CLASS BREAK 97 BLUE EXCL.	
433943303	MERCEDES C-CLASS DTM ASCH OLD BODY	1994
433943304	MERCEDES C-CLASS DTM SCHNEIDER OLD BODY	1994
433943307	MERCEDES C-CLASS DTM LUDWIG OLD BODY	1994
433943308	MERCEDES C-CLASS DTM LOHR OLD BODY	1994
433943314	MERCEDES C-CLASS DTM THIIM OLD BODY	1994
433943315	MERCEDES C-CLASS DTM V.OMMEN OLD BODY	1994
436943303	MERCEDES C-CLASS DTM ASCH NEW BODY	1994
436943304	MERCEDES C-CLASS DTM SCHNEIDER NEW BODY	1994
436943307	MERCEDES C-CLASS DTM LUDWIG NEW BODY	1994
436943308	MERCEDES C-CLASS DTM LOHR NEW BODY	1994
436943314	MERCEDES C-CLASS DTM THIIM NEW BODY	1994
436943315	MERCEDES C-CLASS DTM V.OMMEN NEW BODY	1994
430030000	MERCEDES C SPORT COUPE 2001 RED	
430030001	MERCEDES C SPORT COUPE '01 GREEN M.	
33038023	MERCEDES CL 500 '99 ALMANDIN BLACK	
430038021	MERCEDES CL COUPE '99 DARK BLUE MET	1999
430038022	MERCEDES CL COUPE '99 BLACK MET	
430038024	MERCEDES CL COUPE '99 BRILL. SILVER	
430038025	MERCEDES CL COUPE '99 BLUE METALLIC	
430038026	MERCEDES CL COUPE 1999 BLUE	
400013101	MERCEDES CLK D2 AMG SCHNEIDER DTM 01	2001
400013102	MERCEDES CLK D2 AMG DUMBRECK DTM 01	2001
400013105	MERCEDES CLK WARSTEINER U.ALZEN DTM 01	2001
400013106	MERCEDES CLK WARSTEINER FAESSLER DTM 01	2001
400013109	MERCEDES CLK ESCHMANN MAYLAENDER DTM 01	2001
400013110	MERCEDES CLK ESCHMANN P.HUISMAN DTM 01	2001
400013193	MERCEDES CLK M.HAKKINEN TESTCAR DTM 01	2001
400013714	MERCEDES CLK PERSSON TH.JAEGER DTM 01	2001
400013715	MERCEDES CLK PERSSON CH.ALBERS DTM 01	2001
400013724	MERCEDES CLK ROSBERG P.LAMY DTM 01	2001
400013742	MERCEDES CLK ROSBERG D.TURNER DTM 01	2001
400013791	MERCEDES CLK D2 AMG M.REUTER DTM 01	2001
400023111	MERCEDES CLK ORIGINAL-T T.JAEGER DTM 02	2002
400023112	MERCEDES CLK ORIGINAL-T DUMBRECK DTM 02	2002
400023116	MERCEDES CLK OASE AMG MAYLAENDER DTM 02	2002
400023117	MERCEDES CLK CEB AMG P.HUISMAN DTM 02	2002
400023124	MERCEDES CLK SERVICE 24H MUECKE DTM 02	2002
400023142	MERCEDES CLK SERVICE 24H ALBERS DTM 02	2002
400023201	MERCEDES CLK VODAF.AMG SCHNEIDER DTM 02	2002
400023202	MERCEDES CLK AMG-MERCEDES ALESI DTM 02	2002
400023205	MERCEDES CLK WARSTEINER U.ALZEN DTM 02	2002
400023206	MERCEDES CLK WARSTEINER FAESSLER DTM 02	2002
400031420	MERCEDES CLK COUPE 2002 BLUE MET.	
400031421	MERCEDES CLK COUPE 2002 BLACK	
403023201	MERCEDES CLK VODAF.AMG SCHNEIDER DTM 02	
403023202	MERCEDES CLK AMG-MERCEDES ALESI DTM 02	
403023205	MERCEDES CLK WARSTEINER U.ALZEN DTM 02	
403031423	MERCEDES CLK 2001 SILVER MET.	
403031424	MERCEDES CLK 01 LOLITH BLUE MT	
403031425	MERCEDES CLK 01 OBS. BLACK MET	
430003701	MERCEDES CLK AMG B.SCHNEIDER DTM 00	2000
430003702	MERCEDES CLK AMG TH.JAEGER DTM 00	2000
430003705	MERCEDES CLK AMG K.LUDWIG DTM 00	2000
430003706	MERCEDES CLK AMG M.FAESSLER DTM 00	2000
430003718	MERCEDES CLK PERSSON M.TIEMANN DTM 00	2000
430003719	MERCEDES CLK PERSSON P.DUMBRECK DTM 00	2000
430003724	MERCEDES CLK ROSBERG P.LAMY DTM 00	2000
430003742	MERCEDES CLK ROSBERG D.TURNER DTM 00	2000
403023206	MERCEDES CLK WARSTEINER FAESSLER DTM 02	
400031500	MERCEDES E-CLASS 2002 BLACK	
400031501	MERCEDES E-CLASS 2002 BLUE	
403031503	MERCEDES E-CLASS 01 SILVER MET	
403031504	MERCEDES E-CLASS '01 BLACK MET	
403031505	MERCEDES E-CLASS '01 BLUE MET	
403031506	MERCEDES E-CLASS 01 SILVER MET	
430033500	MERCEDES E-CLASS LIMOUSINE BLUE-BLACK MET	1994
430033501	MERCEDES E-CLASS LIMOUSINE BLUE METALLIC	1994
430033502	MERCEDES E-CLASS LIMOUSINE RED	1994
430033520	MERCEDES E-CLASS COUPE BLUE-BLACK MET.	1994
430033521	MERCEDES E-CLASS COUPE BLUE METALLIC	1994
430033522	MERCEDES E-CLASS COUPE BORNITE	1994
430033530	MERCEDES E-CLASS CABRIO BLUE-BLACK MET.	1994
430033531	MERCEDES E-CLASS CABRIO BLUE METALLIC	1994
430033532	MERCEDES E-CLASS CABRIO ROSEWOOD	1994
430033540	MERCEDES E-CLASS BREAK BLUE-BLACK MET.	1994
430033541	MERCEDES E-CLASS BREAK BLUE METALLIC	1994
430033542	MERCEDES E-CLASS BREAK GREEN	1994
430033595	MERCEDES E-CLASS LIM. 1994 TAXI	1994
430033596	MERCEDES E-CLASS KOMBI 1994 TAXI	1994
433033503	MERCEDES E-CLASS SAL BLUE BLACK MET	
433033523	MERCEDES E-CLASS COUPE SILVER	
433033533	MERCEDES E-CLASS CABRIO SMOKESILVER	
430003001	MERCEDES EVO1 DTM 90 AMG KOENIG/THIIM	1990
430003002	MERCEDES EVO1 DTM 90 AMG KOENIG/LUDWIG 7	1990
430003010	MERCEDES EVO1 DTM 90 SNOBECK/ASCH NR. 14	1990
430003011	MERCEDES EVO1 DTM 90 SNOBECK/CUDINI NR.15	1990
430003020	MERCEDES EVO1 DTM 90 MS-JET/BIELA NR. 16	1990
430003021	MERCEDES EVO1 DTM 90 MS-JET/V.OMMEN NR.17	1990
430003030	MERCEDES EVO1 DTM 90 AMG KAERCHER WENDLG.	1990
430003031	MERCEDES EVO1 DTM 90 AMG KAERCHER KREUTZP	1990
430U03001	MERCEDES EVO1 DTM 90 AMG KOEN UNDECORATED	1990
430U03002	MERCEDES EVO1 DTM 90 AMG KOEN UNDECORATED	1990
430U03010	MERCEDES EVO1 DTM 90 SNOBECK/ UNDECORATED	1990
430U03011	MERCEDES EVO1 DTM 90 SNOBECK/ UNDECORATED	1990
430U03020	MERCEDES EVO1 DTM 90 MS-JET/B UNDECORATED	1990
430U03021	MERCEDES EVO1 DTM 90 MS-JET/V UNDECORATED	1990
430U03030	MERCEDES EVO1 DTM 90 AMG KAER UNDECORATED	1990
430U03031	MERCEDES EVO1 DTM 90 AMG KAER UNDECORATED	1990
430003040	MERCEDES EVO1 RG RACING 1990	1990
430093010	MERCEDES EVO1 AEG SNOBECK 1989	1989
430003101	MERCEDES EVO2 DTM 90 AMG KOENIG/THIIM	1990
430003102	MERCEDES EVO2 DTM 90 AMG KOENIG/LUDWIG	1990
430003110	MERCEDES EVO2 DTM 90 SNOBECK/ASCH	1990
430003111	MERCEDES EVO2 DTM 90 SNOBECK/CUDINI	1990
430003120	MERCEDES EVO2 DTM 90 MS-JET/BIELA	1990
430003121	MERCEDES EVO2 DTM 90 MS-JET/V.OMMEN	1990
430003130	MERCEDES EVO2 DTM 90 AMG KAERCHER WENDLG.	1990
430003131	MERCEDES EVO2 DTM 90 AMG KAERCHER KREUTZP	1990
430003140	MERCEDES EVO2 CAMEL/R.ASCH 1.PL.	1990
430013110	MERCEDES EVO2 SNOBECK CUDINI 1. VERS.	1991
430013111	MERCEDES EVO2 SNOBECK LAFFITE 1. VERS.	1991
430013112	MERCEDES EVO2 SNOBECK CUDINI 2. VERS.	1991
430013113	MERCEDES EVO2 SNOBECK LAFFITE 2. VERS.	1991
430013120	MERCEDES EVO2 MS KAERCHER SCHMICKLER	1991
430013121	MERCEDES EVO2 MS KAERCHER V. OMMEN	1991
430013122	MERCEDES EVO2 MS-JET MASS NO. 24	1991
430013130	MERCEDES EVO2 AMG-WEST THIIM NO. 7	1991
430013131	MERCEDES EVO2 AMG-WEST LOHR NO. 78	1991
430013132	MERCEDES EVO2 AMG-EAST THIIM NO. 7	1991
430013133	MERCEDES EVO2 AMG-EAST LOHR NO. 78	1991
430013134	MERCEDES EVOII ANDORA	1991
430013140	MERCEDES EVO2 ZAKSPEED GIROIX 1. VERS.	1991
430013141	MERCEDES EVO2 ZAKSPEED ASCH 1. VERS.	1991
430013142	MERCEDES EVO2 ZAKSPEED GIR/SCHU 2.VERS	1991
430013143	MERCEDES EVO2 ZAKSPEED ASCH 2.VERS	1991
430013150	MERCEDES EVO2 BAS BERNHARD NO. 50	1991
430023120	MERCEDES EVO2 LAFFITTE/KAERCHER DTM 92	1992
430023121	MERCEDES EVO2 V. OMMEN/KAERCHER DTM 92	1992
430023130	MERCEDES EVO2 ELLEN LOHR DTM 92	1992
430023131	MERCEDES EVO2 K. ROSBERG DTM 92	1992
430023132	MERCEDES EVO2 E.LOHR BERLIN 2000 MAC92	1992
430023133	MERCEDES EVO2 E.LOHR/BERLIN 2000 MACAU 92	1992
430023140	MERCEDES EVO2 ASCH/ZAKSPEED DTM 92	1992
430023141	MERCEDES EVO2 THIIM/ZAKSPEED DTM 92	1992
430933101	MERCEDES EVO2 SCHNEIDER/AMG DTM 93	1993
430933102	MERCEDES EVO2 ASCH/AMG DTM 93	1993
430933110	MERCEDES EVO2 GRAU/DTM JUNIOR TEAM	1993
430933111	MERCEDES EVO2 AMTHOR/JUNIOR TEAM 93	1993
430933130	MERCEDES EVO2 BERLIN 2000 LUDWIG/A.	1993
430933131	MERCEDES EVO2 BERLIN 2000 LOHR/AMG	1993
430933140	MERCEDES EVO2 THIIM/ZAKSPEED DTM 93	1993
430933141	MERCEDES EVO2 V.OMMEN/ZAKSPEED 93	1993
430933150	MERCEDES EVO2 MANTHEY/PERSSON 93	1993
430933151	MERCEDES EVO2 O.MANTHEY DEKRA 93	1993
430933160	MERCEDES EVO2 ALZEN/PERSSON	1993
433023130	MERCEDES EVO2 ELLEN LOHR DTM 92	1992
430933201	MERCEDES EVO3 ASCH/SONAX DTM 93	1993
430933202	MERCEDES EVO3 SCHNEIDER/SONAX 93	1993
430933230	MERCEDES EVO3 LOHR/BERLIN 2000 93	1993
430933231	MERCEDES EVO3 LUDWIG/BERLIN 2000 93	1993
430933240	MERCEDES EVO3 THIIM/DIEBELS DTM 93	1993
430933241	MERCEDES EVO3 V.OMMEN/DIEBELS 93	1993
430943131	MERCEDES EVO3 BERNHARD/BAS DTM 94	1994
433032113	MERCEDES W 202, TYP C 200	1996
430038020	MERCEDES S-CLASS COUPE '99 GREY MET	
400031030	MERCEDES SL 2001 BLUE METALLIC	2001
400031031	MERCEDES SL 2001 BLACK	2001
403031033	MERCEDES SL CABRIO 2001 SILVER EXC	
403031034	MERCEDES SL CABRIO 01 OBSIDIAN EXC	
403031035	MERCEDES SL CABRIO 01 BRILL.SILVER	
403031036	MERCEDES SL CABRIO 01 BRILL.SILVER	
400031110	MERCEDES SPRINTER BREAK TURQUOISE	
400031160	MERCEDES SPRINTER VAN 2001 NOBIS	
403031113	MERCEDES SPRINTER BREAK PEARL BLUE	
403031163	MERCEDES SPRINTER VAN WHITE 2001	
403031164	MERCEDES SPRINTER VAN 'HERMES'	
403031213	MERCEDES SPRINTER BREAK 2002 SILVER	
403031214	MERCEDES SPRINTER BREAK 02 MATT GREEN	
403031263	MERCEDES SPRINTER VAN 2002 RED	
400031200	MERCEDES VANEO 2001 BLACK MET.	2001
403031203	MERCEDES VANEO '01 JASPIS BLUE	
430032200	MERCEDES W 123 LIM 200 D 1975-85 YELLOW	1975
430032201	MERCEDES W 123 LIM 230 E 1975-85 WHITE	1975
430032202	MERCEDES W 123 LIM 280 E 1975-85 SILVER	1975
430032210	MERCEDES W 123 BREAK 200 T 1975-85 RED	1975
430032211	MERCEDES W 123 BREAK 230 TE 75-85 SILVER	1975
430032212	MERCEDES W 123 BREAK 280 TE BLUE METALLIC	1975
430032220	MERCEDES W 123 COUPE 230 CE 1977-85 GOLD	1975
430032221	MERCEDES W 123 COUPE 280 C 1977-85 SILVER	1977
430032222	MERCEDES W 123 COUPE 280 CE BLUE METALLIC	1977
430032290	MERCEDES W 123 LIMOUSINE POLIZEI	1975
430032291	MERCEDES W 123 KOMBI POLIZEI	1975
430032295	MERCEDES W 123 LIMOUSINE TAXI	1975
430032296	MERCEDES W 123 KOMBI TAXI	1975
430003800	MERCEDES W 124 250 D TAXI	
432543018	MERCEDES W 196 GP FRANCE FANGIO 1.PL 54	1954
432543020	MERCEDES W 196 GP FRANCE K.KLING 1954	1954
432543022	MERCEDES W 196 GP FRANCE ST. MOSS 1954	1954
430032100	MERCEDES W 202 1993 C-CLASS GREEN M	1993
430032101	MERCEDES W 202 1993 ESPRIT RED	1993
430032102	MERCEDES W 202 1993 SPORT SILVER	1993
430032103	MERCEDES W 202 EXCLUSIV	1993
430032105	MERCEDES W 202 IAAF LTD. ED. 4444 PCS.	1993
430032160	MERCEDES W 202 1993 AMG BLUE BLACK	1993
430032161	MERCEDES W 202 1993 AMG YELLOW	1993
430032162	MERCEDES W 202 1993 AMG SILVER	1993
430943300	MERCEDES W 202 DTM KL.1 IAA 1993	1994
430943301	MERCEDES W 202 GR. A (MODIFY)	1994
433032106	MERCEDES W 202 EXCL. BRILL.SILVER/BLACK	1993
433032107	MERCEDES W 202 EXCL. IMPERIALROT	1993
433032163	MERCEDES W 202 1993 AMG SILVER	1993
433032203	MERCEDES W 123 SALOON NEW COLOUR	1975
433032213	MERCEDES W123 BREAK NEW COLOUR	1975
433032223	MERCEDES W 123 COUPE NEW COLOUR	1975
433943301	MERCEDES W 202 GR. A (MODIFY)	1994
430131030	MG B CABRIOLET 62/69 BLACK	1962
430131031	MG B CABRIOLET 62/69 RACING GREEN	1962
430131032	MG B CABRIOLET 62/69 RED	1962
430131040	MG B SOFTTOP 1962-69 CREAM	1962
430131041	MG B SOFTTOP 1962-69 RACING GREEN	1962
430131042	MG B SOFTTOP 1962-69 RED	1962
433131033	MG B CABRIOLET LUGG.RACK WHITE EXCL	1962
400010020	MINARDI EUROPEAN PS 01 F.ALONSO '01	2001
400010021	MINARDI EUROPEAN PS 01 T.MARQUES 01	2001
400010120	MINARDI EUROPEAN PS 01 A.YOONG '01	2001
400010121	MINARDI EUROPEAN PS 01 C.ALBERS '01	2001
400010220	MINARDI EUROPEAN PS 01 A.YOONG INDIAN.01	2001
400010221	MINARDI EUROPEAN PS 01 F.ALONSO INDIA.01	2001
400020072	MINARDI F1 A.YOONG LAUNCH VERS.2002	2002
400020073	MINARDI F1 M.WEBBER LAUNCH VERS.'02	2002
430990070	MINARDI F1 M.GENE PRES. 1999	1999
430990071	MINARDI F1 ITALIAN DRIVER PRES.1999	1999
430000020	MINARDI FONDMETAL M02 M.GENE 2000	2000
430000021	MINARDI FONDMETAL M02 MAZZACANE '00	2000
430010070	MINARDI F.ALONSO PRES. 2001	2001
430000071	MINARDI G.MAZZACANE PRES. 2000	2000
430000070	MINARDI M.GENE PRES. 2000	2000
430980022	MINARDI M 198 S.NAKANO 1998	1998
430980023	MINARDI M 198 E.TUERO 1998	1998
430990020	MINARDI M01 FORD ITALIAN DRIVER 99	1999
430990021	MINARDI M01 FORD M.GENE 99	1999
430010071	MINARDI T. MARQUES PRES. 2001	2001
430163370	MITSUBISHI PAJERO SWB BLUE MET	1991
430163371	MITSUBISHI PAJERO SWB GREEN MET	1991
430163372	MITSUBISHI PAJERO SWB RED MET	1991
430163470	MITSUBISHI PAJERO LWB BLUE MET	1991
430163471	MITSUBISHI PAJERO LWB BLACK	1991
430163472	MITSUBISHI PAJERO LWB RED MET	1991
433163473	MITSUBISHI PAJERO LWB 2800 TD RED	1991
433163474	MITSUBISHI PAJERO LWB 2800 TD BLUE	1991
433163763	MITSUBISHI PAJERO SWB HUNTER GREEN EXCL	
433163764	MITSUBISHI PAJERO SWB MARITIM BLUE EXCL.	
433163773	MITSUBISHI PAJERO LWB HUNTER GREEN EXCL	
433163774	MITSUBISHI PAJERO LWB MARITIM BLUE EXCL.	
430015200	NSU 1000 L 1964 BLUE	1964
430015201	NSU 1000 L 1964 RED	1964
430015202	NSU 1000 L 1964 DARK BLUE	
430015400	NSU RO 80 SALOON BLUE MET.	1967
430015401	NSU RO 80 SALOON TARGA ORANGE	
430015402	NSU RO 80 SALOON IBERIC RED	
430015404	NSU RO 80 SALOON SPANISH GREEN	
430015405	NSU RO 80 SALOON SILVER	
433015403	NSU RO 80 SALOON RALLY YELLOW	
433015404	NSU RO 80 SALOON BAHAMA BLUE MET.	
433015405	NSU RO 80 SALOON SAGUNTO BLUE MET.	1971
430019230	NSU SPIDER 1964-67 GEMINI BLUE MET.	
430019231	NSU SPIDER 1964-67 SILVER	
430019220	NSU SPORT PRINZ 1959-67 SILVER MET.	
430019221	NSU SPORT PRINZ '59-67 MUSCARI BLUE	
433019223	NSU SPORT PRINZ 1959-67 RED	
433019224	NSU SPORT PRINZ 1959-67 WHITE	
430015300	NSU TT SALOON 67/72 ORANGE	1967
430015301	NSU TT SALOON 67/72 SILVER	1967
430015302	NSU TT SALOON 67/72 BLUE MET.	1967
433019233	NSU WANKEL SPIDER 1964-67 RED	
433019234	NSU WANKEL SPIDER 1964-67 WHITE	
430145600	OLDSMOBILE AURORA IMSA GTS	
430145601	OLDSMOBILE AURORA IMSA GTS1 WINNER DAYT96	1996
430145605	OLDSMOBILE AURORA PEZZA/GOOD.. DAYT 96	1996
430046060	OPEL ADMIRAL SAL. '69-77 DARK BLUE	1969
430046061	OPEL ADMIRAL '69-77 ICELAND GREEN	
430049000	OPEL AGILA 2000 SILVER	
430049001	OPEL AGILA 2000 MAGMA RED	
433049003	OPEL AGILA 2000 KIWI GREEN EXCL.	
433049004	OPEL AGILA 2000 ARDEN BLUE EXCL.	
430049130	OPEL ASTRA CABRIO 2000 SILVER	
430049131	OPEL ASTRA CABRIO 2000 RED	
430049120	OPEL ASTRA COUPE 2000 BLUE	
430049121	OPEL ASTRA COUPE 2000 BLACK	
433049134	OPEL ASTRA CABRIO '00 BLACK EXCL.	
433049135	OPEL ASTRA CABRIOLET 2000 MIRAGE EXCL.	
433049133	OPEL CABRIOLET 2000 MIRAGE EXCL.	
430934101	OPEL CALIBRA K. ROSBERG DTM 1993	1993
430934102	OPEL CALIBRA M. REUTER DTM 1993	1993
430934103	OPEL CALIBRA -OPEL EXCLUSIV-	1993
430934105	OPEL CALIBRA DTM 94 REUTER/JOEST	1993
430934106	OPEL CALIBRA ROSBERG/JOEST DTM 94	1993
430934117	OPEL CALIBRA WINTER/JOEST DTM 94	1993
430944105	OPEL CALIBRA REUTER/JOEST DTM 94	1994
430944106	OPEL CALIBRA ROSBERG/JOEST DTM 94	1994
430944117	OPEL CALIBRA WINTER/JOEST DTM 94	1994
430954120	OPEL CALIBRA 94 JOEST J.LEHTO DTM95	1995
430954121	OPEL CALIBRA 94 JOEST AMORIM DTM 95	1995
430954190	OPEL CALIBRA TEAM ROSB. PRES. ROSB/LUDW.	1995
430954191	OPEL CALIBRA TEAM ROSB.PRES. LUDWIG	1995
430954192	OPEL CALIBRA TEAM ROSB.PRES.ROSBERG	1995
430954201	OPEL CALIBRA ROSBERG K.LUDWIG DTM95	1995
430954202	OPEL CALIBRA ROSBERG K.ROSBERG 95	1995
430954209	OPEL CALIBRA JOEST M.REUTER DTM 95	1995
430954210	OPEL CALIBRA JOEST Y.DALMAS DTM 95	1995
430954271	OPEL CALIBRA FRANCE K.LUDWIG DTM95	1995
430954272	OPEL CALIBRA FRANCE K.ROSBERG DTM95	1995
430954282	OPEL CALIBRA BYE BYE K.ROSBERG 4444	1995
430964213	OPEL CALIBRA GIUDICI/GIUDICI ITC 96	1996
430964216	OPEL CALIBRA ZAKSPEED ALZEN PRES.	1996
430964217	OPEL CALIBRA ZAKSPEED LUDWIG PRES.	1996
430964224	OPEL CALIBRA JOEST DALMAS ITC 96	1996
430964225	OPEL CALIBRA JOEST WURZ ITC 96	1996
430964243	OPEL CALIBRA ROSB MCDONALD LEHTO	1996
430964244	OPEL CALIBRA ROSB MCDONALD STUCK	1996
430964270	OPEL CALIBRA DESIGN VERSION STUCK	1996
430964271	OPEL CALIBRA CLIFF DESIGN ST. LEHTO	1996
430964307	OPEL CALIBRA JOEST REUTER ITC 96	1996
430964316	OPEL CALIBRA ZAKSPEED ALZEN ITC 96	1996
430964317	OPEL CALIBRA ZAKSPEED LUDWIG ITC 96	1996
430964323	OPEL CALIBRA MOTORSP.STRYCEK ITC 96	1996
430964325	OPEL CALIBRA TEAM JOEST WURZ ITC 96	1996
430964343	OPEL CALIBRA ROSBERG LEHTO ITC 96	1996
430964344	OPEL CALIBRA ROSBERG STUCK ITC 96	1996
430964374	OPEL CALIBRA M.SEKIYA ITC SUZUKA 96	1996
430964388	OPEL CALIBRA JOEST GAVIN ITC 96	1996
430994188	OPEL CALIBRA V.STRYCEK VEEDOL 1999	1999
430994300	OPEL CALIBRA V.STRYCEK NUERBGRG 99	1999
433964307	OPEL CALIBRA JOEST REUTER ITC 96	1996
400042000	OPEL COMBO BREAK 2002 BLUE	
400042070	OPEL COMBO VAN 2002 RED	
403042003	OPEL COMBO TOUR 2002 BREEZE BLUE	
403042004	OPEL COMBO TOUR GM AFTER SALES SILV	
403042073	OPEL COMBO VAN 2002 MAGMA RED	
403042074	OPEL COMBO VAN 2002 WHITE	
403042075	OPEL COMBO VAN GM AFTER S. YELLOW	
430046160	OPEL COMMODORE A 66/71 GREEN MET.	1966
430046161	OPEL COMMODORE A 66/71 DARK RED	
430040300	OPEL CORSA 2000 CITY RED	
430040301	OPEL CORSA 2000 STAR SILVER	
433040303	OPEL CORSA 2000 SPACE GREEN	
433040304	OPEL CORSA 2000 BREEZE BLUE	
433040305	OPEL CORSA 2000 PETROL BLUE EXCL.	
430049122	OPEL COUPE 2000 GREEN	
430049124	OPEL COUPE 2000 DARK RED METALLIC	
433049123	OPEL COUPE CAPRI YELLOW EXCL.	
433049124	OPEL COUPE STAR SILVER EXCL.	
430046070	OPEL DIPLOMAT 1968 BLACK	1969
430046071	OPEL DIPLOMAT 1968 WHITE	
433046073	OPEL DIPLOMAT B TEAM COLL. GOLD EX.	
433046074	OPEL DIPLOMAT B CAR COLL. RED EXCL.	
430043000	OPEL KADETT A LIM 1962/65 YELLOW	1962
430043001	OPEL KADETT A LIM 1962/65 BLUE GREY	1962
430043002	OPEL KADETT A LIM 1962/65 RED	1962
430043004	OPEL KADETT A SALOON 1962/65 IVORY	
430043005	OPEL KADETT A 62/65 ROYAL BLUE	
430043006	OPEL KADETT A 62/65 DARK RED	
430043010	OPEL KADETT A CARAVAN 1962/65 GREY	1962
430043011	OPEL KADETT A CARAVAN 1962/65 BLUE	1962
430043012	OPEL KADETT A CARAVAN 1962/65 WHITE	1962
430045600	OPEL KADETT C SALOON 73/77 BLUE	1973
430045601	OPEL KADETT C SALOON 73/77 RED	1973
430045602	OPEL KADETT C SALOON 73/77 ORANGE	
430045604	OPEL KADETT C SALOON 73/77 BABYBLUE	1973
430045605	OPEL KADETT C SWINGER YELLOW 1973	
430045610	OPEL KADETT C CARAVAN 73/77 CASHM.	1973
430045611	OPEL KADETT C CARAVAN 73/77 RED	1973
430045612	OPEL KADETT C CARAVAN 73/77 BLUE	
430045614	OPEL KADETT C CARAVAN 73/77DARK RED	
430045615	OPEL KADETT C CARAVAN 1973/77 GREEN	
430045619	OPEL KADETT C CARAVAN 73/77 WHITE	
430045620	OPEL KADETT C COUPE 73/77 GREEN	1973
430045621	OPEL KADETT C COUPE 73/77 RED	1973
430045622	OPEL KADETT C COUPE YELLOW/BLACK	1973
430045624	OPEL KADETT C COUPE YELLOW/BLACK	
430043300	OPEL KAPITAEN 1951/53 DARK RED	1951
433043303	OPEL KAPITAEN 1951/53 DARK BLUE	1951
430043301	OPEL KAPITAEN 1951/53 BLACK	1951
430043302	OPEL KAPITAEN 1951/53 GREY	1951
430043304	OPEL KAPITAEN 1951/53 SAVONA GREEN	
430043305	OPEL KAPITAEN 1951/53 IVORY	
430046000	OPEL KAPITAEN SALOON 1969-77 WHITE	1969
430046001	OPEL KAPITAEN 1969-77 BLACK	
430040000	OPEL KAPITAEN P2 SAL. '59-63 BLACK	
430040001	OPEL KAPITAEN P2 SAL. '59 TURQUOISE	
430040400	OPEL OLYMPIA SALOON 1952 BLACK	1952
430040401	OPEL OLYMPIA SALOON 1952 IRISH GREY	1952
430040430	OPEL OLYMPIA CABRIO 1952 BLUE GREY	
430040431	OPEL OLYMPIA CABRIO 1952 BEIGE	
433040433	OPEL OLYMPIA CABR. TEAM C.SAND GREY	
433040434	OPEL OLYMPIA CABR. CAR C.IRISH GREY	
430004000	OPEL OMEGA EVO STREET SILBER	
430004001	OPEL OMEGA EVO STREET BLACK MET.	
430004002	OPEL OMEGA EVO STREET ROT	
430014000	OPEL OMEGA 4000 WEISS OHNE DECALS	1991
430014001	OPEL OMEGA DTM 91 EGGENB/NIEDZWIEDZ	1991
430014002	OPEL OMEGA DTM 91 EGGENB/FERTE N.26	1991
430014010	OPEL OMEGA DTM 91 IRMSCHER/ENGSTLER	1991
430014011	OPEL OMEGA DTM 91 IRMSCHER/STRYCEK	1991
430014012	OPEL OMEGA EVO 3000 STRYCEK TESTCAR	1991
430014020	OPEL OMEGA DTM 91 SCHUEBEL/OBERNDF.	1991
430014030	OPEL OMEGA CRICKET SPA 1991	1991
430934012	OPEL OMEGA EVO 500 STRYCEK/KISSLING	1993
400041000	OPEL REKORD A SALOON 1963-65 SILVER	
400041001	OPEL REKORD A SALOON 1963-65 BLUE	
400041010	OPEL REKORD A BREAK 1962 RED	1962
400041011	OPEL REKORD A BREAK 1962 GREY	1962
400041020	OPEL REKORD A COUPE 1963 AEROBLUE	1963
400041021	OPEL REKORD A COUPE 1963 SILVER	1963
430046100	OPEL REKORD C 2D SALOON GREEN MET.	1966
430046101	OPEL REKORD C 2D SALOON GOLD	
430046102	OPEL REKORD C 2D SALOON LAGO BLUE	
430046104	OPEL REKORD C 2D SALOON COSMOS BLUE	
430046110	OPEL REKORD C BREAK 1966/71 WHITE	1966
430046111	OPEL REKORD C BREAK 1966/71 BLUE	
430046112	OPEL REKORD C BREAK 66/71 BEIGE	
430046114	OPEL REKORD C BREAK 66/71 SIR. BLUE	
430046120	OPEL REKORD C COUPE 1966/71 BLUE MT	1966
430046121	OPEL REKORD C COUPE 1966/71 SILVER	
430046122	OPEL REKORD C COUPE 66/71 BRONCE M.	
430046124	OPEL REKORD C COUPE 66/71 CARDI.RED	
433040223	OPEL REKORD COUPE 61-62 WHITE/GREEN	
433040224	OPEL REKORD COUPE 61-62 RED/BLACK	
430043200	OPEL REKORD P1 LIM 1958 GREEN	1958
430043201	OPEL REKORD P1 LIM 1958 BLAU	1958
430043202	OPEL REKORD P1 LIM 1958 GRAU	1958
430043204	OPEL REKORD P1 LIM 1958 RED/WHITE	1958
430043205	OPEL REKORD P1 LIM 1958 BLACK/WHITE	1958
430043206	OPEL REKORD P1 LIM 1958 BLUE/WHITE	
430043207	OPEL REKORD P1 SAL.1958 BROWN/WHITE	1958
430043208	OPEL REKORD P1 SAL.1958 DARK BLUE	1958
430043209	OPEL REKORD P1 SAL.58 BERMUDA GREEN	
430043210	OPEL REKORD P1 CARAVAN YELLOW	1958
430043211	OPEL REKORD P1 CARAVAN BLUE	1958
430043212	OPEL REKORD P1 CARAVAN RED	1958
430043214	OPEL REKORD P1 CARAVAN BLUE/WHITE	1958
430043215	OPEL REKORD P1 CARAVAN GREY/WHITE	
430043216	OPEL REKORD P1 CARAVAN CLASSICWHITE	1958
430043217	OPEL REKORD P1 CARAVAN ROYAL BLUE	
430043218	OPEL REKORD P1 CARAVAN BURGUNDY RED	
430043260	OPEL REKORD P1 SALOON '58 TURQUOISE	
433043213	OPEL REKORD P1 CARAVAN POST	1958
430040200	OPEL REKORD P2 1960 WHITE/BLUE	
430040201	OPEL REKORD P2 SALOON RED/GREY	
430040210	OPEL REKORD P2 CARAVAN 1960 GREY	
430040211	OPEL REKORD P2 CARAVAN 1960 WHITE	
430040220	OPEL REKORD P2 COUPE 60-62 SILVER	
430040221	OPEL REKORD P2 COUPE 60-62 WHITE	
430964280	OPEL TEAM ROSBERG DESIGN ST. STUCK	1996
430964281	OPEL TEAM ROSBERG DESIGN ST. LEHTO	1996
400014103	OPEL V8 HOLZER J.WINKELHOCK DTM 01	2001
400014104	OPEL V8 HOLZER T.SCHEIDER DTM 01	2001
400014107	OPEL V8 PHOENIX M.REUTER DTM 01	2001
400014111	OPEL V8 HOLZER M.BARTELS DTM 01	2001
400014116	OPEL V8 EUROTEAM A.MENU DTM 01	2001
400014190	OPEL V8 DTM '01 TEST STRYCEK W.FIG.	2001
400014808	OPEL V8 PHOENIX Y.OLIVIER DTM 01	2001
400014817	OPEL V8 EUROTEAM H.HAUPT DTM 01	2001
400014820	OPEL V8 MAMEROW P.MAMEROW DTM 01	2001
400014897	OPEL V8 PHOENIX B.SCHNEIDER DTM 01	2001
430004803	OPEL V8 HOLZER U.ALZEN DTM 2000	2000
430004804	OPEL V8 HOLZER WINKELHOCK DTM 2000	2000
430004807	OPEL V8 PHOENIX M.REUTER DTM 2000	2000
430004808	OPEL V8 PHOENIX M.BARTELS DTM 2000	2000
430004811	OPEL V8 HOLZER E.HELARY DTM 2000	2000
430004812	OPEL V8 IRMSCHER C.MENZEL DTM 2000	2000
430004816	OPEL V8 EUROTEAM S.MODENA DTM 2000	2000
430004817	OPEL V8 HOLZER T.SCHEIDER DTM 2000	2000
430004890	OPEL V8 DTM '00 TEST STRYCEK W.FIG.	2000
433004812	OPEL V8 IRMSCHER C.MENZEL DTM 2000	
433004882	OPEL V8 IRMSCHER C.MENZEL DTM 2000	

158 MINICHAMPS

ITEM-No	ITEM	YEAR
433994820	OPEL VECTRA R.ASCH/IRMSCHER STW '99	1999
433994870	OPEL VECTRA R.ASCH/IRMSCHER STW '99	1999
430040510	OPEL VIVARO BREAK 2001	2001
430040511	OPEL VIVARO BREAK 2001	2001
430040560	OPEL VIVARO DELIVERY VAN 2001	2001
430040561	OPEL VIVARO DELIVERY VAN 2001	2001
433040513	OPEL VIVARO BREAK 2001 STAR SILVER	
433040514	OPEL VIVARO BREAK 2001 SPACE GREEN	
433040563	OPEL VIVARO VAN 2001 MAGMA RED EXCL	
433040564	OPEL VIVARO VAN 2001 INK BLUE EXCL.	
433040565	OPEL VIVARO VAN STAR SILVER	
430048000	OPEL ZAFIRA 1999 PREMIUM BLUE	
430048001	OPEL ZAFIRA 1999 MAGMA RED	
430048002	OPEL ZAFIRA 1999 SILVER	
430048004	OPEL ZAFIRA 1999 GREEN	
433048003	OPEL ZAFIRA 1999 MIRAGE	
433048004	OPEL ZAFIRA 1999 MIDNIGHT BLACK	
433048005	OPEL ZAFIRA 1999 BLUE MET. EXCL.	
433008822	PANOZ LMP 2000 TSUCHIYA DRAGON	
AC4008811	PANOZ LMP BRABHAM 16TH LM '00	2000
AC4008823	PANOZ LMP DRAGON SUZUKI 6TH LM '00	2000
AC4008812	PANOZ LMP KATOH/O'CONNELL 5. LM '00	2000
AC4028800	PANOZ LMP-1 JACKSON/.. SEBRING 2002	2002
AC4978952	PANOZ ESPERANTE GTR BERNARD LM '97	
AC4978954	PANOZ ESPERANTE GTR WEAVER/. LM '97	1997
AC4978955	PANOZ ESPERANTE GTR BRABHAM LM '97	1997
AC4998811	PANOZ LMP O'CONNELL LM '99	
AC4998812	PANOZ LMP BRABHAM LM '99	
540924304	PENSKE 1992 AYRTON SENNA	1992
520934304	PENSKE 93 CHEVY NR.4 E.FITTIPALDI	1993
520934404	PENSKE 93 CHEVY NR.4 E.FITTIPALDI	1993
520934412	PENSKE 93 CHEVY NR.12 P.TRACY	1993
520944416	PENSKE PC22 BETTENH. NO.16 S.JOHANS	1994
520944331	PENSKE PC23 MARLBORO NO.31 A.UNSER	1994
520944602	PENSKE PC23 MERCEDES NO.2 E.FITTIP.	1994
520944603	PENSKE PC23 MERCEDES NO.3 P.TRACY	1994
520944631	PENSKE PC23 MERCEDES NO.31 A.UNSER	1994
523944631	PENSKE PC23 MERCEDES NO.31 A.UNSER	1994
430112531	PEUGEOT 306 CABRIOLET 1995 BLACK	1995
430112532	PEUGEOT 306 CABRIOLET 1995 RED	1995
430112830	PEUGEOT 306 CABRIO 98 RED METALLIC	
430112831	PEUGEOT 306 CABRIO 98 BLUE METALLIC	
430112500	PEUGEOT 306 2-DOOR SAL. 95 GREEN M.	1995
430112502	PEUGEOT 306 2-DOOR SALOON 1995 RED	1995
430112800	PEUGEOT 306 2-DOOR 1998 SILVER	
430112801	PEUGEOT 306 2-DOOR 1998 RED MET.	
430112570	PEUGEOT 306 4-DOOR SALOON 95 GREY M	1995
430112571	PEUGEOT 306 4-DOOR SALOON 95 BLUE M	1995
430112870	PEUGEOT 306 4-DOOR 98 GOLD METALLIC	
430112871	PEUGEOT 306 4-DOOR 98 BLUE METALLIC	
433112890	PEUGEOT 306 4-DOOR 98 GENDARMERIE	
433112891	PEUGEOT 306 4-DOOR POLICE	
430112620	PEUGEOT 406 COUPE 1996 LUCIFER RED	1996
430112621	PEUGEOT 406 COUPE 1996 BLUE MET	1996
430112622	PEUGEOT 406 COUPE 1996 SILVER MET	
430112624	PEUGEOT 406 COUPE 1996 GREEN MET	1996
430112625	PEUGEOT 406 COUPE 1996 ECARLAT RED	
430112626	PEUGEOT 406 COUPE 1996 COSMOS GREY	
430971109	PEUGEOT 406 ESSO J.V.OMMEN STW 97	1997
430971110	PEUGEOT 406 ESSO L.AIELLO STW 97	1997
430981201	PEUGEOT 406 PEUGEOT/AIELLO STW 98	1998
430981202	PEUGEOT 406 PEUGEOT/V.OMMEN STW 98	1998
433112622	PEUGEOT 406 COUPE 1996 SILVER MET	
400112120	PEUGEOT 504 COUPE 1974 GREEN MET.	1974
400112121	PEUGEOT 504 COUPE 1974 RED	1974
400112130	PEUGEOT 504 CABRIOLET 1974 BLACK	1974
400112131	PEUGEOT 504 CABRIOLET '74 COPPER MT	1974
433516746	PORSCHE 356 LIGHT METAL COUPE 1951	1951
430065530	PORSCHE 356 A SPEEDSTER 1956 BLACK	1956
430065531	PORSCHE 356 A SPEEDSTER 1956 IVORY	1956
430065532	PORSCHE 356 A SPEEDSTER 1956 RED	
430065534	PORSCHE 356 A SPEEDSTER 1956 GREEN	
430065535	PORSCHE 356 A SPEEDSTER 1956 YELLOW	
430065536	PORSCHE 356 A SPEEDST.56 TERRACOTTA	
433065533	PORSCHE 356 A SPEEDSTER EXCL.	1956
430062361	PORSCHE 356 C CARRERA 2 BLACK	1963
430062362	PORSCHE 356 C CARRERA 2 RED	1963
430062330	PORSCHE 356 C CABRIOLET SILVER	1963
430062332	PORSCHE 356 C CABRIOLET RED	1963
430062334	PORSCHE 356 C CABRIOLET 1965 BLUE	
430062335	PORSCHE 356 C CABRIOLET 1965 BLACK	
430062336	PORSCHE 356 C CABRIOLET 1965 BLUE	
430062320	PORSCHE 356 C COUPE DARK BLUE	1963
430062321	PORSCHE 356 C COUPE SILVER	1963
430062322	PORSCHE 356 C COUPE 1965 RED	1963
430062324	PORSCHE 356 C COUPE 1965 GREEN	
430062325	PORSCHE 356 C COUPE 1965 IVORY	
430060333	PORSCHE 356 D CABRIOLET SILVER	
433566628	PORSCHE 550 A STOREZ/POLENSKY LM 56	
430066033	PORSCHE 550 SPIDER EXCL.	
433606542	PORSCHE 718 RS 60 WINNER SEBRING 60	
433596503	PORSCHE 718 RS 60 1959 EXCL.	1959
433067123	PORSCHE 911 1964 SILVER/RED EXCL.	1964
433067124	PORSCHE 911 1964 YELLOW	1964
430067120	PORSCHE 911 1964 WHITE	1964
433067121	PORSCHE 911 1964 RED	1964
433067122	PORSCHE 911 1964 CONDA GREEN	
433067124	PORSCHE 911 1964 YELLOW	
433067126	PORSCHE 911 1964 BLUE	
433067127	PORSCHE 911 1964 GREEN	
433067129	PORSCHE 911 1964 PURPLE	
433067127	PORSCHE 911 1964 SILVER POLISHED	
433062023	PORSCHE 911 1974/89 SILVER/RED EXCL	1974
433062123	PORSCHE 911 1989/93 SILVER/RED EXCL	1989
433946109	PORSCHE 911 1994 NIEDZWIEDZ ADAC-C.	1994
400061070	PORSCHE 911 4S 2001 BLACK	2001
400061071	PORSCHE 911 4S 2001 YELLOW	2001
433062033	PORSCHE 911 CARR CABRIO 74/89 EXCL.	1974
433062121	PORSCHE 911 C. 2/4 1992 ANTHRACITE	1992
433062122	PORSCHE 911 C. 2/4 1992 LILA MET.	1992
433736926	PORSCHE 911 C. RSR MARTINI DIJON'73	
433736959	PORSCHE 911 C. RSR BRUMOS DAYTONA73	
433736999	PORSCHE 911 C. RSR HELMICK SEBRING73	
400061030	PORSCHE 911 CABRIOLET '01 BLUE MET.	2001
400061031	PORSCHE 911 CABRIOLET '01 BLACK	2001
430065100	PORSCHE 911 CARRERA RS 1995 YELLOW	1995
430065101	PORSCHE 911 CARRERA RS 1995 BLACK	1995
430065102	PORSCHE 911 CARRERA RS 1995 RED	1995
430746910	PORSCHE 911 CARRERA RSR LIENHARD 74	1974
430062120	PORSCHE 911 CARRERA 2/4 1992 YELLOW	1992
403061023	PORSCHE 911 CARRERA COUPE SILVER	
403061024	PORSCHE 911 CARRERA COUPE BLUE MET.	
403061025	PORSCHE 911 CARRERA 4 COUPE GREEN M	
403061026	PORSCHE 911 CARRERA 4 COUPE BLACK	
430062030	PORSCHE 911 CARRERA CABRIO 74-89 WHITE	1974
430062031	PORSCHE 911 CARRERA CABRIO 1983 RED	
430062032	PORSCHE 911 CARRERA CABRIO 83 BLUE MET	
403061033	PORSCHE 911 CARRERA CABRIO MERIDIAN	
403061034	PORSCHE 911 CARRERA CABRIO ORANGE	
433063035	PORSCHE 911 CARRERA CABRIO 993 EXCL	1994
433067333	PORSCHE 911 CARRERA 2 CABRIO 964 EXCL.	
403061035	PORSCHE 911 CARRERA 4 CABRIO SILVER	
403061036	PORSCHE 911 CARRERA 4 CABR.BLACK MT	
403061073	PORSCHE 911 CARRERA 4S BLACK MET	
403061074	PORSCHE 911 CARRERA 4S SEAL GREY MT	
430061363	PORSCHE 911 CARRERA TARGA 1990	
430736900	PORSCHE 911 CARRERA RSR 73 WHITE/RED	1973
430736901	PORSCHE 911 CARRERA RSR 73 BLACK/RED	
433736903	PORSCHE 911 CARRERA RSR 73 BLACK/RED	
433736904	PORSCHE 911 CARRERA RSR 73 MAGENTA/BLK	
430063030	PORSCHE 911 CABRIO 1994 SILVER	1994
430063031	PORSCHE 911 CABRIO 1994 BLACK	1994
430063032	PORSCHE 911 CABRIO 1994 RED	1994
430063034	PORSCHE 911 CABRIO 1994 ARENA RED	1994
430063040	PORSCHE 911 CABRIO SOFTTOP GREEN	1994
430063041	PORSCHE 911 CABRIO SOFTTOP BLUE	1994
430063042	PORSCHE 911 CABRIO SOFTTOP RED	1994
433063007	PORSCHE 911 COUPE 1993 RED	1993
430063008	PORSCHE 911 COUPE 1993 BLUE	1993
400061020	PORSCHE 911 COUPE 2001 GREY MET.	2001
400061021	PORSCHE 911 COUPE 2001 BLUE MET.	2001
430062020	PORSCHE 911 COUPE 1978/88 RED	1978
430062021	PORSCHE 911 COUPE 1978/88 WHITE	1978
430062022	PORSCHE 911 COUPE 1978/88 BLACK	1978
433996922	PORSCHE 911 COUCERIO S.CUP '99	
433976501	PORSCHE 911 CUP BRAUN MUELLER	
433976502	PORSCHE 911 CUP BRAUN BASSENG	
400016801	PORSCHE 911 GT1 SCHUMACHER/.DAYT'01	2001
400016876	PORSCHE 911 GT1 JEANNETTE/. DAYT'01	2001
400026800	PORSCHE 911 GT1 BYTZEK DAYTONA 2002	2002
430966625	PORSCHE 911 GT1 STUCK LE MANS 1996	1996
430966626	PORSCHE 911 GT1 DALMAS LM 1996	1996
430976601	PORSCHE 911 GT1 EXXON GTS-1 GT 97	
430976606	PORSCHE 911 GT1 AG STUCK/B. FIA 97	1997
430976627	PORSCHE 911 GT1 BMS/ITALIA LM 1997	1997
430976628	PORSCHE 911 GT1 KONRAD MSP LM 1997	1997
430976629	PORSCHE 911 GT1 JB RACING LM 1997	1997
430976630	PORSCHE 911 GT1 FIA GT BLUE CORAL 97	
430976632	PORSCHE 911 GT1 ROCK RACING LM 1997	1997
430976633	PORSCHE 911 GT1 SCHUEBEL LM 1997	1997
430976825	PORSCHE 911 GT1 AG HJ STUCK LM 1997	1997
430976826	PORSCHE 911 GT1 AG DALMAS LM 1997	1997
433986801	PORSCHE 911 GT1 ROHR 2ND DAYTONA 98	
433966600	PORSCHE 911 GT1 1996	1996
433966603	PORSCHE 911 GT1 BLUE METALLIC EXCL	1996
433966625	PORSCHE 911 GT1 STUCK LE MANS 1996	1996
433966626	PORSCHE 911 GT1 DALMAS LM 1996	1996
433976800	PORSCHE 911 GT1 LE MANS 1997	1997
433986925	PORSCHE 911 GT1 LE MANS WHITE	
433986926	PORSCHE 911 GT1 WINNER LE MANS 1998	
433986999	PORSCHE 911 GT1 98 W/O REAR SPOILER	
430986838	PORSCHE 911 GT1 TEAM CHAMP DAYT. 98	
430986925	PORSCHE 911 GT1 2ND LE MANS 1998	
430986926	PORSCHE 911 GT1 WINNER LE MANS 1998	
430060120	PORSCHE 911 GT2 2001 RED	2001
430060121	PORSCHE 911 GT2 2001 SPEED YELLOW	2001
433065003	PORSCHE 911 GT2 STREET YELLOW EXCL	1995
430065000	PORSCHE 911 GT2 STREET 1995 WHITE	1995
430065001	PORSCHE 911 GT2 STREET 1995 BLUE	1995
430065002	PORSCHE 911 GT2 STREET 1995 RED	1995
430966774	PORSCHE 911 GT2 STUCK DAYTONA 1996	1996
430976773	PORSCHE 911 GT2 EVO ROOK BREY.LM 97	1997
430976774	PORSCHE 911 GT2 EVO ROOK AHRL.LM 97	1997
430976777	PORSCHE 911 GT2 EVO CHEREAU LM 97	1997
430976778	PORSCHE 911 GT2 WINNER GT2 LM 97	1997
430976779	PORSCHE 911 GT2 EVO KONRAD MSP LM97	1997
430976784	PORSCHE 911 GT2 EVO STADLER LM 97	1997
430986760	PORSCHE 911 GT2 PLAYSTATION LM 98	
430986765	PORSCHE 911 GT2 ROOCK LM 98	
430986768	PORSCHE 911 GT2 ELF HABERTHUR LM 98	
430986797	PORSCHE 911 GT2 1ST 24H DAYTONA 98	
430996761	PORSCHE 911 GT2 FREISINGER 1999	
430996767	PORSCHE 911 GT2 LARBRE/JARIER 1999	
433060123	PORSCHE 911 GT2 2000 ARTIS SILVER	2000
433956595	PORSCHE 911 GT2 RACING EXCL.	1995
430068004	PORSCHE 911 GT3 DIAMOND BLACK MET.	
430068005	PORSCHE 911 GT3 GREEN	
430068006	PORSCHE 911 GT3 GOLD	
400016931	PORSCHE 911 GT3 R LUHR/.. DAYT. '01	2001
433068003	PORSCHE 911 GT3 INDIA RED	
400016943	PORSCHE 911 GT3 R BARON/. DAYT. '01	2001
400016957	PORSCHE 911 GT3 R BUTTIERO DAYT.'01	2001
400016974	PORSCHE 911 GT3-R ALPHAND LM 2001	
400016976	PORSCHE 911 GT3-RS JEANN.DAYTONA'01	
400016977	PORSCHE 911 GT3-RS JEANNETTE LM '01	
400016983	PORSCHE 911 GT3-RS G.ROSA LM 2001	
400026907	PORSCHE 911 GT3 RWS DAYTONA 2002	2002
400026944	PORSCHE 911 GT3 ORBIT DAYTONA 2002	2002
400026966	PORSCHE 911 GT3 RACERS GR DAYT. '02	2002
403016901	PORSCHE 911 GT3 BERNHARD SUP.CUP 01	
403016911	PORSCHE 911 GT3 C.MENZEL SUP.CUP 01	
403026900	PORSCHE 911 GT3 OECHER BEND 2002	
403026981	PORSCHE 911 GT3-RS LE MANS 24H 2002	
433006907	PORSCHE 911 GT3 R QUESTER DAYT. '00	
433006959	PORSCHE 911 GT3 R BARTH DAYTONA '00	
430006972	PORSCHE 911 GT3 R REPSOL/SAL. LM'00	2000
430006975	PORSCHE 911 GT3 R CHAMPION DAYT.'00	
430006978	PORSCHE 911 GT3 R NOEL/LARIB. LM'00	2000
430006979	PORSCHE 911 GT3 R PERSPECTIVE LM'00	2000
433986991	PORSCHE 911 GT3 CUP VERSION 1998	
433996905	PORSCHE 911 GT3 KAERCHER-MATHAI 99	
433006900	PORSCHE 911 GT3 R WHITE	
433006901	PORSCHE 911 GT3 CUP 2000	
433006912	PORSCHE 911 GT3 DAVISON NO. 12 2000	
433006981	PORSCHE 911 GT3 R WHITE NO.81	
433006983	PORSCHE 911 GT3 R 2000	
430956502	PORSCHE 911 H.GROHS 1. P-CUP 1995	1995
430956524	PORSCHE 911 J.P.MALCHER 1.S-CUP '95	1995
430986996	PORSCHE 911 NO.26 MOWLEM S-CUP98	1998
430946300	PORSCHE 911 PRES. IAA 1993 CUP 94	1994
433946300	PORSCHE 911 PRES. IAA 1993 CUP 94	1994
430986910	PORSCHE 911 P.HUISMAN S-CUP CHAMP98	1998
433736908	PORSCHE 911 RSR 1973	
433746945	PORSCHE 911 RSR 1974	
433956502	PORSCHE 911 RS CUP 1995	
433065103	PORSCHE 911 RS STREET RIVIERA BLUE	1995
430061263	PORSCHE 911 SC TARGA 1977	
403786214	PORSCHE 911 SC SAFARI RALLYE 1978	
430066130	PORSCHE 911 SPEEDSTER 1988 RED	1988
433066133	PORSCHE 911 SPEEDSTER EXCL.	1988
403686710	PORSCHE 911 T RALLYE MC 1968	
400061060	PORSCHE 911 TARGA 2001 RED	
400061061	PORSCHE 911 TARGA 2001 BLACK	
400061160	PORSCHE 911 TARGA 1965 RED	
400061161	PORSCHE 911 TARGA 1965 ORANGE	
400061260	PORSCHE 911 TARGA 1977 BLUE	
400061261	PORSCHE 911 TARGA 1977 GREEN MET.	
430061360	PORSCHE 911 TARGA 1990 BLACK	
400061361	PORSCHE 911 TARGA 1990 TURQUOISE	
403061063	PORSCHE 911 TARGA 2001 RED METALLIC	
403061064	PORSCHE 911 TARGA 2001 SILVER MET.	
433063065	PORSCHE 911 TARGA 1996	
403061065	PORSCHE 911 TARGA 2001	
403061163	PORSCHE 911 TARGA 1965	
403061164	PORSCHE 911 TARGA '65 SILV.POLISHED	
430063060	PORSCHE 911 TARGA 1995 GREEN MET.	1995
430063061	PORSCHE 911 TARGA 1995 RED	1995
430063062	PORSCHE 911 TARGA 1995 BLACK MET.	1995
430069000	PORSCHE 911 TURBO 1977 RED	
430069001	PORSCHE 911 TURBO 77 DARK GREEN MET	1977
430069002	PORSCHE 911 TURBO 77 G.P. WHITE	
430069004	PORSCHE 911 TURBO 77 METEOR MET.	
430069005	PORSCHE 911 TURBO 77 LIGHT GREEN MT	
430069100	PORSCHE 911 TURBO 1990 BLUE MET.	
430069101	PORSCHE 911 TURBO 1990 BLACK	1990
430069102	PORSCHE 911 TURBO 1990 TURQUOISE M.	
430069104	PORSCHE 911 TURBO 1990 INDIA RED	
430069105	PORSCHE 911 TURBO 1990 GREEN	
430069106	PORSCHE 911 TURBO 1990 RED MET.	
430069200	PORSCHE 911 TURBO 1995 BLACK	
430069201	PORSCHE 911 TURBO 1995 SPEED YELLOW	1995
430069202	PORSCHE 911 TURBO '95 FIR GREEN MET	
430069204	PORSCHE 911 TURBO '95 RIVIERA BLUE	
430069205	PORSCHE 911 TURBO '95 RED	
430069206	PORSCHE 911 TURBO 1995 TURQUOISE	
430069300	PORSCHE 911 TURBO '99 RED METALLIC	
430069301	PORSCHE 911 TURBO'99 BLUE METALLIC	1999
430069302	PORSCHE 911 TURBO'99 FROSTY BLUE	
430069304	PORSCHE 911 TURBO'99 RED	
430069305	PORSCHE 911 TURBO'99 PURPLE MET.	
430069306	PORSCHE 911 TURBO 2000 RED	
433069003	PORSCHE 911 TURBO 1977 SILVER	
433069103	PORSCHE 911 TURBO 1990 SILVER	
433069203	PORSCHE 911 TURBO 1995 SILVER	
433069303	PORSCHE 911 TURBO 1999 SILVER	
433069304	PORSCHE 911 TURBO 99 LAPIS BLUE MET	
433069305	PORSCHE 911 TURBO 1999 SPEED YELLOW	
430956501	PORSCHE 911 VIP-CAR P-SUPERCUP 1995	1995
433966501	PORSCHE 911 VIP-CAR P-SUPERCUP 1996	1996
430065660	PORSCHE 914 1969/73 YELLOW	1969
430065661	PORSCHE 914 1969/73 ORANGE	1969
430065662	PORSCHE 914 1969/73 GREEN	1969
430065664	PORSCHE 914 1969/73 SILVER MET.	
430065665	PORSCHE 914 1969/73 RED	
430065666	PORSCHE 914 1969/73 BLACK	
430065650	PORSCHE 914 HARDTOP 69/73 BLUE MET.	
433706723	PORSCHE 917 K 1970	1970
430706701	PORSCHE 917 K GULF DAYTONA 1970	
430706702	PORSCHE 917 K GULF WINNER DAYTONA 70	1970
430706703	PORSCHE 917 KH MARTINI 1ST SEBR. 70	
430706712	PORSCHE 917 K J.NEUHAUS 1970	
430706793	PORSCHE 917 K AUSTR. ELFORD/A.DAYT70	
433716721	PORSCHE 917 L 1971	1971
430716717	PORSCHE 917 L GULF SIFFERT/BELL 71	1971
430716718	PORSCHE 917 L GULF RODRIGUEZ/. LM71	1971
430716721	PORSCHE 917 LH LE MANS TRIALS 1971	1971
430716923	PORSCHE 917 PINK PIG JOEST/K. 1971	1971
436736006	PORSCHE 917/30 SUNOCO 1973	
433786701	PORSCHE 935 MOBY DICK 1978	1978
430816766	PORSCHE 935 MOBY DICK JOEST DRM 81	1981
433776704	PORSCHE 936 SPIDER 1977	1977
430776707	PORSCHE 936 3RD PLACE LE MANS 1978	1978
430786905	PORSCHE 936/78 MARTINI LM 78 ICKX	
430786906	PORSCHE 936/78 MARTINI LM 78 BARTH	
430796912	PORSCHE 936/78 ESSEX LM 79 ICKX	
430796914	PORSCHE 936/78 ESSEX LM 79 WOLLEK	
430816911	PORSCHE 936/81 JULES LM 81 ICKX	
430816912	PORSCHE 936/81 JULES LM 81 MAAS	
433826501	PORSCHE 956 L ICKX/BELL 1.LM 1982	1982
430826501	PORSCHE 956 L ICKX/BELL 1.LM 1982	1982
430836503	PORSCHE 956 L SCHUPPAN/H/H 1.LM 1983	1983
430836516	PORSCHE 956 LH SKOAL 5TH LE MANS 83	1983
430836601	PORSCHE 956 K WARSTEINER WOLLEK 1983	1983
430836602	PORSCHE 956 K BELL/BELLOF 1.NBRG. 83	1983
430836608	PORSCHE 956 K WOLLEK/JOHANSS. 1983	1983
430836612	PORSCHE 956 K BOSS ROSBERG 1983	1983
430836614	PORSCHE 956 K ROSBERG/L./P. NBGRG 83	1983
430846507	PORSCHE 956 L LUDWIG/PESC. 1.LM 1984	1984
430846547	PORSCHE 956 L BOSS 1984	1984
430846601	PORSCHE 956 K ICKX/MASS 1. NBGRG '84	1984
430846610	PORSCHE 956 K WINKELH 1.NORISRING 84	1984
430846691	PORSCHE 956 KH JAEGERM. NORISR. 84	1984
430856507	PORSCHE 956 L LUDWIG/W./B 1.LM 1985	1985
430856619	PORSCHE 956 K BELLOF/BOUTSEN 1985	1985
540844307	PORSCHE 956 K 1984 AYRTON SENNA	1984
430866508	PORSCHE 956 L STARS+STRIPES 1986	1986
403866286	PORSCHE 959 GR.B PARIS-DAKAR 1986	
433063004	PORSCHE 993 WAP020001 BLUE MET.EXCL	1993
430946305	PORSCHE 993 U.ALZEN SUPER CUP 94	1994
430946306	PORSCHE 993 H.HAUPT SUPER CUP 94	1994
430946310	PORSCHE 993 L.BRYNER SUPER CUP 94	1994
430946317	PORSCHE 993 D.DUPUY SUPER CUP 94	1994
430946319	PORSCHE 993 JP.JARRIER SUPER CUP 94	1994
430946324	PORSCHE 993 JP.MALCHER SUPER CUP 94	1994
430063000	PORSCHE 993 COUPE 1993 SCHWARZ	1993
430063001	PORSCHE 993 COUPE 1993 ROT METALLIC	1993
430063002	PORSCHE 993 COUPE 1993 MINT GRUEN	1993
430063003	PORSCHE 993 COUPE EXCL.	1993
433063003	PORSCHE 993 COUPE SILVER/GREY EXCL.	1993
433063004	PORSCHE 993 WAP020001 BLUE MET.EXCL	1993
433063005	PORSCHE 993 SILVER/RED EXCLUSIV	1993
433063033	PORSCHE 993 CABRIOLET EXCLUSIV	1994
433063063	PORSCHE 993 TARGA EXCL. POR. ORANGE	1995
433063064	PORSCHE 993 TARGA BLUE-TURQUOISE	1995
403062033	PORSCHE BOXSTER 2002 BLACK	
403062034	PORSCHE BOXSTER 2002 SPEED YELLOW	
403062073	PORSCHE BOXSTER S '02 MERIDIAN MET.	
403062074	PORSCHE BOXSTER S '02 LAPIS BLUE	
430063130	PORSCHE BOXSTER 1993 SILVER	1993
430063131	PORSCHE BOXSTER 1993 DUNKELBLAU MET	1993
430063132	PORSCHE BOXSTER 1993 ROT	1993
430063133	PORSCHE BOXSTER 1993 EXCL.	1993
433063130	PORSCHE BOXSTER 1993 SILVER	1993
433063133	PORSCHE BOXSTER 1993 EXCL.	1993
430068030	PORSCHE BOXSTER S 1999 SILVER	
430068031	PORSCHE BOXSTER S 99 OCEAN BLUE MET	
430068032	PORSCHE BOXSTER S 1999 RED	
430068034	PORSCHE BOXSTER S 1999 BLUE	
433068033	PORSCHE BOXSTER S 99 BLACK METALLIC	
433068034	PORSCHE BOXSTER S 1999 WHITE	
400061080	PORSCHE CAYENNE TURBO 2002 BLACK MT	
400061081	PORSCHE CAYENNE TURBO 2002 BEIGE MT	
400061000	PORSCHE CAYENNE S 2002 BLUE MET.	
400061001	PORSCHE CAYENNE S 2002 BLACK MET.	
403061003	PORSCHE CAYENNE S'02 LAGO GREEN MET	
403061004	PORSCHE CAYENNE S '02 LAPIS BLUE MT	
403061083	PORSCHE CAYENNE TURBO 2002 RED MET.	
403061084	PORSCHE CAYENNE TURBO '02 TITAN MET	
403061085	PORSCHE CAYENNE TURBO F.OFFROAD-SET	
403061086	PORSCHE CAYENNE TURBO CHROMED	
433946008	PORSCHE CARRERA 2 NO. 8 D.PFEIL CUP 94	1994
430946001	PORSCHE CARRERA 2 NO. 1 W.LAND CUP 94	1994
430946003	PORSCHE CARRERA 2 NO. 3 MAYLAENDER 94	1994
430946007	PORSCHE CARRERA 2 NO. 7 MATCHULL 94	1994
430946016	PORSCHE CARRERA 2 NO.16 KAMPS CUP 94	1994
430946024	PORSCHE CARRERA 2 NO.24 J.V.GARTZEN 94	1994
433060233	PORSCHE CARRERA GT 2000 SILVER EXCL	
430926001	PORSCHE CARRERA CUP 1992 NO 1 MOBIL	1992
430060230	PORSCHE CARRERA GT 2001 BLACK	
430926006	PORSCHE C.CUP 1992 NO 6 EICHMANN	1992
430926015	PORSCHE C.CUP 1992 NO 15 ALZEN	1992
430926016	PORSCHE C.CUP 1992 NO 16 MANTHEY	1992
430926022	PORSCHE C.CUP 1992 NO 22 GARTZEN	1992
430926024	PORSCHE C.CUP 1992 NO 24 W.LAND	1992
430926029	PORSCHE C.CUP 1992 NO 29 T.SEILER	1992
430926042	PORSCHE C.CUP 1992 NO 42 E.WALCHER	1992
430064001	PORSCHE DAUER 962 STREET YELLOW	1994
430946435	PORSCHE DAUER 962 GT 3RD PL LM 1994	1994
430946436	PORSCHE DAUER NO. 36 WINNER LM 1994	1994
430068000	PORSCHE GT3 STREET CAR SILVER	
430068001	PORSCHE GT3 SPEED YELLOW	
430068002	PORSCHE GT3 SAUBER BLUE	
430986990	PORSCHE GT3 STREET CAR	1998
433016923	PORSCHE GT3 SOFTWARE AG 2001 WHITE	
430936001	PORSCHE NR. 1 CALDERARI CUP 1993	1993
430936008	PORSCHE NR. 8 LAND CUP 1993	1993
430936009	PORSCHE NR. 9 HEZEMANS CUP 1993	1993
430936010	PORSCHE NR. 10 GROHS CUP 1993	1993
430936013	PORSCHE NR. 13 A.FUCHS CUP 1993	1993
430936015	PORSCHE NR. 15 HEGER CUP 1993	1993
433065433	PORSCHE NO. 1 1948 EXCL.	1948
433065104	PORSCHE RS 1998 SILVER	
400010022	PROST ACER AP04 J.ALESI 2001	2001
400010122	PROST ACER AP04 H.H.FRENTZEN 2001	2001
400010123	PROST ACER AP04 L.BURTI 2001	2001
400010223	PROST ACER AP04 T.ENGE 2001	2001
403010222	PROST ACER AP04 J.ALESI W.FIG. 2001	2001
430980011	PROST AP 01 O.PANIS 1998	1998
430980012	PROST AP 01 J.TRULLI 1998	1998
430980041	PROST AP 01 O.PANIS TOWER WING 1998	1998
430980042	PROST AP 01 J.TRULLI TOWER W. 1998	1998
430980081	PROST AP 01 PEUGEOT O.PANIS PRES.98	1998
430980082	PROST AP 01 PEUGEOT J.TRULLI PRES.98	1998
430990018	PROST AP 02 PEUGEOT O.PANIS 1999	1999
430990019	PROST AP 02 PEUGEOT J.TRULLI 1999	1999
430990118	PROST AP 02 PEUGEOT N.HEIDFELD TEST'99	1999
430970014	PROST F1 MUGEN O.PANIS 1997	1997
430970015	PROST F1 MUGEN JAPANESE DRIVER 1997	1997
430970024	PROST F1 MUGEN HONDA J.TRULLI 1997	1997
430990088	PROST F1 O.PANIS PRES. 1999	1999
430990089	PROST F1 J.TRULLI PRES. 1999	1999
430000014	PROST PEUGEOT AP03 J.ALESI 2000	2000
430000015	PROST PEUGEOT AP03 N.HEIDFELD 2000	2000
430010073	PROST G. MAZZACANE PRES. 2001	2001
430000084	PROST J. ALESI PRES. 2000	2000
430010072	PROST J. ALESI PRES. 2001	2001
433970084	PROST MUGEN HONDA O.PANIS	1997
430000085	PROST N.HEIDFELD PRES. 2000	2000
400113100	RENAULT 16 1965 WHITE	
400113101	RENAULT 16 1965 GOLD METALLC	
430113600	RENAULT ALPINE A 110 63/67 BLUE MET	1963
430113602	RENAULT ALPINE A 110 63/67 RED	1963
430113604	RENAULT ALPINE A 110 FRENCH BLUE	1963
430781101	RENAULT ALPINE A 443 DEPAILLER LM 1978	
430781102	RENAULT ALPINE A 442B 1ST LM 1978	
400020084	RENAULT F1 J.TRULLI LAUNCH VERS '02	2002
400020085	RENAULT F1 J.BUTTON LAUNCH VERS '02	2002
400020185	RENAULT F1 TESTCAR J.BUTTON 2002	2002
400020014	RENAULT R202 J.TRULLI 2002	2002
400020015	RENAULT R202 J.BUTTON 2002	2002
408020014	RENAULT R202 J.TRULLI 2002	2002
408020015	RENAULT R202 J.BUTTON 2002	2002
430113550	RENAULT R8 GORDINI 1964/68 BLUE	1964
430113552	RENAULT R8 GORDINI 1964/68 YELLOW	1964
520944407	REYNARD 941 GALLES NO.7 A.FERNANDEZ	1994
520944408	REYNARD 941 CHIP G. NO.8 M.ANDRETTI	1994
520944412	REYNARD 941 FORSYTHE NO.12 J.VILLE.	1994
510430007	REYNARD F3 DT. MEISTER 1990	1990
510904303	REYNARD F3 M.S. 1ST GP MACAU 1990	
520954315	REYNARD 95 FORD WALKER/CH. C.FITTIP.	1995
520954427	REYNARD 95 FORD GREEN/PLAYERS J.VILLEN	1995
521964304	REYNARD 95 FORD GOODYEAR R.HEARN 96	1996
521964312	REYNARD 95 FORD FIREST.B.CALKINS 96	1996
520954331	REYNARD 95 HONDA TASMAN/LCI A.RIBEIRO	1995
520964305	REYNARD 96 FORD VALVOLINE R.GORDON	1996
520964317	REYNARD 96 FORD Hollywood M.Gugelmin	1996
520964308	REYNARD 96 HONDA PENNZOIL G.D.FERRAN	1996
520964312	REYNARD 96 HONDA TARGET J.VASSER	1996
523974316	REYNARD 96 MERCEDES P.CARPENTIER CART97	1997
520974304	REYNARD TARGET GANASSI/A.ZANARDI	1997
433138103	MINI COOPER 2000 DAKAR YELLOW	2001
433138104	MINI COOPER 2000 COSMOS BLACK	2001
433138105	MINI COOPER 2000 SOLAR RED	2001
433138106	MINI COOPER 2000 BRIT. RACING GREEN	2001
433138107	MINI COOPER 2000 BLACK	2001
431138100	MINI COOPER 2001 BLUE METALLIC	2001
431138101	MINI COOPER 2001 BLACK	2001
431138108	MINI COOPER ONE BLUE METALLIC	2002
433138140	MINI COOPER ONE LHD CHILI RED	2002
433138141	MINI COOPER ONE LHD BLACK	2002
433138142	MINI COOPER ONE LHD LIQUID YELLOW	2002
433138143	MINI COOPER ONE LHD BRITISH RACING GREEN	2002
433138144	MINI COOPER ONE LHD COSMOS BLACK	2002
433138145	MINI COOPER ONE LHD INDI BLUE	2002
433138146	MINI COOPER ONE LHD PURE SILVER	2002
433138147	MINI COOPER ONE LHD SILK GREEN	2002
433138148	MINI COOPER ONE LHD PEPPER WHITE	2002
433138149	MINI COOPER ONE LHD VELVET RED	2002
433138166	MINI COOPER ONE RHD CHILI RED	2002
433138167	MINI COOPER ONE RHD BLACK	2002
433138168	MINI COOPER ONE RHD LIQUID YELLOW	2002
433138169	MINI COOPER ONE RHD BRITISH RACING GREEN	2002
433138170	MINI COOPER ONE RHD COSMOS BLACK	2002
433138171	MINI COOPER ONE RHD INDI BLUE	2002
433138172	MINI COOPER ONE RHD PURE SILVER	2002
433138173	MINI COOPER ONE RHD SILK GREEN	2002
433138174	MINI COOPER ONE RHD PEPPER WHITE	2002
433138175	MINI COOPER ONE RHD VELVET RED	2002
433138150	MINI COOPER LHD CHILI RED	2002
433138151	MINI COOPER LHD BLACK	2002
433138152	MINI COOPER LHD LIQUID YELLOW	2002
433138153	MINI COOPER LHD BRIT. RACING GREEN	2002
433138154	MINI COOPER LHD COSMOS BLACK	2002
433138155	MINI COOPER LHD INDI BLUE	2002
433138156	MINI COOPER LHD SILK GREEN	2002
433138157	MINI COOPER LHD VELVET RED	2002
433138158	MINI COOPER LHD CHILI RED	2002
433138159	MINI COOPER LHD LIQUID YELLOW	2002
433138160	MINI COOPER LHD BRIT. RACING GREEN	2002
433138161	MINI COOPER LHD INDI BLUE	2002
433138162	MINI COOPER LHD PURE SILVER	2002
433138163	MINI COOPER LHD SILK GREEN	2002
433138164	MINI COOPER LHD PEPPER WHITE	2002
433138165	MINI COOPER LHD VELVET RED	2002
433138176	MINI COOPER RHD CHILI RED	2002
433138177	MINI COOPER RHD BLACK	2002
433138178	MINI COOPER RHD LIQUID YELLOW	2002
433138179	MINI COOPER RHD BRIT. RACING GREEN	2002
433138180	MINI COOPER RHD COSMOS BLUE	2002
433138181	MINI COOPER RHD INDI BLUE	2002
433138182	MINI COOPER RHD SILK GREEN	2002
433138183	MINI COOPER RHD VELVET RED	2002
433138184	MINI COOPER RHD CHILI RED	2002
433138185	MINI COOPER RHD LIQUID YELLOW	2002
433138186	MINI COOPER RHD BRIT. RACING GREEN	2002
433138187	MINI COOPER RHD INDI BLUE	2002
433138188	MINI COOPER RHD PURE SILVER	2002
433138189	MINI COOPER RHD SILK GREEN	2002
433138190	MINI COOPER RHD PEPPER WHITE	2002
433138191	MINI COOPER RHD VELVET RED	2002
430170820	SAAB 9-3 COUPE YELLOW	
433170833	SAAB 9-3 AERO CABRIO LASER RED EXCL	
430170830	SAAB 9-3 AERO CABRIO 2001 BLUE MET.	
430170831	SAAB 9-3 AERO CABRIO 2001 SILVER	
430170860	SAAB 9-3 VIGGEN BLACK	
433170803	SAAB 9-3 SALOON CAYENNE RED EXCL.	
433170823	SAAB 9-3 3-DOOR COUPE BLACK/BEIGE	
430170800	SAAB 9-3 5-DOOR SALOON '99 BLUE MET	
430170640	SAAB 9-5 SALOON 1997 GREEN MET.	
430170810	SAAB 9-5 BREAK 1999 SILVER	
430170811	SAAB 9-5 BREAK 1999 IMOLA RED	
433170813	SAAB 9-5 BREAK 1999 BLACK/BEIGE	
433170643	SAAB 9-5 SALOON SILVER	1997
433170644	SAAB 9-5 SALOON MIDNIGHT BLUE EXCL.	
430170643	SAAB 640 SALOON SILVER	1997
430170530	SAAB 900 CABRIOLET 1995 BLACK	1995
430170531	SAAB 900 CABRIOLET 1995 BLUE	1995
430170532	SAAB 900 CABRIOLET 1995 RED	1995
430170500	SAAB 900 SALOON 1995 BLACK	1995
430170501	SAAB 900 SALOON 1995 AUBERGINE	1995
433170523	SAAB 900 COUPE TALLADEGA RECORD EXC	1997
433170524	SAAB 900 COUPE SILVER EXCL.	1997
433170533	SAAB 900 CABRIOLET 1995 RED	1995
433170534	SAAB 900 CABRIOLET 1995 BLACK	1995

ITEM-No	ITEM	YEAR
433170535	SAAB 900 CABRIOLET 1995 SILVER	1995
433170536	SAAB 900 CABRIOLET 1995 YELLOW	1995
433170863	SAAB VIGGEN 3-DOOR LIGHTNING BLUE	
430930011	SAUBER C12 93 H.H.FRENTZEN BARCELONA	1993
430930011	SAUBER C12 F1 WENDLINGER 1993	1993
430930010	SAUBER C12 F1 LEHTO 1993	1993
433930009	SAUBER C12 F1 WENDLINGER IND. 1993	1993
433930010	SAUBER C12 F1 LEHTO HOCKENHEIM 1993	1993
430940229	SAUBER C13 A.DE CESARIS GP GERM. 94	1994
430980014	SAUBER C17 PETRONAS V10 ALESI 98	1998
430980015	SAUBER C17 PETRONAS V10 HERBERT 98	1998
430980044	SAUBER C17 ALESI TOWER WING 98	1998
430980045	SAUBER C17 J.ALESI TOWER WING 98	1998
430990011	SAUBER C18 PETRONAS J.ALESI 1999	1999
430990012	SAUBER C18 PETRONAS P.DINIZ 1999	1999
430960084	SAUBER F1 HERBERT PRESENTATION '96	1996
430990081	SAUBER F1 J.ALESI PRES. 1999	1999
430990082	SAUBER F1 P.DINIZ PRES. 1999	1999
430950129	SAUBER FORD C14 J.C.BOULLION 1995	1995
511964330	SAUBER FORD C14 H.H. FRENTZEN 1995	1995
445950030	SAUBER FORD H.H. FRENTZEN 1995	1995
430950029	SAUBER FORD K. WENDLINGER 1995	1995
430960014	SAUBER FORD ZETEC C15 J.HERBERT 96	1996
511964315	SAUBER FORD ZETEC C15 H.FRENTZEN 96	1996
430000116	SAUBER PETRONAS C19 P.DINIZ GP MALAYSIA 00	2000
430000117	SAUBER PETRONAS C19 M.SALO GP MALAYSIA '00	2000
430000016	SAUBER PETRONAS C19 P.DINIZ 2000	2000
430000017	SAUBER PETRONAS C19 M.SALO 2000	2000
400010016	SAUBER PETRONAS C20 K.HEIDFELD 2001	2001
400010017	SAUBER PETRONAS C20 K.RAIKKONEN 01	2001
400010116	SAUBER PETRONAS C20 N.HEIDFELD MALAYSIA 01	2001
400010117	SAUBER PETRONAS C20 K.RAIKK. AUSTRALIA 01	2001
403010217	SAUBER PETRONAS C20 K.RAIKK. AUSTRALIA 01	2001
400010216	SAUBER PETRONAS C20 HEIDFELD AUSTRALIA 01	2001
400020007	SAUBER PETRONAS C21 N.HEIDFELD 2002	2002
400020008	SAUBER PETRONAS C21 F.MASSA 2002	2002
430000086	SAUBER PETRONAS DINIZ PRES. 2000	2000
430000087	SAUBER PETRONAS M.SALO PRES. 2000	2000
400010086	SAUBER PETRONAS N.HEIDFELD PRES. 2001	2001
400010087	SAUBER PETRONAS K.RAIKKONEN PRES. 2001	2001
400020097	SAUBER PETRONAS F1 N.HEIDFELD LAUNCH 2002	2002
400020098	SAUBER PETRONAS F1 F.MASSA LAUNCH 2002	2002
432001003	SAUBER MERCEDES C9 SHORT DIST. NO. 61	1989
432001004	SAUBER MERCEDES C9 SHORT DIST. NO. 62	1989
432001005	SAUBER MERCEDES C9 AEG LM 88 NO. 61	1988
432001006	SAUBER MERCEDES C9 AEG LM 88 NO. 62	1988
432001007	SAUBER MERCEDES C9 KOUROS LM 87 NO. 61	1987
432001008	SAUBER MERCEDES C9 KOUROS LM 87 NO. 62	1987
430940029	SAUBER MERCEDES C13 C.WENDLINGER 94	1994
430940030	SAUBER MERCEDES C13 H.H.FRENTZEN 94	1994
430940129	SAUBER MERCEDES C13 A.DE CESARIS GP CANAD	1994
430940230	SAUBER MERCEDES C13 FRENTZEN GP GERM. 94	1994
433057103	SEAT AROSA 1997	1997
430057100	SEAT AROSA 1997 RED	
430057101	SEAT AROSA 1997 GREEN METALLIC	1997
436050503	SEAT SHOWCAR CHROMED	
430058400	SEAT TOLEDO 1999 FLASH RED	
430058401	SEAT TOLEDO 1999 STEEL GREY	
430058403	SEAT TOLEDO SALOON SILVER EXCL.	
430058404	SEAT TOLEDO SALOON PEARL BLUE EXCL.	
430940031	SIMTEK FORD D. BRABHAM 1994	1994
430940032	SIMTEK FORD R.RATZENBERGER 1994	1994
430950011	SIMTEK FORD D.SCHIATTARELLA 1995	1995
430950012	SIMTEK FORD J.VERSTAPPEN 1995	1995
430039000	SMART CABRIOLET 2000 SILVER/BLUE	
430039001	SMART CABRIOLET 00 DARK GREY/SILVER	2000
430039002	SMART CABRIOLET '00 HELLO YELLOW	
430039004	SMART CABRIOLET '00 LITE WHITE	
430039005	SMART CABRIOLET '00 GREEN	
430039006	SMART CABRIOLET '00 BLACK	
433039003	SMART CABRIOLET JACK BLACK/LITE WHITE	
433039004	SMART CABRIOLET RED/GREY	
430039005	SMART CITY CABRIO BLACK/GREEN	
430039006	SMART CITY CABRIO SILVER/RED	
430039007	SMART CITY CABRIO SILVER/BLACK	
403032123	SMART ROADSTER COUPE SILVER/BLUE	
400032133	SMART ROADSTER '03 SILVER/CHAMPAIGN	
430970022	STEWART FORD SF 1 R.BARRICHELLO 97	1997
430970023	STEWART FORD SF 1 J.MAGNUSSEN 97	1997
430980018	STEWART SF2 R.BARRICHELLO 1998	1998
430980019	STEWART SF2 J.MAGNUSSEN 1998	1998
430980029	STEWART SF2 R.BARRICHELLO PRES.98	1998
430980089	STEWART SF2 J.MAGNUSSEN PRES.98	1998
433980029	STEWART SF2 J.VERSTAPPEN 1998	1998
430830020	TOLEMAN TG 183 B J.CECOTTO 1984	1983
430830035	TOLEMAN TG 183 CANDY D WARWICK 1983	1983
430830036	TOLEMAN TG 183 B CANDY B.GIACOMELLI 83	1983
540844319	TOLEMAN TG 183 B AYRTON SENNA	1984
430840020	TOLEMAN TG 184 J.CECOTTO 1984	1984
540844399	TOLEMAN TG 184 AYRTON SENNA	1984
403026204	TOYOTA AVENSIS SILVER MET. EXCL.	
403166204	TOYOTA AVENSIS BLACK MET. EXCL.	
403166213	TOYOTA AVENSIS BREAK SILVER MET.	
403166214	TOYOTA AVENSIS BREAK BLACK MET.EXCL	
430168920	TOYOTA CELICA 2000 SILVER	
430168921	TOYOTA CELICA 2000 BLACK	
430166404	TOYOTA CELICA AURIOL-OCELLI ARG '94	1994
430166502	TOYOTA CELICA RALLYE CATALUNYA 1995	1995
430166620	TOYOTA CELICA SS-II COUPE 94 BLACK	1994
430166622	TOYOTA CELICA SS-II COUPE 94 RED	1994
433168923	TOYOTA CELICA 1999 SILVER	
433168924	TOYOTA CELICA 1999 DARK BLUE MET.	
433168925	TOYOTA CELICA SILVER DUNLOP	
400166100	TOYOTA COROLLA 2-DOOR '01 BLUE MET.	2001
400166101	TOYOTA COROLLA 2-DOOR '01 BLACK MET	
403166103	TOYOTA COROLLA 3-DOOR 2001 SILVER	
400166170	TOYOTA COROLLA 5-DOOR '01 GREEN MET	2001
400166171	TOYOTA COROLLA 5-DOOR '01 RED	2001
403166173	TOYOTA COROLLA 5-DOOR 2001 SILVER	
403166174	TOYOTA COROLLA 5-DOOR 2001 BLACK	
400020074	TOYOTA F1 M.SALO LAUNCH VERS. 2002	2002
400020075	TOYOTA F1 A.MCNISH LAUNCH VERS. 2002	2002
403020074	TOYOTA F1 M.SALO LAUNCH VERS. 2002	2002
403020075	TOYOTA F1 A.MCNISH LAUNCH VERS.2002	2002
400020174	TOYOTA F1 SHOWCAR 2002	2002
343100065	TOYOTA McNISH DIORAMA W.CAR PS'02	2002
343100066	TOYOTA M.SALO DIORAMA W.CAR PS'02	2002
430981627	TOYOTA GT-ONE KATAYAMA/.. LM '98	1998
430981628	TOYOTA GT-ONE BRUNDLE/.. LM '98	1998
430991601	TOYOTA GT-ONE BOUTSEN/.. LM '99	1999
430991602	TOYOTA GT-ONE BRUNDLE/.. LM '99	1999
430991603	TOYOTA GT-ONE KATAYAMA/.. LM '99	1999
430166273	TOYOTA LANDCRUISER '02 SILVER MET.	
430166960	TOYOTA MR2 CABRIOLET 2000 BLUE MET.	
430166961	TOYOTA MR2 CABRIOLET 2000 SILVER	
433166962	TOYOTA MR2 CABRIOLET 2000 SILVER	
433166963	TOYOTA MR2 CABRIOLET '99 RED MET.	
430166000	TOYOTA RAV4 2000 GREEN METALLIC	
430166001	TOYOTA RAV4 2000 BLACK	
433166003	TOYOTA RAV4 SILVER MET.	
433166004	TOYOTA RAV4 BLUE MET.	
400020024	TOYOTA TF102 M.SALO 2002	2002
400020025	TOYOTA TF102 A.McNISH 2002	2002
400020124	TOYOTA TF102 M.SALO 1ST POINT AUS.	2002
408020024	TOYOTA TF102 M.SALO 2002	2002
403020024	TOYOTA TF102 M.SALO 2002	2002
408020025	TOYOTA TF102 A.McNISH 2002	2002
409020024	TOYOTA TF102 M.SALO 2002	2002
409020025	TOYOTA TF102 A.McNISH 2002	2002
433166053	TOYOTA YARIS TS 2000 GREY METALLIC	
430166060	TOYOTA YARIS TS 2001 BLACK	
430166061	TOYOTA YARIS TS 2001 BLUE MET.	
430132571	TRIUMPH TR 6 1968-76 RACING GREEN	1968
430132572	TRIUMPH TR 6 1968-76 RED	1968
430710009	TYRRELL F.CEVERT 1971	1971
430710011	TYRRELL 003 J.STEWART WORLDCH. 1971	1971
430730005	TYRRELL 006 J. STEWART WORLDCH. 1973	1973
430730006	TYRRELL 006 F.CEVERT 1973	1973
433970018	TYRRELL 025 FORD J.VERSTAPPEN 1997	1997
430970019	TYRRELL 025 FORD J.VERSTAPPEN 1997	1997
430970028	TYRRELL 025 WITH WINGLETS J.V. 1997	1997
430970029	TYRRELL 025 WITH WINGLETS M.SALO 97	1997
430980021	TYRRELL 026 T.TAKAGI 1998	1998
430980021	TYRRELL 026 R.ROSSET 1998	1998
430980050	TYRRELL 026 R.ROSSET TOWER W. 1998	1998
430980051	TYRRELL 026 T.TAKAGI TOWER W. 1998	1998
430980070	TYRRELL 026 T.TAKAGI PRES.98	1998
430980071	TYRRELL 026 R.ROSSET PRES.98	1998
433980021	TYRRELL 026 T.TAKAGI 1998	1998
430760003	TYRRELL P34 6-WH. J.SCHECKTER 1976	1976
430760004	TYRRELL P34 6-WH. P.DEPAILLER 1976	1976
430770003	TYRRELL P34 FNCB R.PETERSON 1977	1977
430770004	TYRRELL P34 FNCB P.DEPAILLER 1977	1977
430940003	TYRRELL YAMAHA 022 U.KATAYAMA 1994	1994
430940004	TYRRELL YAMAHA 022 M.BLUNDELL 1994	1994
430950003	TYRRELL YAMAHA U. KATAYAMA 1995	1995
430960018	TYRRELL YAMAHA U.KATAYAMA 96	1996
430960019	TYRRELL YAMAHA 024 M.SALO 96	1996
433048006	VAUXHALL ZAFIRA 1999 EXCL.	1999
430171000	VOLVO 121 AMAZON SALOON RED	
430171001	VOLVO 121 AMAZON SALOON GREY	
430171010	VOLVO 121 AMAZON BREAK WHITE	
430171011	VOLVO 121 AMAZON BREAK BLUE	
433171003	VOLVO 121 AMAZON SALOON PEARL WHITE	
430171401	VOLVO 350 SALOON 1994 SILVER	1996
430171410	VOLVO 350 BREAK 1994 RED	1996
430171411	VOLVO 350 BREAK 1996 RED	1996
430941714	VOLVO 350 BREAK J.LAMMERS BTCC 94	1994
430941715	VOLVO 350 BREAK R.RYDELL BTCC 94	1994
430951709	VOLVO 350 SALOON T.HARVEY BTCC 1995	1995
430951733	VOLVO 350 SALOON R.RYDELL BTCC 1995	1995
430961703	VOLVO 350 SALOON R.RYDELL BTCC 96	1996
430961706	VOLVO 350 SALOON BROCK AUSTRALIAN TC 1996	1996
430961708	VOLVO 350 SALOON K.BURT BTCC 96	1996
433057104	VOLVO C70 COUPE DARK PURPLE MET.	
433171723	VOLVO C70 COUPE BLACK EXCL.	
433171733	VOLVO C70 CABRIO '98 DARK OLIVE MET	
433171734	VOLVO C70 CABRIOLET SILVER EXCL.	
430171720	VOLVO C70 COUPE 1998 GREY METALLIC	1997
433171721	VOLVO C70 COUPE 1998 RED METALLIC	
433171722	VOLVO C70 COUPE 1998 INDIANA RED	
433171730	VOLVO C70 CABRIOLET 98 RED METALLIC	
430171731	VOLVO C70 CABRIOLET 98 BLUE METALLIC	1998
433171732	VOLVO C70 CABRIO '98 TURQUOISE MET.	
430171610	VOLVO P1800 ES 1971 ICE BLUE MET.	1971
430171611	VOLVO P1800 ES 1971 DARK BLUE	
430171612	VOLVO P1800 ES 1971 GOLD MET.	
430171614	VOLVO P1800 ES 1971 DARK RED	
430171615	VOLVO P1800 ES 1971 RED	
430171616	VOLVO P1800 ES 1971 GREEN	
430171617	VOLVO P1800 ES 1971 YELLOW	
430171620	VOLVO P1800 COUPE 1969 WHITE	1969
430171621	VOLVO P1800 COUPE'69 SAFARI YELLOW	
430171622	VOLVO P1800 COUPE'69 GREY	
430171624	VOLVO P1800 COUPE'69 GREEN	
430171625	VOLVO P1800 COUPE'69 SILVER	
430171626	VOLVO P1800 COUPE'69 BLACK	
430171627	VOLVO P1800 COUPE'69 TURQUOISE	
430171101	VOLVO S40 2000 RED METALLIC	
430171103	VOLVO S40 2000 BLUE	
430171104	VOLVO S40 2000 TURQUOISE MET. EXCL.	
430171500	VOLVO S40 SALOON 1996 BLUE	1996
430171501	VOLVO S40 SALOON 1996 SILVER	1996
430171503	VOLVO S40 SALOON 1996 RED	1996
430171504	VOLVO S40 SALOON 1996 BLACK MET.	1996
430171505	VOLVO S40 SALOON 1996 GREEN MET.	1996
433171506	VOLVO S40 SALOON 1996 NATURE RED	
430171260	VOLVO S60 2000 ICEBLUE METALLIC	
430171261	VOLVO S60 2000 GOLD METALLIC	
430171262	VOLVO S60 DUTCH POLICE	
433171263	VOLVO S60 2000 MAJA YELLOW MET.	
433171264	VOLVO S60 2000 RED SOLID	
433171265	VOLVO S60 BLACK METALLIC EXCL.	
430171800	VOLVO S80 SALOON 98 RED METALLIC	
433171801	VOLVO S80 SALOON 98 BLUE METALLIC	
430171802	VOLVO S80 SALOON 98 SILVER	1998
433171804	VOLVO S80 SALOON 98 INDIANA RED	
433171890	VOLVO S80 POLICE NETHERLAND	
433171891	VOLVO S80 POLICE NETHERLAND	
433171803	VOLVO S80 SILVER METALLIC, EXCL.	
433171900	VOLVO S80 SALOON 1999 SILVER MET.	
433171901	VOLVO S80 SALOON 1999 CASSIS MET.	
433171903	VOLVO S80 SALOON 99 ROYAL BLUE MET	
433171905	VOLVO S80 SALOON 1999 SILVER	
433171906	VOLVO S80 SALOON 1999 BLACK METALLIC	
433171113	VOLVO V40 2000 SILVER MET. EXCL.	
433171114	VOLVO V40 2000 SILVER MET. EXCL.	
433171110	VOLVO V40 2000 CHILI RED	
433171111	VOLVO V40 BREAK 2000 RED	
430171511	VOLVO V40 BREAK 2000 BLACK METALLIC	
433171512	VOLVO V40 BREAK 1996 BLACK	1996
433171513	VOLVO V40 BREAK 1996 RED METALLIC	1996
433171514	VOLVO V40 BREAK 1996 BLUEGREEN MET.	1996
433171515	VOLVO V40 BREAK 1996 SILVER SAND	
433171516	VOLVO V40 BREAK 1996 AUBERGINE MET.	1996
433171517	VOLVO V40 BREAK 1996 BLACK MET.	
433171210	VOLVO V70 BREAK 2000 BLACK	
430171211	VOLVO V70 BREAK 2000 SILVER	
433171270	VOLVO V70 XC 2000 BLACK	
430171271	VOLVO V70 XC 2000 SILVER	
430171810	VOLVO V70 BREAK 98 GREEN MET.	
433171811	VOLVO V70 BREAK 98 SILVER MET.	1998
433171813	VOLVO V70 BREAK 98 INDIANA RED	
430171814	VOLVO V70 BREAK POLICE GENEVE	
433171213	VOLVO V70 BREAK 2000 BLUE METALLIC	
433171214	VOLVO V70 BREAK 2000 SILVER MET.	
433171273	VOLVO V70 XC 2000 GOLD METALLIC	
433171274	VOLVO V70 XC 2000 BROWN METALLIC	
433171891	VOLVO V70 BREAK FACELIFT 98	
433171892	VOLVO V70 BREAK 98 ROYAL BLUE MET.	
433171893	VOLVO V70 BREAK TRAFFIC PATROL	
433171894	VOLVO V70 BREAK ARMED RESPONSE	
430050030	VW 181 KUEBELWAGEN 1969-79 ORANGE	
430050031	VW 181 KUEBELWAGEN 69-79 OLIVE	
400051100	VW 411 LE SALOON 1969 BLUE	1969
400051101	VW 411 LE SALOON 1969 ORANGE	1969
400051110	VW 411 LE BREAK 1969 GREEN	1969
400051111	VW 411 LE BREAK 1969 RED METALLIC	1969
430052100	VW 1200 BEETLE 1953-57 GREEN GREY	1953
430052101	VW 1200 BEETLE 1953-57 BLUE	1953
433052101	VW 1200 BEETLE OVAL WINDOW GREY	
430052000	VW 1200 BEETLE SPLIT WINDOW BLACK	1949
430052001	VW 1200 BEETLE SPLIT WINDOW 49 GREY	1949
430052002	VW 1200 BEETLE SPLIT WINDOW 49 GREEN	1949
430052030	VW 1200 CABRIOLET 1951/52 GREEN	1951
430052031	VW 1200 CABRIOLET 1951/52 BLUE	1951
430052032	VW 1200 CABRIOLET 1951/52 GREY	1951
430052034	VW 1200 CABRIOLET 1951/2 ANTHR.MET/CR.	1951
430052040	VW 1200 CABRIOLET SOFTTOP 1951/52 RED	1951
430052041	VW 1200 CABRIOLET SOFTTOP '51/52 RED	1951
430052042	VW 1200 CABRIOLET SOFTTOP '51/52 BLUE	1951
430052043	VW 1200 CABRIOLET SOFTTOP '51/52 GREEN	1951
430052103	VW 1200 DER 1.MILLIONSTE KAEFER	1949
430052003	VW 1200 GOEDE KAEFER BREZEL KAEFER	1949
430052000	VW 1200 SPLIT WINDOW OPEN ROOF BLACK	1949
430055030	VW 1302 CABRIOLET 1970/72 YELLOW	1970
430055031	VW 1302 CABRIOLET 1970/72 RED	1970
430055032	VW 1302 CABRIOLET 1970/72 SILVER	1970
430055034	VW 1302 CABRIOLET 70/72 SAPHIR BLUE	
430055035	VW 1302 CABRIOLET 70/72 SHA. YELLOW	
430055036	VW 1302 CABRIOLET 70/72 MARINA BLUE	
430055037	VW 1302 CONVERTIBLE 70/72 GREEN	
430055000	VW 1302 SALOON 1970/72 ORANGE	1970
430055001	VW 1302 SALOON 1970/72 RED	1970
430055002	VW 1302 SALOON 70/72 GEMINI MET.	1970
430055004	VW 1302 SALOON 70/72 WILLOW GREEN	
430055130	VW 1303 CABRIOLET 1972/80 BLACK	1972
430055131	VW 1303 CABRIOLET 1972/80 RED	1972
430055132	VW 1303 CABRIOLET 72/80 SATURN YELLOW	
430055134	VW 1303 CABRIOLET 72/80 BROWN MET.	
430055135	VW 1303 CABRIOLET 72/80 MARIN YELLOW	
430055136	VW 1303 CABRIOLET 72/80 SUMATRA GREEN	
430055137	VW 1303 CONVERTIBLE 72/80 WHITE	
430055100	VW 1303 SALOON 1972/74 BLUE MET.	1972
430055101	VW 1303 SALOON 1972/74 GREEN	1972
430055102	VW 1303 SALOON 1972/74 LIGHT GREEN	1972
430055104	VW 1303 SALOON 72/74 MOSS MET.	
430055105	VW 1303 SALOON 72/74 MIAMI BLUE	
430055106	VW 1303 SALOON 72/74 RED	
430055108	VW 1303 SALOON 1972/74 BIG GOLD MET	
433055107	VW 1303 SALOON 72/74 YELLOW/BLACK	1972
430055300	VW 1600 SALOON 1966 CREAM	
430055301	VW 1600 SALOON 1966 REGATTA BLUE	
430055302	VW 1600 SALOON 1966 PEARL WHITE	
430055304	VW 1600 SALOON 1966 SEA SAND	
430055310	VW 1600 TL FASTBACK 1966 RED	
430055311	VW 1600 TL FASTBACK 1966 DELTA GREEN	
430055320	VW 1600 TL FASTBACK 1966 BLUE	
430055321	VW 1600 TL FASTBACK 66 DIAMOND BLUE	
430058200	VW BORA 1999 RED	
430058201	VW BORA 1999 JAZZ BLUE	1999
430058203	VW BORA 1999 BORDEAUX RED	
430058204	VW BORA 1999 BLACK	
430058205	VW BORA 1999 INDIGO PEARL	
430058206	VW BORA 1999 INDIGO PEARL	
430058275	VW BORA 1999 INDIGO PEARL	
430058210	VW BORA BREAK 1999 BLUE METALLIC	
430058213	VW BORA VARIANT 1999 SILVER	
430058215	VW BORA VARIANT 1999 BLACK	
430058211	VW BORA VARIANT 1999 GREEN METALLIC	1999
433054003	VW CONCEPT CAR 1994 SALOON ORANGE	1994
430054000	VW CONCEPT CAR 1994 SALOON YELLOW	1994
430054001	VW CONCEPT CAR 1994 SALOON RED	1994
430054030	VW CONCEPT CAR 1994 CABRIO BLUE	1994
430054031	VW CONCEPT CAR 1994 CABRIO YELLOW	1994
430054032	VW CONCEPT CAR 1994 CABRIO RED	1994
430051006	VW D1 2001 DUST BUG FLAKE BLUE EXCL.	
430052200	VW DELIVERY VAN BLUE	1963
430052201	VW DELIVERY VAN LIGHT GREY	1963
430052202	VW DELIVERY VAN LIGHT GREEN	1963
436056070	VW GOLF IV ABT TUNING RED	
430056001	VW GOLF IV SALOON 1997 BLUE	1997
430056002	VW GOLF IV SALOON 1997 BLACK MET.	
430056008	VW GOLF IV 1997 GOLD METALLIC	
430056009	VW GOLF IV 1997 DARK BLUE METALLIC	
430056010	VW GOLF IV BREAK 1999 BLACK MET.	
430058330	VW GOLF IV CABRIO BLACK	
430058331	VW GOLF IV CABRIO BR. GREEN	
430058332	VW GOLF IV CABRIO 1999 BLUE	
430058336	VW GOLF IV SALOON 1997 GREEN MT EX.	1997
430058304	VW GOLF IV SALOON 1997 GREEN MT EX.	1997
430058005	VW GOLF IV SAL. 97 FLASH RED EXCL.	1997
430058006	VW GOLF IV SAL. 97 JAZZ BLUE EXCL.	1997
430058007	VW GOLF IV SAL. 97 BLACK EXCL.	1997
430058333	VW GOLF CABRIOLET RED EXCL.	
430058334	VW GOLF CABRIOLET DARK BLUE EXCL.	
430058335	VW GOLF CABRIOLET SATIN SILVER EX.	
430058013	VW GOLF VARIANT 1999 SILVER	
430058014	VW GOLF VARIANT 1999 INDIGO PEARL	
430058001	VW GOLF VARIANT 1999 BLACK	
430052130	VW HEBMUELLER CABRIOLET 1949/50 BLACK/RED	1949
430052131	VW HEBMUELLER CABRIOLET 1949/50 SCHW./CREME	1949
430052134	VW HEBMUELLER CABRIOLET 1949/50 BLUE	1949
430052140	VW HEBMUELLER SOFTTOP 1949/50 SCHW./BEIGE	1949
430052141	VW HEBMUELLER SOFTTOP 1949/50 BLUE	1949
430052142	VW HEBMUELLER SOFTTOP 1949/50 RED/BLACK	1949
430005000	VW KARMANN GHIA COUPE SCHW.-BLACK	1970
430005001	VW KARMANN GHIA COUPE BLAU-LIGHT BLUE	1970
430005002	VW KARMANN GHIA COUPE ROT-RED	1970
430005003	VW KARMANN GHIA COUPE RED/WHITE	1970
430005005	VW KARMANN GHIA COUPE BLUE/CREAM	1970
430005030	VW KARMANN GHIA CABRIO OFFEN SCHW.	1970
430005031	VW KARMANN GHIA CABRIO OPEN L.BLUE	1970
430005032	VW KARMANN GHIA CABRIO OFFEN ROT	1970
430005060	VW KARMANN GHIA CABRIO GESCHL GRUEN	1970
430005061	VW KARMANN GHIA CABRIO CLOSED CREAM	1970
430005062	VW KARMANN GHIA CABRIO GESCHL ROT	1970
430050220	VW KARMANN GHIA 1600 1966 WHITE	1966
430050221	VW KARMANN GHIA 1600 '66 LIGHT BLUE	1966
430051020	VW KARMANN GHIA COUPE '57 BEIGE/BLACK	1957
430051021	VW KARMANN GHIA COUPE '57 DIAM.GREEN M	1957
430051023	VW KARMANN GHIA COUPE '57 CORN SNOW BLUE	1957
430051024	VW KARMANN GHIA COUPE 1957 BLACK	1957
516974303	VW KARMANN GHIA COUPE '57 BLUE GREY M	1957
430051034	VW KARMANN GHIA CABRIO '57 GREEN MET.	1957
430051035	VW KARMANN GHIA CABRIOLET '57 BLUE	1957
430051036	VW KARMANN GHIA CABRIO '57 PACIFIC BL.	
430051037	VW KARMANN GHIA CABRIO '57 GREEN MET.	
430051038	VW KARMANN GHIA CABRIO '57 BRONCE MET.	
430051039	VW KARMANN GHIA CONVERTIBLE 1957 WHITE	
430051040	VW KARMANN GHIA CONVERTIBLE 1957 GREEN	
433051035	VW KARMANN GHIA CABRIOLET 1957 SILVER	
430058100	VW LUPO 1998 JAZZBLUE	1998
430058101	VW LUPO 1998 GREEN	
430058102	VW LUPO 1998 BLACK	
430058103	VW LUPO 1998 YELLOW	
433058103	VW LUPO SALOON 98 FLASH RED EXCL.	
433058104	VW LUPO 1998 SOFTBLUE EXCL.	
433058105	VW LUPO 1998 JAZZ BLUE EXCL.	
430058000	VW NEW BEETLE 1998 YELLOW	1998
430058001	VW NEW BEETLE SALOON 1998 RED	
430058002	VW NEW BEETLE SALOON 1998 BLACK	
430058003	VW NEW BEETLE SALOON 1998 BLUE	
430058003	VW NEW BEETLE SALOON CYBER GREEN MET 98	
430058004	VW NEW BEETLE SALOON SILVER MET 1998	
430058005	VW NEW BEETLE SALOON BLUE MET 1998	
430058006	VW NEW BEETLE SALOON 1998 LEMON YELLOW	
400051000	VW PHAETON 2002 BLUE METALLIC	
400051001	VW PHAETON 2002 AUBERGINE MET.	
403051003	VW PHAETON 2001 SILVER MET.EXCL.	
403051004	VW PHAETON 2001 BLACK EXCL.	
403051005	VW PHAETON 2001 PEARL GREEN EXCL.	
430050500	VW POLO 1975 RED	1975
430050501	VW POLO 1975 YELLOW	1975
430052300	VW SAMBA REISEBUS GREY	1958
430052301	VW SAMBA REISEBUS GREEN	1958
430052302	VW SAMBA REISEBUS RED	1958
430052303	VW SAMBA REISEBUS GREY/BLUE	
430050420	VW SCIROCCO I 1974 GREEN METALLIC	
430050421	VW SCIROCCO I 1974 BLUE	
403052003	VW TOUAREG 2002 PIANO BLACK EXCL.	
403052004	VW TOUAREG 2002 RAVENNA BLUE MET.	
403052005	VW TOUAREG 2002 REFLEX SILVER EXCL	
403052006	VW TOUAREG 2002 SALT LAKE GREY MET	
403052007	VW TOUAREG 2002 COLORADO RED PEARL	
403052008	VW TOUAREG '02 VENETIAN GREEN PEARL	
403052103	VW TOURAN INDIA BLUE	
403052104	VW TOURAN BLACKMAGIC PEARL EFFECT	
403052105	VW TOURAN AMAZONAS GREEN PEARL EFF.	
403052106	VW TOURAN REFLEX SILVER	
403052108	VW TOURAN GOLD METALLIC	
430015900	WARTBURG 311 SALOON BLACK	
430015930	WARTBURG A311 CABRIOLET BEIGE	1958
430015931	WARTBURG A311 CABRIOLET RED/WHITE	
430015932	WARTBURG A311 CABRIOLET BLUE	
430015900	WARTBURG A312 SALOON BLUE	
430015901	WARTBURG A312 SALOON CORALL/WHITE	1958
430015902	WARTBURG A312 SALOON SILK GREEN	1958
430015920	WARTBURG A312 COUPE GREY/WHITE	
430015921	WARTBURG A312 COUPE BLACK/WHITE	
430015934	WARTBURG A312 CABRIOLET CREAM/GREEN	
430000009	WILLIAMSF1 BMW FW22 R.SCHUMACHER '00	2000
430000010	WILLIAMSF1 BMW FW22 J.BUTTON 2000	2000
430000029	WILLIAMSF1 BMW FW22 R.S. GP BRAZIL 2000	2000
430000030	WILLIAMSF1 BMW FW22 J.B. 1ST POINT 2000	2000
400010005	WILLIAMSF1 BMW FW23 R.SCHUMACHER 01	2001
400010006	WILLIAMSF1 BMW FW23 J.P.MONTOYA 2001	2001
400010025	WILLIAMSF1 BMW FW23 R.S.1ST GP WIN'01	2001
400010026	WILLIAMSF1 BMW FW23 JPM MALAYSIA'01	2001
400010125	WILLIAMSF1 BMW FW23 R.S. KEEP DIST. 2001	2001
400010126	WILLIAMSF1 BMW FW23 JPM 1ST GP WIN	2001
403010006	WILLIAMSF1 BMW FW23 R.SCHUMACHER '01	2001
403010006	WILLIAMSF1 BMW FW24 J.P.MONTOYA 2001	2001
400020019	WILLIAMSF1 BMW FW24 R.SCHUM. '02	2002
400020006	WILLIAMSF1 BMW FW24 BORDEAUX RED	2002
400020105	WILLIAMSF1 BMW FW24 HP R.SCHUM. '02	2002
400020106	WILLIAMSF1 BMW FW24 HP MONTOYA '02	2002
403020105	WILLIAMSF1 BMW FW24 J.P.MONTOYA '02	2002
403020106	WILLIAMSF1 BMW FW24 HP MONTOYA '02	2002
408020005	WILLIAMSF1 BMW FW24 R.SCHUM. '02	2002
408020006	WILLIAMSF1 BMW FW24 JPM MONTOYA '02	2002
430000079	WILLIAMSF1 BMW SHOWCAR R.SCHUMACHER F1'00	2000
430000080	WILLIAMSF1 BMW SHOWCAR J.BUTTON F1 '00	2000
430000099	WILLIAMSF1 BMW SHOWCAR 2000	2000
403020095	WILLIAMSF1 BMW R.SCHUMACHER LAUNCH 2002	2002
400010095	WILLIAMSF1 BMW R.SCHUMACHER PRES. 2001	2001
400010096	WILLIAMSF1 BMW J.P.MONTOYA PRES. 2001	2001
400020095	WILLIAMSF1 BMW R.SCHUMACHER LAUNCH 2002	2002
400020096	WILLIAMSF1 BMW J.P.MONTOYA LAUNCH 2002	2002
403100045	WILLIAMSF1 BMW PIT STOP DIO. LAUNCH 2002	2002
430990098	WILLIAMSF1 FW21 TESTCAR MICHELIN '00	2000
433000199	WILLIAMSF1 FW21 SHOWCAR NO.9 00	
433000009	WILLIAMSF1 FW22 BMW R.SCHUMACHER '00	2000
433000010	WILLIAMSF1 FW22 BMW J.BUTTON 2000	2000
433000029	WILLIAMSF1 FW22 R.S. GP BRAZIL 200	2000
433000030	WILLIAMSF1 FW22 J.B. 1ST POINT 2000	2000
433010095	WILLIAMSF1 R.SCHUMACHER PRES. 2001	2001
436000199	WILLIAMSF1 PROMOTIONAL SHOWCAR F1 '00	2000
430990095	WILLIAMS FW SUPERTEC A.ZANARDI PRES.99	1999
430990096	WILLIAMS FW R. SCHUMACHER PRES.99	1999
430790027	WILLIAMS FW07 A.JONES 1979	1979
430790028	WILLIAMS FW07 C.REGAZZONI 1979	1979
430820006	WILLIAMS FW08 K.ROSBERG W.C. 1982	1982
430820005	WILLIAMS FW08 D.DALY 1982	1982
430830001	WILLIAMS FW08C FORD K.ROSBERG 1983	1983
430830002	WILLIAMS FW08C FORD J.LAFFITE 1983	1983
540834301	WILLIAMS FW08C FORD 1983 A. SENNA	1983
430920005	WILLIAMS FW14B N.MANSELL 1992	1992
430920006	WILLIAMS FW14B R.PATRESE 1992	1992
430930005	WILLIAMS FW15 RENAULT D.HILL 1993	1993
430930006	WILLIAMS FW15 RENAULT A.PROST 1993	1993
430941001	WILLIAMS FW15 D.HILL PRESENT 1994	1994
430941002	WILLIAMS FW15 A.SENNA PRESENT. 94	1994
433930001	WILLIAMS FW15 D.HILL HOCKENHEIM 93	1993
433930002	WILLIAMS FW15 A. PROST HOCKENH. 93	1993
430940001	WILLIAMS FW16 D.HILL 1994	1994
430940002	WILLIAMS FW16 RENAULT A.SENNA 94	1994
430940102	WILLIAMS FW16 N.MANSELL 1994	1994
430940103	WILLIAMS FW16 D.COULTHARD 1994	1994
430940104	WILLIAMS FW16 D.HILL GP ENGLAND 94	1994
430940101	WILLIAMS FW16 D.HILL 1ST GP GB 94	1994
430950095	WILLIAMS FW16 TESTCAR D.HILL 1995	1995
430950096	WILLIAMS FW16 D.COULTH. 95	1995
540944302	WILLIAMS FW16 1994 AYRTON SENNA	1994
430950005	WILLIAMS FW17 D. HILL 1995	1995
430950006	WILLIAMS FW17 J.VILLENEUVE 1995	1995
430950096	WILLIAMS FW17 J.VILLEN. PRES. 1996	1996
430960005	WILLIAMS FW18 J.VILLENEUVE 1996	1996
430960006	WILLIAMS FW18 D.HILL SUZUKA 1996	1996
430960025	WILLIAMS FW18 D.HILL 1996	1996
430960026	WILLIAMS FW18 D.HILL 1ST GP D 1996	1996
445960006	WILLIAMS FW18 J.VILLENEUVE 1996	1996
430970075	WILLIAMS FW19 1996 D.HILL	1996
430970004	WILLIAMS FW19 GERMAN DRIVER 1997	1997
430970005	WILLIAMS FW19 J.VILLEN. PRES. 1997	1997
430970094	WILLIAMS FW19 GERM.DRIVER PRES.97	1997
516974303	WILLIAMS FW19 J.VILLEN. WORLDCH 97	1997
430980001	WILLIAMS FW20 J.VILLENEUVE 1998	1998
430980025	WILLIAMS FW20 J.VILLEN. PRES.98	1998
511984301	WILLIAMS FW20 H.H.FRENTZEN 1998	1998
511984302	WILLIAMS FW20 H.H.FRENTZEN PRES.98	1998
430990025	WILLIAMS FW21 SUPERT. A.ZANARDI 99	1999
430990006	WILLIAMS FW21 S. R.SCHUMACHER 1999	1999